AMERICA'S 400TH ANNIVERSARY

The Quadricentennial Commemoration
of the Founding of Jamestown
1607-2007

FINAL REPORT
OF THE
JAMESTOWN 400TH
COMMEMORATION COMMISSION

For sale by the Superintendent of Documents, U.S. Government Printing Office
Internet: bookstore.gpo.gov   Phone: toll free (866) 512-1800;   DC area (202) 512-1800
Fax: (202) 512-2104 Mail: Stop IDCC, Washington, DC 20402-0001

ISBN 978-0-16-082096-0

CONTENTS

FOREWORD

A Singular Honor

The following letter accompanied the transmittal of this Final Report to the President of the United States and the United States Congress upon the conclusion of the Commission's work on December 31, 2008.

It is our privilege to submit the Final Report of the Jamestown 400th Commemoration Commission, created by Act of Congress (Public Law 106-565) and signed into law by the President of the United States on December 23, 2000.

Our report summarizes the extraordinary story of *America's 400th Anniversary,* an 18-month program of commemorative activities and events that afforded Americans the opportunity to honor their nation's beginning at Jamestown and reflect upon the vision and values that define the world's oldest republic. The anniversary program was a resounding success. We wish to express our appreciation to the President and the Congress, and ultimately to the American People, for the vigorous support we received throughout the course of planning and executing the commemorative program. We are especially grateful for the singular honor of serving on the Commission.

We wish also to call attention to the wide-ranging contributions of the Commonwealth of Virginia—the Governor, the General Assembly, and the Jamestown 2007 organization—and to thank our colleagues on the Jamestown 2007 Management and Steering Committees, with whom we have collaborated closely and productively on virtually every aspect of this endeavor. As this report details, the unparalleled success of *America's 400th Anniversary* resulted not only from an unusually effective federal-state partnership, but from the energy and effort of many dedicated staff members, selfless volunteers, and generous supporters in the public and private sectors, at home and abroad, who worked together over many months.

The 400th anniversary commemoration produced stunning new discoveries, significant new scholarship, impressive new interpretive facilities, and illuminating new educational initiatives that will continue to enhance our understanding of the remarkably consequential convergence of man and nature in the Chesapeake region four centuries ago. Anniversary-related programs and activities increased public awareness of the foundational importance of the Jamestown settlement and Virginia colony in our nation's history. The activities enhanced appreciation for the ties that bind Americans through common language, culture, values, a shared past, and an interdependent future. The programs also featured a timely and profound international dialogue on the foundations and future of democracy—a wide-ranging assessment of the free institutions that have prospered worldwide in our time, and on which the aspirations of people everywhere depend.

Not least among its legacies, the anniversary program also afforded a timeless lesson about the value of telling the truth and telling it well. The commemoration could have highlighted only part of our past, selectively celebrating Jamestown's positive legacies in the manner of preceding observances. Or, the commemoration could have dwelled on hardships and misdeeds, on sad legacies of dispossession and oppression, in a manner calculated only to stoke grievance and resentment. Instead, federal and state commemoration planners and partners eschewed such self-defeating extremes and enthusiastically embraced the whole community in an honest, unifying, and uplifting reflection on the obstacles overcome and progress achieved during our nation's 400-year-old journey toward fulfillment of its founding ideals.

This Final Report is intended to complement the similar report by the Commonwealth of Virginia's Jamestown 2007 organization. It also complements the forthcoming *Jamestown Commentaries on the Foundations and Future of Democracy* and the materials available online at *www.JamestownDemocracy. org*. Together, these and other first-hand accounts will create a complete portrait of *America's 400th Anniversary*, a poignant period of celebration, remembrance, and renewal inspired by the boundless promise of a still-young America.

INTRODUCTION

E Pluribus Unum

A question posed frequently to those leading *America's 400ᵗʰ Anniversary* was how it all came to be: an 18-month commemoration, 13 impressive "signature events," an array of local, national, and international partners, hundreds of community programs and partner-sponsored events, daily discoveries at Jamestown and new scholarship, educational programs and classroom resources disseminated nationwide, state-of-the-art new facilities at Jamestown and nearby Williamsburg, extensive national and international media attention, a parade of top dignitaries, and so much more!

Throughout our history, Americans—and America's friends around the world—have joined Virginians in commemorating the vital beginning at Jamestown on May 13, 1607, when 104 courageous men and boys founded the first permanent English settlement in America. Each of the major commemorations has reflected the character of its time.[1]

The bicentennial anniversary in 1807 came during the administration of President Thomas Jefferson. Designated the "Grand National Jubilee," this commemoration was a five-day affair that included a parade, tent bazaar, theatrical productions, a regatta of sailing vessels in the James River, recitations of odes and orations by College of William and Mary students, religious observances in the Jamestown church graveyard, and a concluding dinner and toasts at Raleigh Tavern in Williamsburg.

In 1857, the celebration theme was America's progress from a tiny colony on the banks of the James River to a nation that stretched the breadth of the continent. Thousands watched as militia companies paraded on Jamestown Island and steamers with bright streamers lay anchored offshore. In keeping with the period's penchant for effusive oratory, former President

---

[1] For additional information on previous Jamestown commemorations, see Appendix 1 (Remarks of Commissioner Rives at the Commission's inaugural meeting on June 12, 2003); see also *The 350ᵗʰ Anniversary of Jamestown, 1607-1957,* Final Report to the President and Congress of the Jamestown-Williamsburg-Yorktown Celebration Commission (Washington, D.C.: U.S. Government Printing Office, 1958), pp. 4-13.

John Tyler, a native of nearby Charles City County, intoned for approximately two and a half hours about Jamestown's and Virginia's glorious history—roughly an hour of speech-making for each history-making century at Jamestown.

The Jamestown 300th anniversary commemoration in 1907 heralded America's emergence as a world power. In the era of the great world fairs, the Jamestown Ter-Centennial Exposition was held in Norfolk on the site of today's Norfolk Naval Base. President Theodore Roosevelt led the ceremonies and used the occasion to launch America's powerful new fleet on a round-the-world tour, signaling our nation's active engagement in international affairs. Other notable speakers during the exposition included Tuskegee Institute's Booker T. Washington and author Mark Twain. Meanwhile, on Jamestown Island, the Association for the Preservation of Virginia Antiquities (APVA)[2] and the federal government worked together to erect a protective seawall, excavate and preserve the sites of early statehouses and other buildings, construct a large obelisk called the "Tercentary Monument," and build a new Memorial Church over the foundation of the 1639 church.

The Jamestown Festival in 1957 yielded close federal and state collaboration in the Historic Triangle[3] and enhanced visitor facilities, including the Colonial Parkway—linking Jamestown, Williamsburg, and Yorktown—and Jamestown Festival Park, now the Commonwealth of Virginia's "Jamestown Settlement." The April-November program featured military reviews and fly-overs, ship and aircraft christenings, community-based heritage programs, an outdoor drama at Cape Henry, and a visit by Vice President Richard M. Nixon. The 1957 commemoration is best remembered for the visit to Jamestown by the youthful monarch of Great Britain, Queen Elizabeth II, who marked the settlement's 350th anniversary with her first state visit to the United States.

With that rich tradition and legacy, commemoration of Jamestown's 400th anniversary presented a rare opportunity and a monumental responsibility. At the state level, the Virginia

---

[2] The organization, founded in 1889, is known today as "APVA Preservation Virginia."

[3] The "Historic Triangle" refers to the compact area in southeastern Virginia that encompasses three crucial venues in American history—Jamestown, Williamsburg, and Yorktown—bordered on the north side by the York River and by the James River to the south.

General Assembly in 1996 designated the Jamestown-Yorktown Foundation as the lead agency for commemoration planning, and Virginia Senator Richard J. Holland, the Foundation chairman, appointed the "Celebration 2007 Steering Committee" chaired by Stuart W. Connock.[4] Virginia Governor George Allen launched the commemoration's 10-year countdown in his 1997 "State of the Commonwealth" address, calling on citizens and communities to become involved and to invite friends and relatives from around the nation and the world to "come home to Virginia."

In July 2000, Congressman Herbert H. Bateman (1-VA) and U.S. Senators John W. Warner and Charles S. Robb introduced legislation to create the federal Jamestown 400th Commemoration Commission. Congress enacted the measure, and President William J. Clinton signed the bill into law on December 23, 2000. In the spring of 2003, Secretary of the Interior Gale Norton appointed the Commission's chairman, Frank B. Atkinson of Hanover, Virginia, and its 15 other members.

The state Steering Committee began its work by holding 20 roundtables across the Commonwealth to hear from Virginia's diverse cultural and geographic communities about what the 400th anniversary commemoration should include. The roundtable meetings brought together more than 1,700 people and 250 organizations and yielded more than 10,000 suggestions. A consensus emerged that the commemoration should last a year or more, be inclusive and educational in character, encompass all parts of Virginia, and have national and international participation and impact.

Working jointly, state and federal planners later developed the thematic focus of the commemoration. The programs, events, and activities became known collectively as *America's 400th Anniversary* and commemorated both the voyage to Jamestown and the 400-year-old American odyssey that began there—truly, a *Journey that Changed the World.*

The dramatic times in which the commemoration occurred seemed to attest daily to the enduring and still-evolving legacies

---

[4] Stuart W. Connock was a former Virginia secretary of finance and longtime member of the Jamestown-Yorktown Foundation Board of Trustees, having served as the board's chairman until shortly before his appointment as chairman of the Jamestown 2007 Steering Committee.

of the Jamestown settlement, supplying the substance of the commemoration's message:

- With democracy advancing worldwide, a focus on representative government's American origins at Jamestown was essential;

- The settlement's entrepreneurial character likewise had special relevance given the contemporary emergence of dynamic global markets;

- The theme of exploration and discovery resonated as rapid-fire technological and scientific breakthroughs transformed life in the early 21st century; and

- The obstacles overcome in the 400 years since America's distinctive cultural diversity began at Jamestown provided an encouraging example of what perseverance and pursuit of principle can yield in an interconnected world.

Democracy, enterprise, exploration, and diversity thus became the primary subjects for illumination and reflection as *America's 400th Anniversary* cast new light upon Jamestown's legacies. This thematic mix ensured that the 400th anniversary program would not merely recall the past, but also would provide useful insights to inform the future.

Consistent with these ideas and messages, the Virginia commemoration committee changed its name from the "Celebration 2007 Steering Committee" to the "Jamestown 2007 Steering Committee," and planning participants referred to the anniversary program as a "commemoration" rather than a "celebration." The change in nomenclature was a gesture of respect for Virginia Indians' perspective on the commemoration, and it also reflected recognition that some aspects of the difficult beginning at Jamestown were appropriately regarded as occasions for solemn remembrance, quiet reflection, or prayerful thanksgiving rather than exuberant celebration. An attitude of solemnity was considered more appropriate, for example, in recalling the settlement's impact on the indigenous peoples of Virginia, the widespread suffering and loss of life among the earliest English settlers, and the oppression of Africans brought to the colony in chains. That these and other hardships, challenges, and threats have been overcome and are being overcome still—through fulfillment of America's founding ideals over the course of our four-centuries-old journey—was deemed a cause for celebration, and the word "celebration" was widely used in that context throughout the commemoration.

The commemoration planning fostered a remarkable array of collaborative relationships and partnerships. A bipartisan succession of Virginia governors, state lawmakers, and members of the Virginia congressional delegation provided indispensable support. Generous corporate sponsors donated resources. Organizations responsible for the Jamestown sites and other local attractions rolled up their sleeves and worked together. Congress, the White House, and a host of federal agencies joined state and local entities in lending expertise and support. An influential organizing committee was formed in the United Kingdom. Virginia's Indian tribes became actively engaged, as did African-American leaders. A rich variety of communities defined by geographic, ancestral, ethnic, and other bonds formed planning groups. Institutional partnerships were created, and a legion of selfless volunteers worked on a plethora of planning committees, task forces, and working groups.

A crucial development for the commemoration was the announcement in February 2006 that the Honorable Sandra Day O'Connor, a retired associate justice of the Supreme Court of the United States, would serve as the honorary chairperson of *America's 400th Anniversary*. A widely respected leader, ardent advocate of civics education and public service, and historic figure in her own right,[5] Justice O'Connor embodied the commemoration's themes and became its tireless champion.

No human enterprise of consequence succeeds without confronting challenges and surmounting hurdles, and this was true of the Jamestown quadricentennial commemoration. As planning began, numerous studies bore witness to the decline in contemporary America's historical literacy, and many national heritage sites reported sagging tourist visitation numbers. In the popular imagination, the most familiar images of early America—the *Mayflower* and Pilgrims—continued to suggest

---

[5] Appointed by President Ronald Reagan in 1981, Justice O'Connor became the first woman to serve on the nation's highest tribunal.

erroneously that English settlement in the New World first took root in New England. Academic content standards for schools across America tended to diminish or overlook events at Jamestown in Virginia.

The commemoration planning process was complicated by the presence of two adjacent Jamestown sites (Historic Jamestowne and Jamestown Settlement) with distinct management structures as well as the existence of multiple public and private commemoration planning groups. Uncertain levels of public and private financial support for the program posed another major challenge, as did the vigorous early debate over the commemoration's meaning and how best to convey it to statewide, national, and international audiences. In addition, Virginia's Indian tribes initially were ambivalent concerning participation in the commemoration.

The tragedies of September 11, 2001, and the ensuing battle against terrorism compelled commemoration planners to confront a host of new security issues and an entirely new dynamic in which to convene major events involving heads of state and other VIPs. Two years later, in September 2003, Hurricane Isabel slashed directly across Jamestown Island and the surrounding area on its way through Virginia, producing the costliest natural disaster in state history. Isabel's highly destructive winds and floodwaters damaged structures and collections at Historic Jamestowne and threatened the tight timeline for major facility improvements scheduled to be completed in time for the commemoration.

Numerous lesser challenges could be added to this list. The crucial fact is that none of this adversity markedly diminished the commemoration. Commemoration planners overcame organizational, logistical, and financial obstacles through goodwill and collaborative effort. Heirs to each of the cultures that came together at Jamestown joined in telling their stories. Neither the storm's fury nor the terrorists' treachery ultimately proved a material impediment. The commemoration's uplifting messages reached audiences in myriad ways: on television and the Internet, through national publications and international conferences, in the inspiring remarks of the President of the United States and Her Majesty, Queen Elizabeth II, and in the lessons of gifted teachers and the renditions of gifted performers.

Among the many indications of the Jamestown commemoration's success was a national survey conducted at the end of the program for the state's Jamestown 2007 organization. Nine of 10 respondents deemed Jamestown's founding to be an important or very important event, and 70 percent said that Jamestown's legacies continue to shape American society. These and other indications of increased awareness were products, at least in part, of intensive media coverage that produced more than 12 billion news impressions in the United States during the year-and-a-half-long commemorative program. The enhanced awareness was complemented by new archaeological discoveries and new scholarship and literature about Jamestown, raising hopes that the settlement's legacies would be treated fully and accurately in future historical and literary works.

Although "the history of our country did not begin on Cape Cod in 1620"—a historical truth that Vice President Richard Cheney observed to spirited applause at Jamestown in early 2007— America's Pilgrim iconography is unlikely to change anytime soon, nor would anyone wish to diminish the importance of the English settlements in New England. It is enough that the *America's 400ᵗʰ Anniversary* program gave people throughout our country a better understanding of Jamestown's pivotal part in our national saga and a truer sense of the profound impact made by the people and ideas that converged in Virginia beginning with the arrival of three small ships in May 1607.

Our national motto, *e pluribus unum*—"out of many, one"— captures the spirit that animated the Jamestown commemoration from the planning phase through the 18 frenzied months of programs and events. America's story is the triumph of unity amid diversity—of shared ideals emerging from varied backgrounds and perspectives. That, too, is the story of *America's 400ᵗʰ Anniversary*. Through the hearts and hands of many, the commemoration accomplished a singular tribute worthy of our past and relevant to our future. In both its planning and execution, the commemoration provided a vivid reminder that the bold journey begun 400 years ago has brought together people of goodwill, and is still changing the world for the better.

CHAPTER 1

America's 400ᵗʰ Anniversary:
Arranging an Extraordinary Commemoration

As this narrative and the companion report of Virginia's Jamestown 2007 organization will reflect, *America's 400ᵗʰ Anniversary* produced many moving moments and memorable images:

- *The President of the United States giving voice to Jamestown's transcendent message of human freedom and then climbing atop the music conductor's platform to lead a 400-person orchestra in a rousing rendition of "The Stars and Stripes, Forever";*

- *Her Majesty, Queen Elizabeth II, addressing the oldest continuous legislative body in the Western Hemisphere and celebrating the world's most consequential collaboration between free nations;*

- *The Chief Justice of the United States and his counterpart from England and Wales, averring the 400-year-old settlement's crucial role in developing the rule of law, and placing a memorial on the banks of the James River to honor that monumental contribution;*

- *Dramatic stories and stunning objects emerging daily from the archaeological dig at Historic Jamestowne, refuting myth after myth, including the biggest myth of all—that the James Fort and its tales were long ago lost to the river.*

- *Thousands of excited school children seeing history come alive aboard replica ships, in a re-created triangular fort, along the nearby streets of revolutionary Williamsburg, and—through the aid of technology—in classrooms across America;*

- *Delegates from around the world, architects and advocates for a new wave of democratic development, optimistically exploring how to bring the 400-year-old journey begun at Jamestown to their own distant lands;*

- *Virginia's Indian tribal representatives on an official visit to England, sharing their Native dress and dance, being received with dignity and affection in a Mother Country that officially recognized the tribes' sovereignty more than three centuries earlier and honors it still;*

- *More than 10,000 African-American leaders and activists from around the United States gathering to reflect on the "State of the Black Union," proudly recalling the presence of "Africans at Jamestown before there were Pilgrims at Plymouth," and illuminating an imprint on America that predated even the founding promise of liberty and justice for all;*

- *The Godspeed, spreading word of the commemoration at portside festivals along the East Coast of the United States, and sailing into New York harbor for Independence Day observances under Lady Liberty's gaze;*

- *The Magna Carta and treasures from the "World of 1607," loaned by leading museums around the globe, inspiring the awe of visitors to Jamestown Settlement's new galleries throughout the anniversary year;*

- *General Washington atop his large white horse, entering majestically as the Williamsburg Symphonia Orchestra and other talented performers pay tribute to America's armed forces on the 225ᵗʰ anniversary of the Yorktown victory;*

- *Artisans, merchants, and dignitaries from Virginia and Kent, England, on the National Mall in Washington, D.C., highlighting their cultural traditions, displaying their crafts and wares, and celebrating their historic and continuing ties as part of the popular annual Smithsonian Folklife Festival;*

- *The* Discovery, *returning to England in time for the 400ᵗʰ anniversary of the three ships' departure on December 19, 1606, and Americans and Britons gathering to mark that milestone in Middle Temple where visionaries created and capitalized the Virginia Company; and*

- *Replicas of the three tiny ships, navigating rough seas and emerging ghost-like from the thick fog off Cape Henry to honor the 400ᵗʰ anniversary of their first landing on April 26, 1607.*

As difficult as it is to describe adequately powerful moments and evocative images such as these and many others, it is harder still to convey the enormous time, talent, energy, and effort invested over a prolonged period in planning them. In this chapter, we strive to summarize those contributions. In keeping with our charge, we focus on the work of the Federal Commission.

When Congress and the President brought the Federal Commission into being in 2000, collaboration already was underway between federal and state commemoration planners. The Federal Commission's creation itself was a product of such cooperation. Aware of the experience of the 1957 Jamestown commemoration, Stuart W. Connock, chairman of the Jamestown 2007 Steering Committee, initiated efforts to have the federal government establish a commemorative commission. Steering Committee members and National Park Service representatives then worked together to craft the legislation, helped coordinate its introduction by U.S. Senators Warner and Robb and Congressman Bateman, and assisted in securing its passage. After consulting with Virginia Governors James Gilmore and Mark Warner and members of the Virginia congressional delegation, Interior Secretary Gale Norton took steps in 2001 and 2002 to constitute the federal Jamestown commission according to its statutory mandate. Interior Department and National Park Service officials acted to secure the Commission's initial financial resources and arranged for the Jamestown-Yorktown Foundation and the Association for the Preservation of Virginia Antiquities to serve as custodians of the appropriated funds while the Commission was in formation.[6]

On January 10, 2003, Secretary Norton announced the membership of the Commission: Frank B. Atkinson (chairman); Stephen R. Adkins; Warren M. Billings; Thomas J. Bliley, Jr.; Nancy N. Campbell; H. Benson Dendy III, Suzanne Owen Flippo, Michael P. Gleason; J. Steven Griles; Ann W. Loomis; Fran P. Mainella; John L. Nau III; Daphne Maxwell Reid; Alexander (Sandy) Rives; M. Jordan Saunders; and Malfourd W. Trumbo.[7] Secretary Norton then convened the members for a swearing-in ceremony and an organizational meeting in Washington, D.C., on June 12, 2003. "In many ways," said Secretary Norton to the commissioners at their first meeting,

> the work of the Commission will be similar to the work of those stalwart explorers nearly four centuries ago (though I expect not to hear reports of 80 percent casualties among you a few years from now).... The 104 who set sail for Virginia in 1606 were comprised of volunteers—citizens who, like you, took up the task of their own free will for the improvement of their lives and the lives of others.... [S]uccess came only with the cooperation and assistance of others, partnerships that you as well will establish. And, of course, the Jamestown colony could not have succeeded

---

[6] Philip G. Emerson, executive director of the Jamestown-Yorktown Foundation, Elizabeth S. Kostelny, executive director of APVA Preservation Virginia, and their capable staffs provided vital early and continuing assistance to the Federal Commission on a range of important administrative and programmatic matters.

[7] Two other commissioners, Mary A. Bomar and P. Daniel Smith, were appointed later to fill vacancies. A list of Federal Commission officers, members, and senior staff, with their periods of service, is provided in Appendix 2. The officers and members of the Jamestown 2007 Steering Committee also are listed in Appendix 2.

without the backing of the Virginia Company of London. So, too, today, four centuries later, will the involvement of the private sector prove to be critical to your efforts.... The road ahead is indeed a challenging one, with the eyes of the nation and indeed the world upon you. I close this morning with a reminder to you, taken from the [Virginia Company's original instructions to the Jamestown settlers]: "Lastly and chiefly, the way to prosper and obtain good success is to make yourselves of one mind for the good of your country and your own."

In drafting the Federal Commission's statutory mandate, commemoration planners were mindful of the significant preparations already underway for several years through the work of the state Steering Committee, and they sought to craft a complementary rather than duplicative role for the new federal panel.[8] Among the 16 appointees to the Federal Commission were persons who had participated prominently in those earlier efforts under the Steering Committee's auspices[9] and others with extensive experience in collaborative public-private and federal-state endeavors related to historical preservation, interpretation, and education.[10] As a result, by legislation and the disposition of its members, the Federal Commission was committed from the outset to an approach that complemented the work of Virginia's commemoration planning organization and other partners

---

[8] The full text of Public Law 106-565 (The Jamestown 400ᵗʰ Commemoration Commission Act of 2000) is set out in Appendix 3.

[9] Commissioners Atkinson, Dendy, Flippo, Rives, and Trumbo were current or former members of the Jamestown 2007 Steering Committee and/or the Jamestown-Yorktown Foundation Board of Trustees. Atkinson was vice chairman of the Steering Committee until March 2004, when he resigned that post to concentrate on his responsibilities as Federal Commission chairman. Flippo chaired the Steering Committee's Program and Events Committee and its Creative Advisory Group throughout the commemoration's planning process.

[10] Commissioner Adkins was Chief of the Chickahominy Indians. Commissioners Billings (APVA Preservation Virginia), Campbell (National Trust for Historic Preservation), Nau (*Preserve America* initiative), and Saunders (Saunders Trust for American History) had extensive experience in the referenced preservation organizations and endeavors, among others. Commissioners Griles, Loomis, Mainella, and Rives (and, later, Bomar and Smith) were federal officials whose work included significant historic preservation and educational activities, often in collaboration with other governmental entities and private organizations. Commissioners Atkinson, Billings, Gleason, and Reid had written or produced print and electronic works concerning history and government and interacted regularly with historical and educational organizations.

while fulfilling the Commission's own distinctive national and international mission.

The Federal Commission devoted its first year to an intensive organizational and strategic planning process that featured five full meetings of the Commission, including a September 2003 joint meeting with the state Steering Committee,[11] and dozens of working group meetings and conference calls. The Commission adopted bylaws, established administrative procedures and financial accounts, elected officers, constituted committees,[12] engaged a planning consultant, and opened an office in Williamsburg.[13] Among the officers, only Chairman Atkinson's position was specified by statute, so the Commission through its bylaws created two vice chairmanships and the positions of secretary and treasurer. Members elected Commissioners Campbell and Dendy as the vice chairs and Commissioners Reid and Gleason as secretary and treasurer, respectively. The Commission engaged H. Edward (Chip) Mann as its planning consultant, and, at the conclusion of the year-long strategic planning process, employed him as the Commission's executive director—a position he retained through the conclusion of the commemoration.

In May 2004, the Commission adopted its Strategic Plan, a detailed blueprint to which it adhered closely for the duration of the commemoration. After noting that Congress had created the Federal Commission to help plan and execute "an anniversary commemoration of national and international scope," the Commission's strategic document summarized the responsibilities that had been assigned to the Commission by statute:

---

[11] At a reception in the Great Hall of the Wren Building at the College of William and Mary following the joint meeting on September 10, 2003, Robert V. Hatcher, Jr., a member of the Jamestown 2007 Steering Committee, presented to Chairman Atkinson the gavel that had been used by his father, Robert V. Hatcher, Sr., when he chaired the federal commission for the Jamestown 350th commemoration in 1957. During the Jamestown 400th Commemoration Commission's final meeting in December 2008, Chairman Atkinson presented the gavel to Commissioner Smith for retention in the Commission's archives at Colonial National Historical Park until the 450th anniversary commemoration.

[12] Appendix 4 contains the Commission's roster of committees and liaison groups.

[13] The Federal Commission's offices were co-located with Virginia's Jamestown 2007 organization at the William Byrd II House at 412 W. Francis Street in Williamsburg from summer 2003 until September 2005, when the Commission's permanent offices were established nearby at 424 Scotland Street. Both offices were leased from the Colonial Williamsburg Foundation.

ensuring a suitable national observance of the Jamestown 2007 anniversary; facilitating international involvement in the anniversary observances; assisting in ensuring that anniversary observances are inclusive and appropriately recognize the experiences of all people present in 17th-century Jamestown; assisting in developing anniversary programs and activities and in ensuring an excellent visitor experience at Jamestown; assisting in the development of heritage tourism and economic benefits resulting from the commemoration; and supporting and facilitating marketing initiatives, such as issuance of commemorative coins and stamps, that raise awareness of Jamestown and the commemoration.

The Commission's planning document also recited commemoration preparations underway under the auspices of the state Steering Committee, including plans for a series of signature events and community-based programs backed by a commitment of significant financial support from the Commonwealth of Virginia.

After evaluating its mission, ongoing planning efforts, and likely resource and partnering opportunities, the Federal Commission adopted a blueprint in May 2004 that embraced six primary program components and specified various organizational partners. That plan contains the most succinct summary of the Commission's intentions and, now, its accomplishments. Accordingly, its major elements are set out here at length:

(A) Securing Jamestown's Legacies through Education

[The Commission will carry out a] set of interrelated, mutually reinforcing national education initiatives designed to heighten awareness and appreciation of the legacies of Jamestown among national and international audiences, [including] development and nationwide dissemination of elementary and secondary school curriculum related to Jamestown and its distinctive role in American history and government. The Commission anticipates reaching agreement for a key strategic partnership with the University of Virginia Center for Politics ("CFP"), which will take primary responsibility for development of elementary and secondary civics-related curriculum linking the origins of representative government and other principles at Jamestown with the founding of United States, the experiences of various cultures and groups in gaining full access to American democracy, and the contemporary practice of politics and governance (including practical application learning). CFP will also facilitate the marketing of these educational materials to school teachers nationwide, including development of a web portal through which approved educational resources relevant to Jamestown in multiple disciplines can be accessed. CFP will play a coordinating role and work collaboratively through a Curriculum Advisory Committee with other Jamestown-related organizations providing educational content. CFP will also coordinate with the Jamestown 2007 office in integrating its civics-related curriculum with the curriculum and programming of [the *Jamestown Live!* national webcast], a Jamestown 2007 signature event planned for fall 2006.

(B) Exploring the Future of Democracy

The Federal Commission will assume lead sponsorship of the "Future of Democracy" conference series. Since America traces its roots to Jamestown, and the advance of democracy in our age traces its roots to America, Jamestown's 400th anniversary is a fitting occasion to engage scholars and practitioners from across America and around the world in a seminal discussion of the future of democracy and an exploration of the values and conditions that make it possible for men and women of varied nationalities, cultures, religions, backgrounds, and ideals to live together in freedom.

A [World] Forum on the Future of Democracy will be held at Jamestown and Williamsburg, Virginia, in the fall of 2007. Plans call for past and present American leaders from the public and private sectors to be joined by foreign dignitaries, architects of emerging democracies, scholars, and practitioners in a multi-day explication of the elements necessary for democracy to prosper in America and around the world in the 21st century. The Federal Commission will partner with Virginia's Jamestown 2007 Steering Committee, the Colonial Williamsburg Foundation, the College of William and Mary, and other organizations to plan and execute this high-profile Forum.

The [World] Forum in Jamestown-Williamsburg will be the culmination of a year-long series of conferences held at other Virginia sites addressing particular topics relevant to the future of democracy. These conferences will be hosted by sponsoring organizations other than the Federal Commission, but the Federal Commission will play a coordinating role. Plans for the series currently include opening the series in fall 2006 with an International Youth Summit on Democracy sponsored by the University of Virginia Center for Politics.... Another conference during the year-long series will focus on the rule of law, constitutionalism, and individual rights.... and will be held at the University of Richmond.... In addition, the Mercatus Center at George Mason University has expressed interest in organizing and hosting a conference on market freedom and democracy as part of the series. Other conference sponsors and sites will be identified through a forthcoming public solicitation by the Democracy Conference Committee. A Democracy Program Planning Council, consisting of the Commission's Democracy Conference Committee plus key sponsors/partners, has already convened to begin planning.

(C) Celebrating the Historic and Continuing US–UK Ties

The Federal Commission will play a prominent role in developing, implementing and coordinating commemorative programs and events that highlight the historic and continuing ties between the United States and the United Kingdom. These ties will be highlighted and reinforced through visits to this country by members of the British Royal Family and British governmental officials as well as other prominent British citizens, and through British-American collaboration on commemorative events on both sides of the Atlantic. This effort is a joint responsibility of the Federal Commission and the state Steering Committee, and to that end a Joint US-UK Planning Committee has been formed and is operational. The Joint Committee will work to enhance the relationship between U.S. commemoration planners and organizations in the U.K. who can provide resources, support, and participation related to commemorative activities, including especially the [democracy] conference series, [an event in] the U.K. in late 2006 commemorating the launch of the voyage to Virginia, the America's Anniversary Weekend program in May 2007, and British participation in the Smithsonian's Folklife Festival 2007. In addition, the Joint Committee is working with the Bush administration, the Warner (Virginia) administration, and appropriate authorities and individuals in the U.K. to establish appropriate government-to-government dialogue, to facilitate formation of an official commemoration planning group in the U.K., and to extend appropriate invitations. An official planning mission to the U.K. by Federal Commission members and other relevant representatives and individuals is envisioned for fall 2004.

(D) Ensuring an Inclusive Commemoration

For the quadricentennial commemoration to be a truly inclusive event, the story of Jamestown needs to reflect a palpable geographic and demographic diversity.   Offering communities who are part of the Jamestown saga an opportunity to tell their stories in their voices will enrich the commemoration and add immeasurably to its historical record and legacies. The goal is to convey all relevant history accurately, not to dwell on mistakes of the past, but to highlight the accomplishments of the past 400 years and call attention to the manner in which hardships were overcome and the extent of the progress that has been achieved.

The Federal Commission will give priority to assisting all planning organizations in reaching out to assure that appropriately varied perspectives relevant to Jamestown and its legacies are represented in the programs, events, projects, and interpretive materials and exhibits developed for the commemoration.   The Commission's outreach initiatives committee has ... proposed that two advisory committees—one comprised of Virginia Indians and the other of African Americans—be created to advise federal and state commemoration planners.   These panels will have as their primary goals to identify effective methods for telling their stories and highlighting their legacies, including developing plans for a Virginia Indian–focused signature event and an African American–focused signature event, as well as providing input to help ensure that all signature events and commemorative programs are appropriately inclusive in content as well as participation. It is envisioned that the Federal Commission and the state Steering Committee will collaboratively assign appropriate staff resources to serve as liaisons to these advisory bodies and other constituent organizations.

(E) Spreading the Word Nationally and Internationally

[The] Federal Commission will focus on the development of proactive national and international media strategies that call attention to commemorative programs, events, and the legacies of Jamestown. The [Commission] will have responsibility for providing media relations and marketing support for the national educational initiatives, the "Future of Democracy" conference series, and the other key programs and projects that are being led by the Federal Commission.

The [Federal Commission's] communications committee has met twice to review the public relations and marketing efforts of the key state and private partners involved in commemoration planning and programs. As a result of this review, the committee has recommended formation of a communications task force that includes representatives from Jamestown 2007, the National Park Service, APVA Preservation Virginia, the Virginia Tourism Corporation, the Jamestown-Yorktown Foundation, the Colonial Williamsburg Foundation, the [Greater Williamsburg Area Chamber and Tourism Alliance], and the [Historic Triangle] Host Committee, among others, plus Federal Commission and state Steering Committee staff. The communications task force will provide the necessary coordination for development of an umbrella plan featuring an effective, interwoven strategy to communicate both the stories and legacies of Jamestown and news about the 400th anniversary commemoration....

(F) Facilitating Federal Cooperation and Support

The Federal Commission ... will take the lead in communicating with decision-makers in federal agencies. The goal is to ensure maximum participation in and optimal support for the commemoration by the three branches of the United States Government, to the benefit of all commemoration planning partners.

Specific tasks associated with this role include close coordination with the state Steering Committee (Jamestown 2007 office) and other key partners in identifying appropriate resources, expertise, and personnel needed in connection with the commemoration. The range of needs includes infrastructure improvements, logistical support, security, programmatic support, and diplomatic outreach, among other topics. The Commission's federal participation committee has undertaken to inventory these commemoration-related needs and match them with resources known to be available from federal departments and agencies. The committee has developed an awareness strategy to communicate commemoration goals and plans to as many components of the federal government as possible through briefings and other methods of communication. The committee is also focused on identifying and cultivating funding sources, and will assist in facilitating the submission of qualified proposals for federal grants, as well as generating research and support for federal appropriations requested on behalf of 2007 commemoration planners.

A related goal of the committee is to promote federal support for the development of the permanent federal and private facilities and programs at Historic Jamestowne as a lasting legacy of the 400ᵗʰ anniversary commemoration, and to assist other federal efforts, such as the issuance of a commemorative coin by the United States Mint, that will inure to the benefit of all of the Jamestown sites and their ongoing education and research programs.

Virginia's commemoration leadership and other Jamestown organizations and partners welcomed the Federal Commission's strategic plan, especially the Commission's assumption of lead responsibility for the democracy forum signature event, educational curriculum/website development, British commemorative initiatives (including the *Royal Visit* invitation), and federal government liaison activities (including coordination with the White House). In 2005, state and federal commemoration planners executed a memorandum of understanding that embodied this division of responsibility. The agreement also recognized shared federal-state responsibility in key areas such as cultural outreach, promotional communications, and fundraising activities. As a structure for ongoing collaboration and coordination, the agreement provided for a Federal Commission member to serve as a representative on the newly formed Jamestown 2007 Management Committee. Chaired by Virginia Senator Thomas K. Norment, Jr., of James City County, the Management Committee provided day-to-day managerial direction to the Commonwealth of Virginia's commemorative planning efforts, including the state's Jamestown 2007 office.[14] These key programmatic and organizational decisions established the essential framework that guided the commemoration to a highly successful conclusion.

As part of its strategic plan, the Federal Commission resolved to keep its administrative costs low, avoid duplication of staff functions already covered by the state's Jamestown 2007 office, and focus available resources on programs to the greatest extent possible. As a result, the Commission created only two major staff positions—the executive director and the democracy conference project director[15]—and worked extensively through experienced vendors and organizational partners to execute its

---

[14] Senator Norment represented the Jamestown-Williamsburg area in the Senate of Virginia and was co-chairman of the Jamestown-Yorktown Foundation, the state agency responsible for planning the commemoration on behalf of the Commonwealth. The other Management Committee members were Stuart W. Connock and Colin G. Campbell, the chair and vice chair, respectively, of the Jamestown 2007 Steering Committee. Federal Commission Chairman Atkinson served on the Management Committee initially and then assumed *ex officio* status, with Vice Chair Dendy taking on responsibility as the Federal Commission's permanent representative. Jeanne Zeidler and H. Edward Mann, the executive directors of Jamestown 2007 and the Federal Commission, respectively, also participated in the Management Committee's meetings.

[15] Drema L. Johnson served as the democracy conference project director. See Chapter 5. In addition, valuable administrative support was provided to the Commission by Mary Jones, Lisa Perez, and April Rudolph.

programmatic plans. As detailed elsewhere in this report, the Commission established significant vendor relationships with the University of Virginia Center for Politics (for educational website and curriculum development), Prosody Creative Services (for creative/production work on the democracy conference project), Broadcast Partners LLC (for nationally broadcast historical vignettes about Jamestown), and several communications firms.

Aside from its comprehensive partnership with Virginia's Jamestown 2007 organization, the Commission's most far-reaching partnering relationships were with the Jamestown 2007 British Committee, the Colonial Williamsburg Foundation, the College of William and Mary, the National Geographic Society, and the nine other colleges and universities in Virginia that hosted democracy-related conferences as part of the Commission's international conference series.[16] The Commission also worked closely with the permanent organizations that administer the adjacent sites at Jamestown (the National Park Service and APVA Preservation Virginia at Historic Jamestowne, and the Jamestown-Yorktown Foundation at Jamestown Settlement) and with Jamestown 2007's Historic Triangle Host Committee and local government representatives.

The Commission's ability to allocate resources to programming rather than administration also was enhanced through commissioners' considerable commitment of their personal time and expertise. Chairman Atkinson and Vice Chairs Campbell and Dendy were extensively involved in the Commission's day-to-day operations and oversight, and Commissioners Gleason and Rives, who co-chaired the administration and planning committee, worked directly with Commission staff on budget, finance, contracting, and other administrative matters. In light of the Interior Department's jurisdiction over the Commission and the National Park Service's special competence in matters related to federal advisory commissions, the Commission relied heavily on those federal entities for guidance on ethics compliance, procurement, budget requests, audit standards, and numerous other administrative matters. Commissioner Rives, who served as the Park Service's Jamestown 400ᵗʰ project

---

[16] For a description of the university-based conferences that comprised the International Conference Series on the Foundations and Future of Democracy, see Chapter 5.

director through September 2007, played an integral role in these activities, and Commissioners Griles, Mainella, Bomar, and Smith also provided assistance at key junctures in their capacities as federal officials. Commissioner Loomis, who served as legislative director and chief of staff to U.S. Senator John Warner during the Commission's work, spearheaded successful efforts on Capitol Hill to secure funding for the Commission. As detailed throughout this report, other members of the Commission assumed substantive responsibilities as co-chairs of the programmatic committees that directed the Commission's work. As a result, the Commission operated less like an advisory body and more as a hands-on working group, with commissioners laboring daily alongside the Commission's able and dedicated executive director, democracy conference project director, administrative support staff, vendors, and partner organizations.

Another important decision made in the Commission's strategic planning process—and endorsed by the Jamestown 2007 Management Committee in its memorandum of understanding with the Commission—was the decision to integrate federal and state fundraising efforts. Before creation of the Federal Commission (albeit with the active support and assistance of various volunteer leaders who later became Federal Commission members), the state Jamestown 2007 organization formed the not-for-profit Jamestown 2007, Inc., to receive and expend donated funds, instituted the "Founding Colony Sponsor" corporate giving program, and began outreach to potential donors. Its efforts yielded success in July 2004, when Norfolk Southern Corporation announced a multimillion-dollar commitment to the commemoration as the first Founding Colony Sponsor.[17] Once the Federal Commission was fully operational, several of its members actively assisted Jamestown 2007's fundraising efforts, including identifying and contacting potential donors. Under the approach adopted by state and federal commemoration planners, the state's Jamestown 2007 organization engaged professional corporate fundraising assistance and managed the program; Federal Commission

---

[17] A member of Norfolk Southern Corporation's executive team, Dr. Robert Martinez, played a leadership role in commemoration planning. A former Virginia secretary of transportation, Martinez chaired Jamestown 2007's Logistics Committee and served as a member of the Federal Commission's Democracy Program Planning Council (see Chapter 5). He was instrumental in Norfolk Southern's decision to become the commemoration's first Founding Colony Sponsor.

Federal Commission members join U.S. Secretary of the Interior Gale Norton (center) for the Commission's inaugural meeting (Washington, DC, June 12, 2003) (from left to right: Suzanne Owen Flippo; Alexander L. (Sandy) Rives; Ann W. Loomis; Fran P. Mainella; J. Steven Griles; Secretary Norton; Frank B. Atkinson (Chairman); Michael P. Gleason (Treasurer); Stephen R. Adkins; H. Benson Dendy III (Vice Chair); Daphne Maxwell Reid (Secretary))

Chairman Atkinson and State Steering Committee Chairman Stuart W. Connock assemble with commemoration leaders on September 18, 2007, following the America's 400th Anniversary finale, the World Forum on the Future of Democracy (first row, from left to right: Federal Commission Executive Director H. Edward (Chip) Mann; Commissioner Flippo; Democracy Conference Project Director Drema L. Johnson; Chairman Atkinson; Chairman Connock; Vice Chair Dendy; back row, from left to right: Federal Commission Office Manager Lisa Perez; Commissioner Warren M. Billings; Federal Commission Vice Chair Nancy N. Campbell; Jamestown 2007 Steering Committee Vice Chair Colin G. Campbell; Commissioner Malfourd Whitney (Bo) Trumbo; Commissioner Adkins; Jamestown 2007 British Committee Treasurer Alex King; Commissioner Reid)

Journalist Gwen Ifill (center), host of the Jamestown Live! educational webcast on November 9, 2006, is joined by commemoration leaders on the program's set at Jamestown Settlement (from left to right: Jamestown 2007 Executive Director Jeanne L. Zeidler, State Senator Thomas K. Norment, Jr. (Chairman of the Jamestown 2007 Management Committee); Vice Chair Dendy; State Steering Committee Vice Chair Campbell)

Chairman Atkinson discusses plans for America's Anniversary Weekend *with President George W. Bush at the White House Correspondents Association dinner on April 21, 2007, as Bob Deans (left), author of* The River Where America Began, *looks on*

Commissioner Rives delivers remarks at Cape Henry, site of the Jamestown settlers' first landing in Virginia, at ceremonies on April 26, 2007, marking the 400th anniversary of the landing

Commissioner Reid speaks during the State of the Black Union signature event (Hampton University, February 9, 2007)

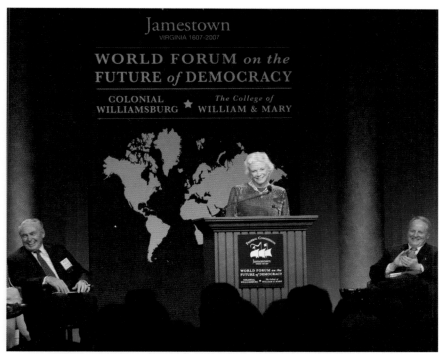

Justice Sandra Day O'Connor, Honorary Chairperson of America's 400th Anniversary, *addresses the opening ceremony of the* World Forum on the Future of Democracy *(Colonial Williamsburg, September 16, 2007)*

Senator Norment addresses the World Forum of the Future of Democracy *(Colonial Williamsburg, September 17, 2007)*

Chief Kenneth Adams of the Upper Mattaponi Indians delivers remarks at America's Anniversary Weekend *(Anniversary Park, May 13, 2007)*

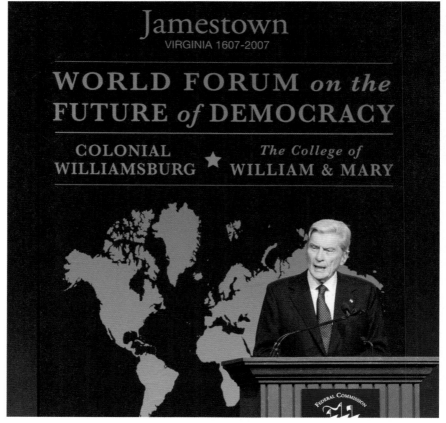

U.S. Senator John W. Warner, sponsor of legislation creating the Federal Commission, addresses the World Forum on the Future of Democracy *(Colonial Williamsburg, September 16, 2007)*

Ken Ashby (center) and Maris Segal, Executive Producers of America's 400th Anniversary, and other senior members of the Prosody Creative Services team celebrate the success of the commemoration's final signature event (Colonial Williamsburg, September 18, 2007)

Representatives of Virginia Indian tribes perform traditional dance in Native regalia for Gravesham festival-goers during the tribes' historic mission and educational outreach in England, July 2006

Her Majesty, Queen Elizabeth II, tours the re-created fort at Jamestown Settlement on May 4, 2007, accompanied by (from left to right) Virginia Governor Timothy M. Kaine, Vice President Richard B. Cheney, and Jamestown-Yorktown Foundation Executive Director Philip G. Emerson

President George W. Bush directs the 400-piece Anniversary Orchestra after delivering remarks at America's Anniversary Weekend *(Anniversary Park, May 13, 2007)*

The Commonwealth of Virginia's replica ship Godspeed sails past the Statue of Liberty on the way to Independence Day ceremonies during its 2006 promotional tour of major East Coast seaports

Commissioner Flippo prepares to honor the original Jamestown voyagers with a memorial wreath at Virginia Quay, near the site from which the first settlers departed 400 years earlier (Blackwall, England, December 19, 2006)

Governor Kaine delivers memorable remarks at Middle Temple in London during the Federal Commission's gala dinner on December 19, 2006, marking the 400th anniversary of the launch of the three ships bound for Jamestown

Federal Commission members and guests on hand for the Democracy Conference Series opening ceremony at the University of Virginia enjoy one of many lighthearted moments during the commemoration (commissioners pictured from left to right: Chairman Atkinson; Commissioner Loomis; Commissioner Adkins (standing); Commissioner Reid; also pictured, seated at right: Democracy Program Planning Council Chairman Timothy J. Sullivan)

members participated in prospective donor outreach; and the Jamestown 2007 Management Committee allocated a portion of the donated funds to help support the Federal Commission's programs.[18]

The joint endeavor proved successful. Two other organizations —the Colonial Williamsburg Foundation, Inc., and Verizon Communications, Inc.—joined Norfolk Southern as Founding Colony Sponsors, and 11 additional organizations lent generous support to Jamestown 2007 at lower giving levels.[19] The Federal Commission played a central role in Verizon's decision in March 2006 to become a top-level sponsor of the commemoration, and the Commission also attracted designated support for its own programs from Lockheed-Martin Corporation, CONSOL Energy and CNX Gas Corporation, and McGuireWoods LLP. The College of William and Mary Foundation, Carnegie Corporation of New York, and Rockefeller Brothers Fund provided grants to support the *World Forum on the Future of Democracy*, and the Colonial Williamsburg Foundation provided expertise and in-kind aid to the *World Forum* in addition to its contributions as a Founding Colony Sponsor. Finally, the Jamestown 2007 British Committee funded commemorative activities in the United Kingdom through a separate fundraising effort. Collectively, corporations and other private organizations provided more than $12,600,000 in funding to *America's 400th Anniversary*, with the resources supporting the programmatic initiatives of all of the planning organizations.[20]

While the commemoration attracted significant backing from the private sector, the Federal Commission nevertheless relied heavily on governmental appropriations and grants for its operations and programming. The Interior Department's

---

[18] Contributions from Jamestown 2007 primarily supported the Federal Commission's democracy conference series and its work with British commemoration planners. Jamestown 2007 also expended funds directly on activities recommended in the Federal Commission's strategic plan, including staff positions that supported the work of the Virginia Indian and African American Advisory Councils, communications services, and administrative activities.

[19] Jamestown 2007 sponsors included: Anheuser-Busch Companies, Inc. (Chesapeake Donor); Philip Morris USA, James City County, AirTran Airways, SunTrust Bank, PLC, Dominion, and Ferguson Enterprises, Inc./Wolseley PLC (Legacy Sponsors); TowneBank, City of Poquoson, Rutherfoord Insurance, and Target Corporation (Participating Sponsors and Contributors).

[20] Apart from the private funds donated for commemoration events and programming, Jamestown-Yorktown Foundation, Inc. and APVA Preservation Virginia conducted highly successful capital campaigns to fund major facilities development and exhibits at Jamestown Settlement and Historic Jamestowne, respectively.

annual appropriation regularly included an allocation for Federal Commission operating costs during 2001-2008. The United States Department of Education made a grant to the Federal Commission in 2005-2006 to support development and dissemination of Jamestown-related curriculum, and the Bureau of Educational and Cultural Affairs of the United States Department of State provided significant grant funding in 2006-2007 for the *World Forum on the Future of Democracy*. In addition to the support of Bush administration officials, this federal funding was made possible through the active efforts of U.S. Senator John Warner, U.S. Representatives JoAnn Davis (1-VA) and Frank Wolf (10-VA), and other members of the Virginia congressional delegation and their staffs. Additional funding for the *World Forum* was provided by the Commonwealth of Virginia in 2007 through legislative appropriations and a discretionary allocation approved by Governor Timothy M. Kaine. Federal, state and local agencies, state colleges and universities, and other governmental instrumentalities also provided extensive expertise and unreimbursed services to the commemoration, including the Federal Commission's initiatives.

During the five-year course of its work, the Federal Commission spent approximately $5.4 million, with the private sector supplying 10 percent of the funding.[21] Independent audits confirmed that the Commission expended all of its funds in accordance with applicable federal guidelines and the Commission's additional procedural safeguards.[22] The Commission also succeeded in completing each of its programmatic undertakings on time and within budget. As it concluded its work in 2008, the Commission issued more than $500,000 in grants to prominent governmental or not-for-profit entities that pledged to continue important aspects of the Commission's work. The funded "Legacy Projects" included ongoing operation and promotion of Jamestown-related websites disseminating educational curriculum and materials on democratic development, publication of the *Jamestown Commentaries on the Foundations and Future of Democracy*, production of print and electronic materials describing the 400th anniversary commemoration, distribution of commemorative

---

[21] Appendix 5 contains a summary of the Commission's receipts and disbursements.

[22] Goodman and Associates provided financial review and audit services to the Commission. Successive reviews were conducted in fall 2006, winter 2007-2008, and at the conclusion of the Commission's work in late 2008.

plaques to island nations visited by the first English voyagers en route to Jamestown, ongoing archaeological investigation of James Fort and Chief Powhatan's headquarters at Werowocomoco, development of plans for ongoing dialogues on democracy and international exchange, and a variety of educational initiatives highlighting lessons from the Jamestown experience, Captain John Smith's voyages of discovery in the Chesapeake watershed, and post-2007 Jamestown anniversaries.

Among the greatest legacies of the Jamestown commemoration was the development of new and dramatically enhanced visitor facilities and related resources at Historic Jamestowne and Jamestown Settlement. Operated by the National Park Service and APVA Preservation Virginia, Historic Jamestowne provided anniversary-year visitors with an eye-popping look at the active archaeological dig on the site of James Fort and a view of Jamestown Island, which served as the Virginia colony's capital from 1607 until 1699. A new visitor center, interpretive "archaearium," and archaeological research and collection facility were among $54 million in federally and privately funded improvements completed in time for the commemoration. Immediately northwest of Jamestown Island, the Commonwealth of Virginia's Jamestown Settlement—itself a legacy of the 350th anniversary commemoration in 1957—treated visitors to a powerful "living history" experience, with replicas of the three ships that brought the first settlers to Jamestown, a riverside interpretive area, and re-creations of the James Fort and a Powhatan Indian village. A new education wing, visitor reception facility, and dramatically expanded museum with collections devoted to each of the cultures that converged at early Jamestown were among the $70 million in Jamestown Settlement improvements accomplished by the Commonwealth and private donors in the run-up to the *America's 400th Anniversary* observances.

Federal Commission members played vital roles in helping to achieve these ambitious and timely capital improvements, which not only impressed anniversary-year event-goers but promised to attract and inform Jamestown visitors for decades to come. As a federal entity, the Commission's purview encompassed the capital improvements at Historic Jamestowne, and several Commission members participated directly in those efforts.[23]   Other commissioners worked with private and state organizations to secure financial support for the enhancements at Jamestown Settlement. Acting in various Jamestown-related capacities over a number of years, commissioners also devoted considerable effort to promoting more effective collaboration between the two Jamestown sites. They assisted significantly in securing ticketing and transportation arrangements that created a more seamless visitor experience by connecting the two complementary attractions and linking them to a new regional visitor center established at Colonial Williamsburg.[24]

Another crucial aspect of commemoration planning that occupied the attention of Federal Commission members was securing the active participation of Native Americans and African Americans. To ensure that the 400th anniversary commemoration was inclusive and highlighted the contributions of all three cultures that converged at Jamestown, commemoration planners formed Virginia Indian and African American advisory councils, allocated funding for signature events planned by those panels, provided staff resources, and involved representatives of both groups in commemoration planning generally. Commissioners Adkins and Reid led outreach efforts for the Federal Commission and provided leadership through the advisory councils and through communications and educational programming committees.

The Federal Commission and state Jamestown 2007 organization shared an unequivocal commitment to historical accuracy and inclusiveness that guided all aspects of commemoration planning. This distinguishing attribute of the 400th anniversary was much remarked throughout the commemoration. "When I visited 50 years ago," recalled Her Majesty, Queen Elizabeth II, in her May 2007 address to the Virginia legislature,

> we celebrated the 350th anniversary largely from the perspective of those settlers, in terms of the exploration of new worlds, the spread of values and of the English language, and the sacrifice of those early pioneers. These remain great

[23] Commissioners Rives, Loomis, Griles, Mainella, Smith, and Bomar played active roles in the development and funding of Historic Jamestowne's new facilities in their capacities as federal employees.

[24] Facility improvements at Historic Jamestowne and efforts to promote operational coordination with Jamestown Settlement are described in Chapter 6 of this report.

attributes and we still appreciate their impact today. But 50 years on we are now in a position to reflect more candidly on the Jamestown legacy. Human progress rarely comes without cost. And those early years in Jamestown, when three great civilizations came together for the first time—Western European, Native American, and African—released a train of impact which continues to have a profound social impact.... The "melting pot" metaphor captures one of the great strengths of your country and is an inspiration to others around the world as we face the continuing social challenges ahead.[25]

Absence of official federal government recognition of the eight organized Virginia Indian tribes posed a particular obstacle as commemoration planning began in earnest after 2003. The sovereignty of the Virginia tribes had been acknowledged in a 1677 treaty with the English Crown, and the Commonwealth of Virginia had belatedly recognized the tribes in the 1980s, but legislative and administrative action to accord the Virginia tribes federal recognition remained stalled in Washington, D.C., as the commemoration neared. Some Virginia Indian leaders spoke publicly of boycotting the Jamestown commemoration in protest, while others saw the approaching anniversary as an opportunity to highlight the tribes' culture, contributions, and continuing relevance. As Chief of the Chickahominy Tribe, Commissioner Adkins was among the most influential proponents of the latter view; he encouraged commemoration planners to afford the Indian community prominent opportunities to tell its story and simultaneously urged his Native colleagues to avail themselves of the unique forum created by the commemoration.[26]

In May 2004, the Federal Commission adopted a resolution expressing its commitment to providing such a forum.[27] After welcoming the decision of tribal leaders to participate actively in the commemoration, the Commission declared that

---

[25] The full text of Queen Elizabeth II's address to the Virginia General Assembly is provided at Appendix 6.

[26] The eight state-recognized tribes are the Chickahominy, Eastern Chickahominy, Mattaponi, Monacan, Nansemond, Pamunkey, Rappahannock, and Upper Mattaponi.

[27] The text of the resolution is included in Appendix 7.

38

> highlighting the culture and distinctive contributions of Virginia Indians before, during and since the 1607 settlement at Jamestown is an important aspect of the Federal Commission's mission. The 400th anniversary commemoration will be enriched through Virginia Indians' telling their own stories in their own voices. It promises to leave a valuable legacy of cross-cultural understanding.

Although precluded by federal ethics laws from endorsing pending legislation, the Commission left no doubt about its views:

> Recognizing the Commission's statutory mandate to ensure an inclusive Jamestown commemoration, and to highlight the contributions of all peoples who came together in 17th century Virginia, the Commission believes that resolution of the differing views surrounding the federal recognition question and the resulting achievement of such recognition by 2007 would constitute an important contribution to the success of Jamestown's 400th anniversary commemoration.

Virginia's Governor and two U.S. Senators already were on record in support of federal recognition, and the Jamestown 2007 Steering Committee and Jamestown-Yorktown Foundation Board of Trustees adopted resolutions of support as well.

"Life has not been easy for Virginia's indigenous peoples," wrote Chief Adkins in a commentary published the week before the Jamestown anniversary in May 2007, "but to the person we are proud to be Virginians and Americans. Most tribal members across the commonwealth are proud to be a part of a commemoration that has provided an opportunity for us to tell our story and to let the world know that descendants of some of the sovereign nations who greeted the settlers on the shores of the Powhatan River (James River) at Tsenacomoco are still here."[28] Although Virginia Indians participated actively in virtually all aspects of the *America's 400th Anniversary* commemoration, the objective of federal recognition was not

---

[28] See Stephen R. Adkins, "Diverse Populace Wove the Fabric of Jamestown," *Richmond Times-Dispatch,* May 6, 2007. The texts of Chief Adkins' May 2007 article and other published commentaries by Commission members are included in Appendix 8.

realized by 2007 as hoped. The House of Representatives approved legislation in May 2007 granting recognition to six of the Virginia tribes, but the Senate had not adopted comparable legislation by the time this report went to press. Nevertheless, events surrounding the *America's 400ᵗʰ Anniversary* commemoration heightened the visibility of Virginia's indigenous people and stirred the hearts and minds of thousands of Virginians and Americans to support federal recognition, making passage of recognition legislation increasingly likely. "Recognition efforts aside," concluded Chief Adkins, "the 400ᵗʰ anniversary commemoration of the first permanent English settlement at Jamestown provided Virginia Indians with the best forum they have had in 400 years to tell their story not only to their fellow Virginians, but to people across America and around the world."

State and federal commemoration leaders also wrestled during the early planning years with the question of how best to communicate Jamestown's importance and its various legacies to national and international audiences. They engaged professional communications consultants, convened numerous work sessions, and at length forged a consensus around *"America's 400ᵗʰ Anniversary: The Journey that Changed the World"* as the primary thematic construct. Sub-themes highlighted the influential ideas that characterized that historic journey: Jamestown's enduring and still-evolving legacies related to democracy, enterprise, exploration, and diversity.

As commemoration planning commenced, some might reasonably have doubted the feasibility of convincingly casting Jamestown's 400ᵗʰ anniversary as *America's* 400ᵗʰ anniversary. Such a portrayal might collide with popular assumptions about the Pilgrims' primacy, cultural preconceptions, general skepticism about marketing claims, and rival assertions of historic preeminence. But as commemorative events unfolded in 2007 to international notice and national acclaim, any lingering doubts swiftly dissipated. The successive visits and remarks by the Queen and the President conveyed the singular magnitude of the occasion, and national publications embraced the commemoration's theme. *TIME* joined several other popular magazines in devoting its cover to the Jamestown commemoration with "America at 400" as its caption,[29] and the White House news release on May 13, 2007, was headlined: "President Bush Celebrates America's 400th Anniversary in Jamestown." Electronic and print news reports across the United States and around the world conveyed the same message. Four hundred years after their venture, Jamestown's English settlers, together with those they encountered and those who soon followed, at last were receiving due acclaim as trailblazers on a journey that changed the world.

Although the joint communications task force recommended in the Federal Commission's strategic plan was never formed, the Jamestown 2007 Management Committee supplied a similar forum for coordinating communications efforts by the federal and state planning organizations and major partners. At that committee's invitation, Federal Commission representatives participated in the selection of Jamestown 2007's communications consultants in mid-2005, and the Federal Commission later engaged the same firm (Ruder Finn) for interim communications services. The Management Committee also served as the primary venue for achieving consensus on communications-related messaging and strategies and for assigning lead responsibility for communications on an event-by-event basis. The state's Jamestown 2007 office, for example, took the lead in handling promotional communications and media relations for the *Godspeed Sail,* the *Jamestown Live!* educational webcast, *America's Anniversary Weekend,* the Virginia Indian and African American signature events, and community-based programs. The Federal Commission spearheaded communications for the *World Forum on the Future of Democracy* and the democracy conference series, the *Jamestown—Journey of Democracy* educational initiatives, and domestic coverage of British commemorative activities. Other partners played leading roles in communications activities for other events, including the Colonial Williamsburg Foundation (*Royal Visit*), Jamestown-Yorktown Foundation (*World of 1607* exhibition), Jamestown 2007 British Committee (United Kingdom–based commemorative events), and the National Park Service and APVA Preservation Virginia

---

[29] "America at 400: How the Jamestown Colony Made Us Who We Are," *TIME,* May 7, 2007; see also "The First Americans: What Really Happened at Jamestown 400 Years Ago," *U.S. News & World Report*, January 29-February 5, 2007, and "Jamestown: The Real Story," *National Geographic*, May 2007.

(Yorktown 225ᵗʰ anniversary and Cape Henry first landing observances).³⁰

The *America's 400ᵗʰ Anniversary* program included 13 signature events³¹ that spanned 18 months from April 2006 to September 2007, as well as a wide array of educational, cultural, and historical programs in communities throughout Virginia. As described in the following chapters, many of the signature events and other major programs involved extensive Federal Commission participation and support:

- Chapter 2 describes the Commission's primary role in coordinating with the White House, Congress and federal agencies in support of virtually all commemorative activities, including four presidential and vice presidential visits to Virginia during the commemoration year.

- Chapter 3 chronicles the Commission's successful initiative to form a British commemorative committee, lay the groundwork for the *Royal Visit*, recruit former Prime Ministers Margaret Thatcher and Tony Blair as honorary co-chairs of the democracy conference series, organize a visit to England by representatives of Virginia's Indian tribes, host a major London event commemorating the departure of the three English ships bound for Jamestown, and facilitate Kent's participation with Virginia in the Smithsonian Folklife Festival.

- Chapter 4 describes the Commission's role in fostering educational activities, such as the *Jamestown—Journey of Democracy* curriculum initiatives, the *Jamestown Live!* educational webcast, and the Virginia Indian and African

---

³⁰ The Federal Commission procured media relations and other communications-related services during successive phases of its work from Ruder Finn, Inc., Siddall, Inc., The Hodges Partnership, and Greystone Partners. Through an in-kind donation of services by participating sponsor McGuireWoods LLP, William R. Allcott served as the Commission's part-time communications director during 2007.

³¹ The signature events were (in sequence): *Godspeed Sail* and "Landing Party" exhibitions at East Coast seaports; Virginia Indian symposium ("400 Years of Survival"); Yorktown 225ᵗʰ anniversary observances; preview gala for the permanent African-American galleries in the Jamestown Settlement museum; *Jamestown Live!* educational webcast; 2007 State of the Black Union national symposium; *World of 1607* special exhibition; *Godspeed* in-state sail and "Journey up the James" portside festivals; *America's Anniversary Weekend*; Smithsonian Folklife Festival ("Roots of Virginia Culture"); American Indian Intertribal Festival; 2007 Virginia Black Cultural and Commerce Expo; and *World Forum on the Future of Democracy.*

American signature events.

- Chapter 5 recounts the Commission's sponsorship of the commemoration's finale, the *World Forum on the Future of Democracy*, and the year-long series of university-based conferences that preceded it.

- Chapter 6 describes the Commission's support for historic preservation, investigation, and interpretation throughout the Chesapeake region, including capital improvements at Jamestown, creation of the Captain John Smith Chesapeake National Historic Trail, and other legacy initiatives.

In some instances, the lead responsibility for carrying out commemorative programs and events resided not with the Federal Commission, but with the state's Jamestown 2007 organization or with key partners, such as the Jamestown-Yorktown Foundation, the National Park Service, APVA Preservation Virginia, and the Colonial Williamsburg Foundation. Acknowledging the contributions of many and the commemoration's inevitable dependence on successful collaboration and partnership are prerequisites for any accurate account of *America's 400th Anniversary*. Nevertheless, as detailed in the chapters that follow, the Federal Commission played an indispensable role at every step of the way in planning and executing what became a truly extraordinary national and international commemoration.

CHAPTER 2

A Commemoration for All Americans:
The Role of the United States Government

From the beginning, those planning *America's 400th Anniversary* understood that a primary measure of the success of their endeavors, and so the commemoration, would be the presence of the President of the United States at Jamestown, leading anniversary observances in May 2007. Like the prominent participation of President Theodore Roosevelt at the Norfolk-based exposition during the 300th anniversary celebration in 1907, the presence of President George W. Bush at the *America's Anniversary Weekend* festivities at Jamestown on May 11-13, 2007, would affirm the national significance of the Jamestown milestone and call broad-based attention to the commemorative events. The responsibility for securing and coordinating this presidential participation, and the involvement of other distinguished national leaders, fell to the Federal Commission.

As it turned out, President Bush not only led the commemorative ceremonies at Jamestown on May 13, 2007. He and First Lady Laura Bush also toured the archaeological dig and surveyed the monuments at Historic Jamestowne, then visited Jamestown Settlement where they boarded *Susan Constant* for the unfurling of her sails and a cannon salute and viewed living-history demonstrations. A spirited welcome from 25,000 visitors greeted President and Mrs. Bush at adjacent Anniversary Park, where the President delivered a major address on Jamestown's legacies. "The story of Jamestown will always have a special place in American history," he declared.

It's the story of a great migration from the Old World to the New. It is a story of hardship overcome by resolve. It's the story of the Tidewater settlement that laid the foundation of our great democracy.... Today democratic institutions are taking root in places where liberty was not imaginable long ago. At the start of the 1980s, there were only 45 democracies on Earth. There are now more than 120 democracies, and more people live in freedom than ever before.... [O]ur shared respect for the rule of law and our deeply held belief in individual liberty ... are more than just American values and British values, or Western values. They are universal values that come from a power greater than any man or any country. These values took root at Jamestown four centuries ago. They have flourished in our land, and one day they will flourish in every land.[32]

The President and First Lady next joined young people in inserting several objects into a time capsule that would be sealed until the 450th anniversary commemoration. The objects included a letter, gold coin, and mementos from Queen Elizabeth II's recent visit. Before departing, President Bush unexpectedly mounted the conductor's platform and—to the amazement of the musicians from around the country who comprised the occasion's 400-piece Anniversary Orchestra— waved the baton vigorously as the orchestra turned in a rousing and seemingly well-timed rendition of "The Stars and Stripes, Forever."

The presidential party departed by helicopter shortly thereafter from the isthmus that connects Jamestown Island to the rest of the Colonial Parkway. But the President was heard to remark in several settings thereafter about the impressive events of that anniversary day, and just before Thanksgiving he returned to the area and delivered another address at historic Berkeley Plantation on the blessings of liberty and the contributions of the Virginia colony.

---

[32] The full text of the President's address as distributed by the White House on May 13, 2007, is found in Appendix 9.

Acclaimed historian Arthur M. Schlesinger, Jr., while a senior member of President John F. Kennedy's administration, had noted the apparent validity of Berkeley's claim as the locus of America's first thanksgiving assemblage, settling for some a point of tiresome debate among northern and southern partisans. But the President's choice of Berkeley as the venue for his Thanksgiving message on November 19, 2007, carried an even stronger imprimatur. With the river-borne *Godspeed* replica as a backdrop, he declared,

> [F]ew Americans … know the story of the Berkeley Thanksgiving. This story has its beginnings in the founding of the colony of Virginia four centuries ago. As the colony grew, settlers ventured beyond the walls of Jamestown, and into the surrounding countryside. The Berkeley Company of England acquired 8,000 acres of nearby land, and commissioned an expedition to settle it. In 1619, a band of 38 settlers departed Bristol, England for Berkeley aboard a ship like the one behind me. At the end of their long voyage, the men reviewed their orders from home. And here's what the orders said: "The day of our ship's arrival shall be yearly and perpetually kept holy as a day of Thanksgiving to Almighty God." Upon hearing those orders, the men fell to their knees in prayer. And with this humble act of faith, the settlers celebrated their first Thanksgiving in the New World.[33]

President Bush also issued a commemoration-year proclamation calling the attention of the American people to the signal contributions of the Virginia colony.[34]

The two anniversary-year presidential visits were the most notable in a remarkable series of Jamestown-related appearances by senior officials of the United States Government during the 2007 commemoration. In January, Vice President Richard B. Cheney joined members of the Virginia General

---

[33] Commissioner Saunders and her husband, Tom Saunders, were among those who helped arrange the presidential visit to Berkeley Plantation. In his remarks, President Bush noted the important role of the Saunders and the Saunders Trust for American History at the New York Historical Society in preserving the plantation site.

[34] The text of the proclamation, and an earlier letter of commendation from President George W. Bush, are included in the presidential documents reprinted in Appendix 10.

Assembly on the opening day of their 2007 session for a memorial gathering in the church at Historic Jamestowne. Near the site where representative government in America began, the Vice President observed,

> It's striking to realize how much of America's story begins with a little three-sided fort, raised on the banks of the James River, four centuries ago.... The history of our country did not begin at Cape Cod in 1620.... A year before that—on July 30, 1619, just a few steps from this sanctuary—the first representative assembly in the new world was called to order. Indeed, so much of what defines our country—its language, legal traditions and institutions—have roots in the community that rose in this corner of Virginia. English liberty and law, private property, the spirit of free enterprise, and commerce—all of these are part of the Jamestown legacy.

Recalling that the Jamestown story "also involves struggle and injustice ..., [men] kept in bondage, their life's labor stolen from them .... [and] native peoples, who were here first, and who would suffer great loss," the Vice President spoke of the progress made during America's 400-year-long odyssey. "On that journey, we have confronted many injustices, and widened the circle of liberty, and become known to the world as freedom's home and defender."

The Vice President's appearance, arranged by the Federal Commission, was the kick-off event for an all-star series of commemoration-year observances, a fact noted in his remarks:

> Standing here in the year 2007, we can draw a straight line from those early days of struggle and fortitude in a tiny settlement to the great nation we know and love today. For that reason, this will be a special year of commemoration and reflection— from *America's Anniversary Weekend* in May to the *World Forum on Democracy* in September. And it will be a particular honor when Queen Elizabeth herself returns to Jamestown, 50 years after she came here on her first visit to America as the British sovereign.

The Vice President and Mrs. Lynne Cheney returned to the Historic Triangle in early May to greet the Queen and

President George W. Bush lauds the "Tidewater settlement that laid the foundation of our great democracy" in remarks delivered at Jamestown *during* America's 400th Anniversary *ceremonies on May 13, 2007*

President Bush poses aboard the replica ship Susan Constant *with Captain Eric Speth (center) and members of the ship's crew (Jamestown Settlement, May 13, 2007)*

President Bush visits the James Fort dig and discusses discoveries with Historic Jamestowne Administrator Ann Berry and Dr. William Kelso, Director of the Jamestown Rediscovery Project (Historic Jamestowne, May 13, 2007)

President Bush and school students wave after depositing items in the time capsule during America's Anniversary Weekend festivities, as First Lady Laura Bush, Governor Kaine, and Virginia First Lady Anne Holton watch (Anniversary Park, May 13, 2007)

More than 25,000 attend 400th anniversary festivities on May 13, 2007, including former U.S. Senator George Allen (left foreground) and former Virginia Lieutenant Governor John Hager (center), both active participants in commemoration planning

President Bush greets platform dignitaries, including Vice Chair Dendy (left), Virginia Attorney General Robert F. McDonnell (center), and Virginia Lieutenant Governor William T. Bolling (right) after concluding Anniversary Weekend *remarks*

President Bush greets U.S. Representative Jo Ann Davis (1-VA), a key supporter of the commemoration, during Anniversary Weekend *festivities as Vice Chairs Colin and Nancy Campbell and other commemoration leaders look on*

President Bush, Governor Kaine, and U.S. Secretary of the Interior Dirk Kempthorne (right) applaud as Justice O'Connor delivers Anniversary Weekend remarks

Marine One *and support helicopters take off from the Jamestown isthmus after the President and First Lady conclude participation in anniversary ceremonies on May 13, 2007*

Astronauts aboard the International Space Station address the Anniversary Weekend *audience as members of the 1607-person Anniversary Choir watch from below giant electronic screens flanking the main stage (Anniversary Park, May 13, 2007)*

Commissioner Reid assists in unveiling the U.S. Postal Service's triangular Jamestown commemorative stamp at Historic Jamestowne on May 11, 2007 (from left to right: Commissioner Reid; Katherine C. Tobin of the U.S. Postal Service Board of Governors; Virginia Attorney General Robert F. McDonnell; Dr. Edwin (Ned) Logan, coordinator of the Jamestown 2007 Stamp and Cachet Project)

Chairman Atkinson greets Vice President Cheney at the Newport News airport on May 4, 2007, before proceeding to Jamestown Settlement for ceremonies honoring Her Majesty, Queen Elizabeth II

Chief Justice of the United States John G. Roberts and Justice Sandra Day O'Connor, Honorary Chairperson of America's 400th Anniversary, listen at Historic Jamestowne on April 14, 2007, as the Lord Chief Justice of England and Wales, Lord Phillips of Worth Matravers, presents a plaque recognizing Jamestown's landmark contributions to the global advance of the rule of law

Vice Chair Dendy, joined by (from left to right) Commissioner Rives, Chief Adams, Commissioner Adkins, and Captain Speth, presides over "Landing Party" ceremonies in Philadelphia during the Godspeed's *summer 2006 promotional tour to East Coast seaports*

Interior Secretary Kempthorne (center) tours the replica ship Godspeed *on the Potomac during its 2006 sail, accompanied by (from left to right) former U.S. Attorney General William P. Barr, Chairman Atkinson, and Commissioner Mainella (Director of the National Park Service) (Alexandria, Virginia, June 1, 2006)*

Before delivering a major address on the role of the United States in exporting democracy, U.S. Secretary of Defense Robert M. Gates (fourth from left) poses with commemoration leaders at the World Forum on the Future of Democracy (Colonial Williamsburg, September 17, 2007) (from left to right: Senator Norment; Planning Council Chairman Sullivan; Chairman Atkinson; Secretary Gates; Justice O'Connor; Chairman Connock; Vice Chair Campbell; Senator John Warner; College of William and Mary President Gene R. Nichol)

Senator John Warner, chairman of the Senate Armed Services Committee, swears in new military recruits during the tribute to American armed forces at the commemoration of the 225th anniversary of the Yorktown victory

Interior Secretary Kempthorne greets platform dignitaries before the Yorktown 225th anniversary ceremonies (from left to right: Secretary Kempthorne; French Ambassador Jean-David Levitte; former Secretary of the Army John O. Marsh, Jr.; Senator John Warner; Senator George Allen)

accompany her as she visited the Jamestown sites and Colonial Williamsburg.[35] But before leaving in January, the Vice President presented state legislative leaders with "the rarest of tributes"— commemorative coins struck by the United States Mint.

> By this extraordinary act of Congress, the nation pays lasting homage to the 400th anniversary of the first English settlement on the North American shore. And we proudly acknowledge Virginia's irreplaceable role in creating the greatest nation on Earth, the United States of America.[36]

The gold and silver coins went on public sale for the first time the next day, January 11, 2007, at Historic Jamestowne and Jamestown Settlement, and 400,000 were sold before the year was out.

Present and former federal Cabinet officials played prominent roles in numerous commemoration events. During his initial week as secretary of the interior in May 2006, former Idaho Governor Dirk Kempthorne attended Jamestown 2007's first signature event, a dockside "Landing Party" festival in Alexandria, Virginia, near Washington, D.C., that coincided with the high-profile visit of the new replica ship *Godspeed*. The Alexandria stop was the first of six ports visited by the *Godspeed* during its 80-day tour up the East Coast, an educational and promotional program that drew nearly half a million visitors— twice the number anticipated—and a bonanza of media coverage in major metropolitan areas.[37] Secretary Kempthorne also delivered a major address at the October 19, 2006 signature event marking the 225th anniversary of the victory at Yorktown and represented the Department of the Interior during the three-day *America's Anniversary Weekend* celebration in May 2007.

---

[35] Reflecting their interest in founding-era history, Vice President and Mrs. Cheney in 2006 made a family visit to the Jamestown sites and hosted archeologist William Kelso and other Jamestown representatives for a dinner at the Vice President's residence.

[36] The full text of the Vice President's address at Historic Jamestowne on January 10, 2007, is found in Appendix 11.

[37] The Jamestown-Yorktown Foundation replaced two replica ships, *Godspeed* and *Discovery,* with newer versions shortly before the commemoration began, and the new *Godspeed* set sail from Jamestown on May 22, 2006, on its East Coast tour. It visited the Washington, D.C. area, Baltimore, Philadelphia, New York City, Boston, and Newport, completing its last port call on July 30, 2006. The event generated more than 830 million media impressions that reached an estimated 335 million people in the United States and around the world. Federal Commissioners Dendy and Flippo were among those leading the welcoming ceremonies at various stops.

Secretary of Defense Robert Gates was on hand in Williamsburg on September 17, 2007, for the *World Forum on the Future of Democracy*, and his remarks traced the history of American efforts to promote democracy. Former Secretary of State Lawrence Eagleburger, former Attorney General William P. Barr, and Admiral James M. Loy, the former deputy secretary of homeland security, also participated in the *World Forum* as speakers. Earlier sessions of the year-long series of university-based conferences on democracy featured such high-profile figures as Undersecretary of State Karen Hughes, former Ambassador to the United Nations Richard Holbrooke, and General Lance L. Smith, Supreme Allied Commander of the North Atlantic Treaty Organization (NATO).

The extent of high-level executive branch involvement in Jamestown commemorative events was a testament to the importance of the anniversary and to the quality of the program, but among the most important factors in facilitating federal VIP participation and agency support was the Federal Commission's early development of a positive working relationship with the White House. From Chairman Atkinson's first West Wing meeting in October 2005 through the final commemorative event in September 2007, Barry Jackson, assistant to the President for strategic initiatives and external affairs, and other members of the White House staff provided crucial support on matters ranging from presidential and vice presidential visits, to federal departmental and agency assistance, to the official invitation to Queen Elizabeth and other international dignitaries to participate in the commemoration.[38] Their influential imprimatur and evident enthusiasm for the project helped set the tone for the rest of the executive branch. A working group consisting of Commissioners Griles and Nau and Executive Director Mann joined Chairman Atkinson in this fruitful high-level engagement, and U.S. Senators John Warner and George Allen and other members of the Virginia congressional delegation also contributed to the dialogue at key junctures.[39] As a result, the messages conveyed by senior executive branch officials resonated strongly with the key themes of *America's 400th*

---

[38] Jackson was designated as the White House's liaison to the commemoration planning effort by Karl Rove, the assistant to the President, deputy chief of staff, and senior advisor.

[39] The Commission's successful liaison with the Bush administration also was aided by Commissioners Loomis, Mainella, Bomar, Rives, Trumbo, and Smith. Ron Christie, a former member of Vice President Cheney's staff, assisted the Commission's efforts.

Anniversary, and the commemoration experienced a degree of presidential, vice presidential, and cabinet-level participation that was apparently without precedent in other national, state, and local commemorations.

Leaders of the federal judiciary also participated prominently in the *America's 400ᵗʰ Anniversary* program. In April, Chief Justice of the United States John G. Roberts came to Historic Jamestowne to accept a plaque presented by his English counterpart, Lord Chief Justice Phillips of Worth Matravers, on behalf of the four English Inns of Court. The plaque and accompanying ceremonies, which were led by Justice Sandra Day O'Connor, the commemoration's honorary chair, and by Virginia Supreme Court Justice Donald W. Lemons, celebrated the Anglo-American legal tradition and the Jamestown settlement's distinctive contributions to the rule of law—a topic that Chief Justice Roberts addressed at length during a democracy conference speech the preceding evening in Richmond.[40] Supreme Court Justice Stephen G. Breyer and Judge J. Harvie Wilkinson III of the United States Court of Appeals for the Fourth Judicial Circuit also participated in the April conference on the rule of law, and were joined there by several high-ranking British jurists. Supreme Court Justice Anthony Kennedy attended activities honoring Queen Elizabeth II during her visit to the Historic Triangle.

Throughout the commemoration, Justice O'Connor spoke eloquently of the Jamestown settlement's foundational role in development of the rule of law—the principles of representative government, individual rights, and an impartial judiciary—on which mankind's opportunity to live in peace and freedom depends. "Our best hope for world peace comes from democracy and the rule of law," she observed in remarks opening the *World Forum on the Future of Democracy* in September 2007. "The challenge that we face in this century is ... to ensure that everyone has an opportunity to have [the rule of law] and its benefits." Justice O'Connor's contributions to the commemoration, however, went far beyond her salient observations about Jamestown's role in the development of America's legal and

---

[40] Chief Justice Roberts was among a notable array of American and British jurists, lawyers, and scholars who participated in the democracy conference hosted by the University of Richmond School of Law on April 10-14, 2007, as part of the Federal Commission's year-long conference series. See Chapter 5.

governmental institutions. A frequent visitor to the Historic Triangle—she also was chancellor of the College of William and Mary and senior trustee of the Colonial Williamsburg Foundation—her service as honorary chair of *America's 400th Anniversary* proved indispensable in elevating the national and international profile of the commemoration and attracting other high-level participants. From February 2006, when she accepted the invitation of Virginia Senator Thomas K. Norment and Colonial Williamsburg President Colin G. Campbell to lead the commemoration, Justice O'Connor's cheerful, encouraging presence and inspiring words provided the glue that made the enterprise whole and were the catalyst for its success beyond all predictions.

Congressional support for the Jamestown 400th commemoration took many forms and was another indispensable ingredient in the *America's 400th Anniversary* mix. As noted throughout this report, members of the Virginia congressional delegation attended commemorative events, patroned bills and appropriation requests, encouraged federal agency cooperation, and helped to ensure that the United States Government was a full partner with the Commonwealth of Virginia and private sponsors in realizing the potential of *America's 400th Anniversary*. In addition to informal forms of assistance, the following actions by the United States Congress aided the Jamestown commemoration and permanent sites directly and significantly:

- Enactment of Public Law 106-565 (Jamestown 400th Commemoration Commission Act of 2000), creating the Federal Commission.

- Funding for operation of the Federal Commission in the Department of the Interior appropriations for fiscal years 2001-2008, resulting in combined resources of $2,645,000.

- Funding for the extensive capital improvements at Historic Jamestowne during fiscal years 1999-2008, resulting in combined appropriations of $33,421,000.

- Funding for the Federal Commission's *Jamestown—Journey of Democracy* educational initiatives through the Department of Education appropriations for fiscal year 2005, resulting in a grant of $100,000.

- Funding for the *World Forum on the Future of Democracy* through the Department of State appropriations for fiscal year 2006, resulting in a grant of $900,000.

- Enactment of Public Law 108-289 (Jamestown 400th Anniversary Commemorative Coin Act) in 2004, directing the United States Mint to issue gold and silver commemorative coins in honor of Jamestown's 400th anniversary, with proceeds to benefit the Jamestown sites and commemoration.

- Enactment of Public Law 109-418 (The Captain John Smith Chesapeake National Historic Trail Designation Act) in 2006, designating the Captain John Smith Chesapeake National Historic Trail under the auspices of the National Park Service.

The members of the Virginia congressional delegation who represented the Historic Triangle and nearby areas were especially active and visible throughout the planning process and anniversary-year program. They included U.S. Senators John W. Warner, George Allen, and James H. Webb, Jr., and U.S. Representatives JoAnn Davis, Robert C. Scott, and J. Randy Forbes. A special acknowledgement and word of appreciation is due Senator Warner, who possessed a distinctive understanding of commemorations from his service as Administrator of the American Revolution Bicentennial in 1976, and who lent his strong personal support and the considerable resources of his experienced staff to many vital aspects of the Commission's work.

Other members of Congress and congressional staff members participated prominently in a wide range of commemorative activities, democracy conference sessions, and other anniversary-related events. An especially important figure in early planning for the democracy conference series was former Speaker of the House of Representatives Thomas S. Foley of Washington, who served with former Attorney General William Barr as the program's honorary vice chair. Former Congressman Lee H. Hamilton of Indiana and former U.S. Senator Charles S. Robb of Virginia, both of whom had recently completed high-profile service as members of the Iraq Study Group, participated in democracy conference series programs.

Finally, it is important to highlight the contributions of the many federal departments, agencies, bureaus, and offices that contributed to the commemoration's success in important— and often unheralded—ways. At least 37 federal agencies and entities assisted the commemoration by carrying out more than three dozen significant initiatives, projects, and tasks. Executive Director Mann performed the crucial liaison function with most of these entities, and throughout the commemoration he was continually impressed by federal officials' receptiveness to requests for assistance and their enthusiasm for the commemoration project as a whole. Many of their contributions are acknowledged elsewhere in this report, and no doubt some have been omitted inadvertently. In addition to those previously discussed in this chapter, we wish to call particular attention to the following entities, officials, and contributions:

- National Park Service; Department of the Interior: Park Service Directors Fran Mainella and Mary Bomar, Park Superintendents F. Alec Gould, Alexandra (Sandy) Rives, and P. Daniel Smith and the Park Service's dedicated employees at Colonial National Historical Park and elsewhere made so many crucial contributions to the commemoration and the Federal Commission's work that a detailed recitation here is impossible. Together with Interior Secretaries Norton and Kempthorne, Deputy Secretary Griles, and other Interior Department officials, their direct assistance to the Federal Commission's administration, funding and legislative efforts proved indispensable to the Commission's success.

- Executive Office of the President: The capable staff of the Executive Office of the President, including senior personnel involved in advance, communications, and speechwriting, were exceedingly cooperative and helpful in preparing for visits to Jamestown by President and Mrs. Bush and Vice President and Mrs. Cheney. As noted above, Barry Jackson, assistant to the President for strategic initiatives and external affairs, served as the Commission's primary point of contact and facilitated crucial expressions of high-level support and other forms of assistance to commemoration planners.

- Bureau of Education and Cultural Affairs; Department of State: The Bureau, through the work of Senior Program Officer Brent Beemer and others, provided a substantial grant and coordinated arrangements for participation by 85 international delegates from emerging democracies in the *World Forum on the Future of Democracy*. Undersecretary Karen Hughes delivered a stimulating keynote address at the International Youth Democracy Summit at the University of Virginia, the opening event of the Commission's democracy conference series. Ambassador Robert H. Tuttle and the American Embassy in London provided crucial support and guidance with respect to the entire program of Anglo-American commemorative activities, and the Office of Protocol advised the Commission on the formal invitation and other aspects of the visit by Her Majesty, Queen Elizabeth II.

- Department of Education: In 2004, Secretary Rodney Paige issued an early letter of endorsement of the Commission's education initiatives that helped engender broad-based interest in the Commission's programs. The Department's Office of Innovation and Improvement provided a $100,000 grant to support development of the Commission's *www. JamestownJourney.org* website and civics-related curriculum, and provided valuable technical assistance throughout the process.

- National Aeronautics and Space Administration (NASA): Administrator Michael Griffin

56

participated in the *America's Anniversary Weekend* program on May 13, 2007, and arranged a broadcast to Jamestown from the International Space Station as part of the ceremonies. NASA transported a Jamestown artifact and commemorative coins on the Space Shuttle, *STS 117 Atlantis*, in June 2007 and called attention to the Jamestown commemoration in other ways, including participation by astronauts in numerous commemorative events. NASA's Langley Research Center was especially active in supporting Jamestown-related educational initiatives, including assisting in curriculum development and staffing exhibits at commemorative events. These and other contributions highlighted the connection between centuries-old voyages of discovery and exploration of today's frontiers in space.

- Department of Defense: Secretary of Defense Robert M. Gates addressed the *World Forum on the Future of Democracy*, and the Department supported many of the commemoration's signature events by having ceremonial units (including honor guards, bands, and fly-over units) provide pomp, pageantry, and a patriotic flair. Hundreds of sailors from the aircraft carrier USS *Carl Vinson* volunteered to assist and staffed activities during *America's Anniversary Weekend*. The Norfolk Naval Base assisted with the transfer of the replica ship *Discovery* to England aboard the British naval auxiliary vessel, RFA *Fort Rosalie*.

- United States Mint, Department of the Treasury: Officials at the Mint provided guidance to the commemorative coin planning team, led by Commissioners Rives and Dendy, on the design, selection, and marketing process for the gold and silver commemorative coins. Director Edmund C. Moy came to Jamestown on January 11, 2007, to participate in public ceremonies on the first day of issuance and to authenticate personally the coin purchases made on that day. Mint officials earlier worked with Virginia officials and commemoration planners on the issuance of Virginia's state quarter featuring the three sailing ships bound for Jamestown in 1607.

- Department of Homeland Security: The Department provided crucial grants to local law enforcement agencies to support security planning and operations related to major commemorative activities, and the United States Secret Service provided security briefings, review, and coordination for the visits of President Bush, Vice President Cheney, and Her Majesty, Queen Elizabeth II. Numerous other components of the Department of Homeland Security provided assistance, including the United States Coast Guard office in Norfolk, which helped expedite the permit issuance for the *Godspeed Sail* in the summer of 2006.

- Chesapeake Bay Office, National Oceanographic and Atmospheric Administration (NOAA), Department of Commerce: The Office supported the development of multiple interpretive water buoys for use as part of the Captain John Smith Chesapeake National Historic (Water) Trail. The Chesapeake Bay Interpretive Buoy System provides technologically sophisticated means through which Water Trail visitors can access geographic, historical, scientific, and educational information along the water route.

- The Center for Folklife and Cultural Heritage, Smithsonian Institution: The Center worked with commemoration planners on arrangements for the showcasing of Virginia at the 2007 Smithsonian Folklife Festival, and guided selection of Virginia and English artisans, craftsman, and performers for inclusion in the Festival. The Smithsonian's National Museum of Natural History assisted the Commission in the identification and development of Jamestown-related educational curriculum.

- United States Postal Service: Through the Citizens' Stamp Advisory Committee, the Postal Service facilitated entries and reviewed designs for the Jamestown commemorative stamp, which was issued on May 11, 2007. The popular stamp ("Settlement of Jamestown") was only the third triangular stamp issued by the Postal Service, and it featured the three-sided James Fort and three ships that brought settlers to Jamestown in 1607.

The Jamestown commemoration's powerful images reached eyes and ears across the country, and its messages touched hearts nationwide, largely because the President, Vice President, Chief Justice, Members of Congress, Associate Justices, Cabinet officers, and other respected national leaders took time to join their state and local counterparts at the events and lend their insights and well-chosen words to the occasions. The commemoration had national reach also because the federal government contributed vital financial resources and agency support to the most visible aspects of the program. Through a forward-looking federal initiative and public-private partnership, visitors to the place where America began enjoyed an awe-inspiring, educational experience in Historic Jamestowne's new facilities and learned about the interrelation of man and nature in the Chesapeake region by traveling the nation's first water-borne historic trail. The Federal Commission expresses its gratitude to the dedicated public servants in the United States Government, and to the people they serve, for making possible these and many other commemoration achievements.

CHAPTER 3

Celebrating the
"Special Relationship":
British Participation
in Anniversary Activities

On November 15, 2006, Her Majesty, Queen Elizabeth II, used the occasion of her annual speech marking the opening session of Parliament to make the announcement that commemoration planners had been anticipating for several years: "The Duke of Edinburgh and I look forward to our state visit to the United States of America in May 2007 to celebrate the 400th anniversary of the Jamestown settlement." With those 30 unadorned words uttered across the sea, planning for *America's 400th Anniversary* suddenly entered a dramatic new phase. The news of the British monarch's participation—punctuated with the poignant reminder that it would be a reprise of her first state visit to the United States 50 years earlier for Jamestown's 350th anniversary commemoration—was flashed across the country, creating palpable excitement and electrifying preparations for anniversary-year observances. There now was no doubt that the Jamestown milestone would command international attention.

At the request of federal and state commemoration planners, President George W. Bush and Governor Timothy M. Kaine invited the Queen and Prince Philip to participate in the *America's Anniversary Weekend* festivities on May 11-13, 2007, or to visit Jamestown at another time of Buckingham Palace's choosing during the anniversary year. Touring the two Jamestown sites and Colonial Williamsburg secretly on October 4, 2006, to explore possible arrangements for a royal visit, a small

British delegation led by Sir Robin Janvrin, Private Secretary to the Queen, and Sir David Manning, Her Majesty's Ambassador to the United States, signaled to Chairman Atkinson and Colonial Williamsburg President Colin Campbell the Queen's probable intention to schedule her state visit during the first days of May, roughly a week before the *Anniversary Weekend* ceremonies. The timing seemed ideal from the commemoration planners' perspective; the *Royal Visit* on May 3-4, 2007, followed by *Anniversary Weekend* on May 11-13, 2007, would place the Jamestown observances in the national and international spotlight for an extended (10-day) period and provide additional opportunities for citizen participation and media coverage.

On May 3, 2007, Queen Elizabeth II and Prince Philip flew directly from London to Richmond, and proceeded to the Executive Mansion for a brief reception hosted by Governor Kaine and First Lady Anne Holton and attended by five former Virginia governors and U.S. Senator John Warner. The royal couple then greeted members of the public during a stroll from the mansion to the east lawn of Capitol Square, where she met the chiefs of the eight state-recognized Indian tribes and viewed a Native American ceremonial dance. The Queen, Prince Phillip, and the Kaines then climbed the steps of the newly restored Virginia Capitol and waved to the assembled thousands from the south portico before entering the seat of government originally designed by Thomas Jefferson, the Commonwealth's second governor after independence.[41] Entering the chamber of the House of Delegates, which traces its lineage to Jamestown's first representative assembly in 1619, the Queen received a rousing welcome and desk-thumping display of affection from Virginia's 21st century solons, who convened in a special joint

---

[41] Two days earlier, on May 1, 2007, the south portico had been the scene of ceremonies marking the reopening of the restored building after a two-year-long renovation. Before his legislative election to the state judiciary in January 2004, Commissioner Trumbo led the Capitol renovation efforts as a member of the Virginia Senate and vice chairman of the Joint Rules Committee of the Virginia General Assembly, and he worked to ensure that the project was completed in time for an anniversary-year visit by the British monarch. Virginia Senator Thomas K. Norment, House of Delegates Speaker William J. Howell, and Governor Timothy M. Kaine were similarly influential in making sure that the Capitol restoration project was completed in time for ceremonies marking Virginia's 400th anniversary.

session for the occasion.[42] She concluded her address by paying tribute to the special bond that unites Americans and Britons:

> This four hundredth anniversary marks a moment to recognize the deep friendship which exists between our two countries. Friendship is a complex concept. It means being able to debate openly, disagree on occasion, surmount both good times and bad, safe in the knowledge that the bonds that draw us together—of history, understanding, and warm regard—are far stronger than any temporary differences of opinion. The people of the United Kingdom have such a relationship with the people of this great nation. It is one of the most durable international collaborations anywhere in the world at any time in history, a friendship for which I certainly in my lifetime have had good cause to be thankful. That is a lasting legacy of Jamestown, that is something worth commemorating, and that is why I am pleased to be here today. [43]

From Richmond, the royal entourage hastened to Duke of Gloucester Street in Colonial Williamsburg, where they were greeted by Colonial Williamsburg President Colin Campbell and Mrs. Nancy Campbell, vice chair of the Federal Commission. The Queen, the Duke, and the Campbells then traveled by horse-drawn carriage down the picturesque colonial avenue to the acclaim of thousands of cheering onlookers, and on to the nearby Williamsburg Inn, where the Queen and her retinue retired for the evening. The stately Inn had played host to Her Majesty 50 years earlier, and its most impressive suite, named in her honor, bore stunning photographs of the 31-year-old monarch who had so enthralled Virginians in 1957.

The next morning, Queen Elizabeth II and Prince Philip toured Jamestown Settlement and Historic Jamestowne, accompanied by Vice President and Mrs. Cheney, Governor Kaine, Justice

---

[42] Commissioners Atkinson, Dendy, and Flippo were present on the House of Delegates floor for the Queen's address by invitation from Speaker William J. Howell. Also present were state Steering Committee Chairman Connock and representatives of the Jamestown 2007 British Committee, including Lord Watson of Richmond, Sir Robert Worcester, Viscount and Viscountess de l'Isle, Alex King, Rebecca Casson, and Amanda Cottrell.

[43] The full text of the address by Queen Elizabeth II is found in Appendix 6.

O'Connor, Senator Norment, Chairman Connock, and other dignitaries. A reception followed at the Governor's Palace in Colonial Williamsburg, where commemoration leaders, including Chairman and Mrs. Atkinson, Vice Chair and Mrs. Dendy, and Commissioner Flippo, were formally presented to the Queen. After exchanging toasts with the Governor at a tented luncheon beside the Governor's Palace gardens, Her Majesty proceeded to the College of William and Mary, where she was made an honorary member of the Class of 2007 and rang the Wren Bell, an honor traditionally reserved for graduating seniors. Before returning to London, the royal party made its way to Louisville for the Kentucky Derby and to Washington, D.C., for a state dinner hosted by President Bush and a wreath-laying at the new World War II memorial. A genuinely warm and often robust welcome, beamed nationally and internationally through wall-to-wall news coverage, greeted the British sovereign at every stop on her tour. In the wake of an American visit that commentators speculated might be the last of her reign, Queen Elizabeth II left a deep reservoir of goodwill and affection along with heightened awareness of Jamestown's importance as the place where America began four centuries ago.

The groundwork for the impressive *Royal Visit* had been laid over many months, beginning with a series of concerted contacts by commemoration planners designed to spark interest in the Jamestown anniversary in England and, particularly, in Buckingham Palace. Federal Commissioner Flippo and state Steering Committee Chairman Connock co-chaired a joint federal-state working group on British participation in the commemoration,[44] and they reached out early in the planning process to well-placed contacts in England who had interacted with the Jamestown-Yorktown Foundation on other occasions.[45] Colonial Williamsburg President Colin Campbell and Federal Commission Vice Chair Nancy Campbell also used their international contacts to stoke interest in a royal visit.

---

[44] The members of the working group, originally called the "Joint US-UK Planning Committee" and later the "Anglo-American Planning Committee," are listed in the Federal Commission's committee roster at Appendix 4.

[45] Among the important contacts occurring before formation of the joint working group were discussions that several Foundation board members had with Lord Tollemache, the lord-lieutenant of Suffolk, and meetings held in Ispwich (near Otley Hall, the family home of the *Godspeed*'s captain, Bartholomew Gosnold) by Connock, Flippo, and Virginia First Lady Roxane Gilmore during a gubernatorial trade mission in May 2001.

Her Majesty, Queen Elizabeth II, begins her state visit to the United States for the Jamestown commemoration with an address to a joint session of the Virginia General Assembly in the newly renovated Virginia Capitol on May 3, 2007 (also pictured: Virginia House of Delegates Speaker William J. Howell (left) and Lieutenant Governor William T. Bolling)

After addressing the Virginia General Assembly in Richmond earlier in the afternoon, Her Majesty greets visitors along Duke of Gloucester Street in Colonial Williamsburg en route to the Williamsburg Inn for the evening

Standing outside the historic Memorial Church, Commissioner Rives presents a gift to Her Majesty during her visit to Historic Jamestowne on May 4, 2007

Allan Willett, Lord-Lieutenant of Kent, welcomes Chief Anne Richardson of the Rappahannock Indian Tribe at Cobham Hall in Kent during the Virginia Indians' July 2006 mission to England

The replica ship Discovery, *bound for a berth at Canary Wharf adjacent to the Museum in Docklands, nears Southampton on October 15, 2006, after a 10-day transatlantic voyage aboard the RFA* Fort Rosalie

Sir Robert Worcester and Alex King, Deputy Leader of the Kent County Council, deposit items contributed by the Jamestown 2007 British Committee to the time capsule during Anniversary Weekend *(Historic Jamestowne, May 11, 2007)*

Lord Watson and Sir Robert Worcester pose with American dignitaries at Guildhall in London during a March 20, 2006 gala celebrating the impending 400th anniversary of the Virginia Company's first charter (from left to right: Virginia Delegate Vincent F. Callahan, Jr. (Co-Chairman of the Jamestown-Yorktown Foundation); Lord Watson; Sir Robert Worcester; U.S. Ambassador Robert H. Tuttle; Mrs. Tuttle; former Speaker of the U.S. House of Representatives Thomas S. Foley; Mrs. Callahan; Michael Snyder)

Leaders and members of the Virginia Indian tribes are joined by representatives of Her Majesty, Queen Elizabeth II, the U.S. Embassy, British and Kentish governments, and British and American commemoration planning committees at Cobham Hall in Kent for the official welcoming ceremony on July 14, 2006

Virginians attending the December 19, 2006 events marking the 400th anniversary of the launch of the Susan Constant, Godspeed, and Discovery prepare to lay wreaths at the Virginia Quay monument honoring the original voyagers

A cadet from Virginia Military Institute serves as a member of the honor guard as Governor Kaine, speaking at the Museum in Docklands on December 19, 2006, transfers ownership of the replica ship Discovery to the Jamestown UK Foundation

Dignitaries gather on December 19, 2006, to view the recently opened "Journey to the New World" exhibition at the Museum in Docklands, near the site of the Jamestown settlers' departure 400 years earlier (from left to right after drummer: Sir Robert Worcester; Hazel Forsyth (Museum of London); Chairman Atkinson; Lord Watson; Governor Kaine; Virginia First Lady Anne Holton; Jim Fitzpatrick (MP - Poplar and Canning Town, Minister for London); Sandra Matthews-Marsh (Chief Executive, Visit Kent Ltd.); David Spence (Director, Museum in Docklands); Amanda Cottrell (High Sheriff of Kent))

Lord Watson of Richmond and Sir Robert Worcester, Co-Chairs of the Jamestown 2007 British Committee, display gifts received from Governor Kaine during ceremonies marking the transfer of the replica ship Discovery *to the Jamestown UK Foundation (Museum in Docklands, December 19, 2006)*

Jamestown 2007 British Committee Executive Director Rebecca Casson (right) and British Committee Treasurer Alex King (center) greet Interior Secretary Kempthorne during the Godspeed Sail *event in Alexandria, Virginia, on June 1, 2006*

Her Majesty speaks with Governor Kaine in the Memorial Church on Jamestown Island as Vice President and Mrs. Cheney (seated at front) and the British Ambassador to the United States, Sir David Manning (standing in doorway), look on (Historic Jamestowne, May 4, 2007)

Her Majesty visits with British Committee representatives Lord Watson (right), Amanda Cottrell (center), and Rebecca Casson (left) while in Williamsburg on May 4, 2007

Lord Phillips of Worth Matravers, the Lord Chief Justice of England and Wales, holds a copy of Lord Watson's new book, Jamestown: The Voyage of English, *as he delivers keynote remarks at Middle Temple during the Federal Commission's gala dinner commemorating the 400th anniversary of the launch of the original voyage to Jamestown (London, December 19, 2006)*

Guests at the packed Great Hall of Middle Temple on December 19, 2006, listen as Governor Kaine delivers remarks on the historic significance of the Jamestown voyage and settlement

Speaker Howell describes plans for the 400th anniversary commemoration at Jamestown, including visits by Her Majesty and the American President, and invites Britons to Virginia for the festivities (Middle Temple, London, December 19, 2006)

Federal Commission representatives on hand for the December 2006 ceremonies in England gather in front of the monument at Virginia Quay in Blackwall following the wreath-laying (from left to right: Commissioner Billings; Commissioner Flippo; Executive Director Mann; Vice Chair Dendy; Chief Adkins in Native regalia; Chairman Atkinson)

In late September 2004, Chairmen Atkinson and Connock led a joint federal-state delegation on an official trip to London, during which the American representatives notified responsible officials in the Foreign and Commonwealth Office, including a senior 10 Downing Street representative, of the impending invitation for a royal visit and briefed high-level government officials on overall plans for the Jamestown commemoration.[46] Members of the American delegation also provided briefings for senior officials at the United States Embassy in London, discussed the Commission's education initiatives with the British education ministry, explored plans for a "rule of law" conference and other democracy-related programs with leading barristers, jurists, foreign ministry officials, and a representative of the Westminster Foundation for Democracy, visited Virginia Quay at Blackwall and other possible commemorative event venues, and took steps to organize a high-level British planning committee for the commemoration.

Shortly after the delegation's return to the United States a meeting was held at the British Embassy in Washington, D.C., with the ambassador, Sir David Manning, and senior members of his staff. Chairmen Atkinson and Connock presented a similar briefing on commemoration plans and requested the Ambassador's endorsement of the invitation for a royal visit.[47] They were joined in the meeting and request by Lord Watson of Richmond, a widely respected Briton who had been introduced to commemoration planners by Virginia Governor Mark Warner and had recently agreed to serve as co-chair of what would become the Jamestown 2007 British Committee.[48] Ambassador Manning reported that Buckingham Palace was now aware of the expected invitation for May 2007, and he provided helpful

---

[46] The trip took place from September 27 to October 1, 2004, and was funded through a contribution from the Jamestown-Yorktown Educational Trust, a not-for-profit affiliate of the Jamestown-Yorktown Foundation. In addition to Chairmen Atkinson and Connock, the delegation included Commissioner Flippo, Executive Director Mann, Justice Donald W. Lemons of the Virginia Supreme Court, and former Virginia Delegate L. Ray Ashworth, chairman emeritus of the Jamestown-Yorktown Foundation. Lemons and Ashworth were members of the Jamestown 2007 Steering Committee.

[47] Commissioner Griles, Justice Lemons, and Executive Director Mann also participated in the briefing.

[48] Among other notable roles, Lord Watson was chairman and then international chairman emeritus of the English Speaking Union, chairman of Burson Marsteller Europe, and, earlier, the host of numerous award-winning British Broadcasting Company (BBC) documentaries and president of the Liberal Party. The author of several works, he published *Jamestown: The Voyage of English* (London 2006) during the course of his work on the Jamestown commemoration.

counsel regarding the steps to be taken and contacts to be made in effecting the invitation and moving toward its acceptance. This important meeting—one of two dozen discussions that the Federal Commission's chairman and executive director held with Ambassador Manning and/or Deputy Ambassador Alan Charlton during the commemoration planning period[49]—proved pivotal in formalizing discussions related to the Queen's visit. Shortly thereafter, Chairman Atkinson and Commissioner Griles reached out to the White House to set in motion the President's issuance of a state visit invitation to Queen Elizabeth II, while Senator Norment and Vice Chair Dendy took steps to secure an invitation from Governor Kaine for a royal visit to the Commonwealth of Virginia.

Formation of an influential Jamestown 2007 British Committee and the group's ensuing efforts to encourage a royal visit to Jamestown also played a vital role in the invitation process. The American delegation that visited the United Kingdom in September 2004 stopped first in Kent County, southeast of London, for discussions with Alex King, of the Kent County Council and other Kentish officials. As Kent's cabinet member for regeneration and later the Council's deputy leader, King was the early catalyst for prominent British participation in the Jamestown commemoration, and he spearheaded efforts to form a British planning committee for that purpose.[50] From these and other discussions in Kent and London, concrete

---

[49] The four-year tenure of Alan Charlton as deputy ambassador in Washington commenced in May 2004 and encompassed the royal visit and numerous other British activities related to the Jamestown commemoration, with Charlton and his embassy colleagues making highly important contributions to all of those activities. Chairmen Atkinson and Connock and Commissioner Griles met with Charlton at the embassy within days after his arrival in May 2004 and briefed him on plans for the commemoration. "[They] walked me through all of their very ambitious plans for activities and events and Her Majesty's visit, and I was somewhat skeptical that it would happen," Charlton recalled in remarks at a 2008 embassy dinner honoring his Washington service, "but, remarkably, virtually everything [they] predicted came true." The Queen's state visit, Charlton declared, was the highlight of his eventful tenure as his country's deputy chief of mission in the American capital.

[50] Collaborative efforts between Kent County in England and New Kent County, Virginia, were underway before this trip and contributed significantly to Kent County's interest in the Jamestown commemoration and its broader interest in developing ongoing economic, educational, cultural, and other ties between Kent and Virginia. Several New Kent County government officials participated in the September 2004 meetings with the American delegation in Kent, and representatives of the Virginia Department of Tourism participated prominently in subsequent discussions. In November 2006, a memorandum of understanding commencing the "Kent-Virginia Development Project" was signed by Sir Sandy Bruce-Lockhart, Leader of the Kent County Council, and Virginia Governor Mark Warner. The agreement formalized Kent-Virginia collaboration on economic development, tourism, cultural exchange, and other matters.

plans for the committee quickly emerged, with another leading resident of Kent, Sir Robert Worcester, agreeing to join Lord Watson as co-chair of the committee.[51] The Kent County Council provided staff and initial financial support to the planning committee; influential British leaders with enthusiasm for the anniversary enterprise soon agreed to serve on it; and within a few months the Jamestown 2007 British Committee's efforts were underway.[52] The American ambassador in London, Robert H. Tuttle, agreed to serve as "patron" of the Jamestown 2007 British Committee, while Ambassador Manning accepted a like position with the Committee's American counterpart. All understood a Jamestown visit by Queen Elizabeth II to be the centerpiece of a plan for wide-ranging—and unprecedented—British participation in the Jamestown 400th commemoration.[53]

As contacts regarding a possible royal visit continued, a series of important gatherings during 2005 helped to lay the foundation for a robust program of British-American activities associated with the Jamestown anniversary. Ambassador Manning hosted a reception at the embassy in February 2005 for British business executives in America, commemoration planners from both countries, senior government officials, and other dignitaries. With the Ambassador's encouragement, the Federal Commission and its partners used the event to raise awareness of the commemoration and generate interest on the part of British business interests. U.S. Senators John Warner and George Allen led the presentation, which provided the guests with an engaging video overview of commemoration plans and improvements underway at the Jamestown sites.

Chief Stephen Adkins in April welcomed Rebecca Casson, executive director of the Jamestown 2007 British Committee, to the Virginia Indian Tribal Alliance for Life (VITAL) Pow-

---

[51] A Kansas native with dual American and British citizenship, Worcester was chairman of the Pilgrims Society. He was well known in England as the founder of MORI, a leading international public opinion research organization, and as a political commentator and patron of various philanthropic causes. During his work on the commemoration, he also became chancellor of the University of Kent.

[52] Alex King agreed to serve as treasurer of the Committee, and Rebecca Casson, head of Kent-Virginia development for the Kent County Council, was designated as its executive director. Both were instrumental in the organization of the Committee and played central roles in all aspects of its work during 2004-2007.

[53] The Final Report of the Jamestown 2007 British Committee, issued in December 2007, is included at Appendix 12. It includes a roster of the British Committee's members.

Wow at the Chickahominy tribal grounds in New Kent County, Virginia. Representing the British Committee and Kent County, Ms. Casson extended an invitation to the Virginia tribes to visit Kent, Gravesend (the resting place of Pocahontas), and London in July 2006. An outgrowth of discussions among Chief Adkins, Executive Director Mann, and British planners, the invitation set the stage for a dramatic gathering a year later that helped galvanize tribal leaders for joint effort on the commemoration and other endeavors.

In summer 2005, key meetings on both sides of the Atlantic solidified plans for commemorative activities in the United Kingdom as well as prominent British participation in anniversary observances in America. Sir Sandy Bruce-Lockhart (later, Lord Bruce-Lockhart of the Weald), the leader of the Kent County Council and a member of the Jamestown 2007 British Committee, and British Committee Treasurer Alex King led a British delegation that participated in the Federal Commission's June 2-3 meeting in Williamsburg and met with Senator Norment, Chairman Connock, and other state commemoration leaders. Two months later, an American delegation that included Federal Commissioners Dendy and Adkins, Executive Director Mann, Virginia House of Delegates Speaker William J. Howell, Justice Donald W. Lemons, Chief Kenneth Adams of the Upper Mattaponi Indians, and President Emeritus Timothy J. Sullivan of the College of William and Mary traveled to London to participate in the British Committee's meeting at the House of Lords and other fruitful planning sessions. The July visit, which occurred just two weeks after a lethal terrorist attack on the London Underground transit system, provided an opportunity for the Americans to express solidarity with the British People. It also served as a sobering reminder of the terrorism backdrop against which commemorative events had to be planned.

As conceived in 2005, the British Committee's agenda of commemorative activities included support for royal participation in the American observances, a range of educational, cultural, tourism, and promotional activities in the United Kingdom, and the following major events:

- Legal Community Observances: Spring 2006 events in London marking the anniversary of the Virginia charter, a series of lectures on the rule of law sponsored by the English Inns of Court, and participation by English jurists and barristers in the "Democracy and the Rule of Law" conference in Richmond in April 2007 as part of the Federal Commission's democracy conference series.

- Virginia Indian Festival: A July 2006 festival in Kent honoring representatives of the Virginia Indian tribes, with educational, cultural, and commemorative components, followed by a visit to Parliament.

- Launch Anniversary Events: December 2006 events in London and at Blackwall marking the 400th anniversary of the launch of the *Susan Constant, Godspeed,* and *Discovery* bound for Jamestown.

- *Discovery* Tour: A visit to multiple English venues by the replica ship *Discovery* and a Jamestown-related exhibition at the Museum in Docklands.

- Smithsonian Folklife Festival: Celebration of Anglo-American and Kentish-Virginian ties at the popular annual festival on the National Mall in Washington, D.C., at which the "Roots of Virginia Culture" would be featured.

The anniversary calendar made 2006 an exceptionally active year for commemoration enthusiasts in the Mother Country. As the 400th anniversary of the formation of the Virginia Company approached, the British Committee on March 20, 2006, hosted a gala fundraising dinner in the Guildhall of the City of London to mark the occasion.[54] Delegate Vincent F. Callahan, Jr., co-chairman of the Jamestown-Yorktown Foundation Board of Trustees, led the Virginia delegation. The main address was delivered by Thomas S. Foley, former Speaker of the U.S. House of Representatives and former Ambassador to Japan, and newly on board as an honorary vice chair of the Federal Commission's International Conference Series on the Foundations and Future of Democracy. Speaker Foley's remarks at the well-attended gathering highlighted British-American ties and the importance of the two nations' partnership in the global advance of democratic ideals.

On April 10, 2006—the 400th anniversary of the charter that brought the Virginia Company into existence—an American delegation that included Ambassador Tuttle, Virginia Chief Justice Leroy R. Hassell, Sr., Chairman Atkinson, and other state and federal officials were honored guests at a banquet that featured stirring toasts and the performance of an original masque about the Jamestown venture. The setting was the historic Great Hall of Middle Temple, whose masters included Sir John Popham, the Lord Chief Justice and principal catalyst for the Virginia Company's formation, as well as many of the Virginia Company's original investors. The previous day, the American visitors attended Palm Sunday services at Temple Church, where they heard the church's master, Reverend Robin Griffith-Jones, deliver a homily on the Jamestown endeavor and its lasting significance, and then were luncheon guests of the venerable Inner Temple.

The four English Inns of Court contributed to the Jamestown anniversary program in a variety of ways. During the American planners' September 2004 visit to London, William Blair, QC, chairman of the English Commercial Bar Association and, later, a member of the Jamestown 2007 British Committee, convened several leading English barristers and jurists at Gray's Inn, where

---

[54] As described in its Final Report (see Appendix 12), the British Committee and its public and private supporters financed the commemorative programs and events in the United Kingdom. The Jamestown UK Foundation, Ltd., chaired by Alex King, was formed in January 2006 to lead the British fundraising efforts. The Federal Commission covered its own administrative and travel costs associated with the British initiatives, and the Commission also funded a gala dinner at Middle Temple on December 19, 2006, that it hosted to mark the anniversary of the three ships' launch for Jamestown. The Federal Commission's costs associated with the British initiatives were fully defrayed by corporate sponsors that donated through Jamestown 2007, Inc., or directly to the Commission.

they heard presentations by Justice Lemons and Chairman Atkinson and discussed ways to highlight the Anglo-American legal tradition during the course of the commemoration. Out of these discussions grew plans for prominent British participation in the "Rule of Law" democracy conference at the University of Richmond, the Inns' presentation of a plaque at Historic Jamestowne (attended by the two countries' chief justices), and a prestigious series of "rule of law" lectures in London between May 2006 and February 2007.[55]

British participation in the Federal Commission's year-long conference series on democracy took several forms. Lord Chief Justice Phillips of Worth Matravers, Lady Justice Mary Arden, and Lord Justice Bernard Anthony Rix were among those exploring shared and divergent aspects of the British and American legal systems at the April 2007 conference at the University of Richmond. During the same month, Ambassador Manning, Admiral Sir Mark Stanhope, and dozens of British military planners were among those who convened in Norfolk for a democracy conference on the transatlantic relationship hosted by Old Dominion University and NATO. Perhaps most important were the high-profile endorsements and visible support given to the democracy conference series by two former British prime ministers widely esteemed in the United States. Former Prime Ministers Margaret Thatcher and Tony Blair agreed to serve as honorary chairs of the conference series, joining former American Presidents George H.W. Bush and William J. Clinton in that role. Both British leaders delivered pre-recorded remarks on democracy's Jamestown roots and global advance at the conference series finale in Williamsburg.[56]

---

[55] The lecture series was sponsored by the English Commercial Bar Association (COMBAR) in association with the English Inns of Court, the American Bar Association, and the Virginia Supreme Court. The lectures are described in the British Committee's Final Report at Appendix 12.

[56] Baroness Thatcher, who served as chancellor of the College of William and Mary during 1993-2000, discussed the democracy series with the College's president emeritus, Timothy J. Sullivan, during the Americans' July 2005 planning trip to London and agreed to serve as honorary chair of the program. Prime Minister Blair was acquainted with the democracy conference series through briefings by British and American commemoration planners in 2005-2006 and through discussions with his elder brother, Jamestown 2007 British Committee member William Blair. Shortly before stepping down as prime minister in June 2007, he accepted an invitation from Justice O'Connor to become the fourth honorary co-chair of the series and to participate in the culminating *World Forum on the Future of Democracy*. See Chapter 5.

On July 14, 2006, a 55-member Virginia Indian delegation that included Chief Adkins, four other tribal chiefs, and representatives of all eight state-recognized tribes arrived in England for nearly a week of educational and cultural activities that drew extensive media coverage there and significant notice in the United States as well. It was thought to be the tribes' first official mission to England in more than two centuries, and it called to mind the dramatic visit of Pocahontas in 1617. The delegation was welcomed at Cobham Hall in the Borough of Gravesham by Allan Willett, Lord-Lieutenant of Kent, who represented Queen Elizabeth II, and by Lord Watson, Sir Robert Worcester, Lord Bruce-Lockhart, Alex King, and other members of the Jamestown 2007 British Committee and governmental representatives. Federal Commission Vice Chair Dendy, Commissioner Billings, and William H. Leighty, chief of staff to Governor Kaine, joined the Virginia Indians in the delegation.[57] After a procession in which the visiting Indians entered the hall in Native regalia bearing the flags of the United States, Virginia, and each of the eight tribes, Chief Anne Richardson of the Rappahannock Tribe spoke movingly of the Virginia Indians' journey over four centuries marked by tragedy, survival, and, more recently, renewed hopefulness. She presented the Lord-Lieutenant with a gold wedding ring, a gift for the Queen that symbolized the tribes' continual relationship with the Crown since the 1677 treaty and their affection for Her Majesty. Later, the tribal delegation went to the town of Gravesend for a private worship service at St. George's Church, the final resting place of Pocahontas.[58] They returned to the church two days later for a public worship service, where they were joined by 250 parishioners, local government leaders, and members of the Jamestown 2007 British Committee.

The Kentish Borough of Gravesham was also the scene of a two-day cultural festival in which the Native visitors donned their traditional regalia, performed songs and dances, held a pow-wow, displayed arts and crafts, and mingled with the estimated 12,000

---

[57] Representatives of Chesterfield County, Virginia, which established a "twinning" relationship with the Borough of Gravesham, also accompanied the group.

[58] Pocahontas died as she, her husband John Rolfe, and their young son Thomas were en route down the Thames on their return voyage to Virginia in March 1617. She was buried in the chancel area of St. George's Church, where stained glass windows donated by the Colonial Dames of America in 1914 still honor her memory. In the churchyard stands a statue of Pocahontas that is identical to the one outside the Memorial Church at Historic Jamestowne.

English visitors who attended the popular event. The Indians continued their educational and cultural outreach for several days thereafter, visiting 16 primary and secondary schools in the borough, participating in a cultural diversity seminar hosted by the Kent County Council, and joining history scholars, including Commissioner Billings, for a University of Kent symposium at Canterbury. The chiefs and other tribal representatives, joined by Commissioner Dendy and other dignitaries, concluded the successful mission on July 19 with a visit to London, where they toured Parliament, viewed Prime Minister's Question Time from the Distinguished Visitors Gallery, visited the British Museum, and attended other significant meetings and functions.

While the Virginia Indians were renewing their ties across the sea, cementing their own intertribal bonds, and garnering positive attention in Kent, London, and Virginia, planning for the British sovereign's American visit continued behind the scenes. Unofficial confirmation that the Queen would be coming to Jamestown reached the Federal Commission leadership in August 2006 through a confidential communication from the White House. It was assumed at first that the British monarch would join the President for the *America's Anniversary Weekend* festivities on May 11-13, 2007. When Sir Robin Janvrin and Ambassador Manning visited Jamestown and Williamsburg in early October and conveyed tentative plans for a slightly earlier visit by Her Majesty, commemoration leaders quietly shifted gears and began developing concepts for a separate royal visit to the Historic Triangle in early May.

The day after the royal advance party surveyed Jamestown, their countrymen aboard the *Fort Rosalie* of the Royal Fleet Auxiliary cast off from the Norfolk Naval Base en route to Southampton, England. On the ship's helicopter deck, partially dismantled for the voyage and secured in a custom-built steel cradle, was the *Discovery*, a replica of the smallest of the three vessels that brought the first settlers to Jamestown. On October 15, 2006, the replica completed its much safer, straighter, and faster return voyage—the trip took 10 days instead of its namesake's five months—and in so doing it fulfilled one of the foremost goals of British commemoration planners. Nothing, they felt, could convey to the British audience the magnitude of the 1607 accomplishment and the courage of their intrepid forebears so well as the sight of that amazingly small ship. In

May 2005, the Jamestown 2007 British Committee sent a letter to the Federal Commission requesting its assistance in securing a replica ship for use in connection with Jamestown-related observances in Britain. The Commission relayed the request to the Jamestown-Yorktown Foundation, whose governing board sought and received authorization from the Virginia General Assembly and Governor Kaine to gift the vessel to the Jamestown UK Foundation. The Virginia government also authorized the expenditure of $150,000 to rehabilitate and stabilize the vessel and to support interpretive programming in England. The ship's legal transfer from the "Official Fleet" of the Commonwealth of Virginia to the Jamestown UK Foundation at length was accomplished, and the vessel was on its way. In its place at Jamestown was a newly built replica of the *Discovery*, which joined the new *Godspeed* there in time to welcome commemoration-year visitors.

In one of the more ironic juxtapositions of the 18-month *America's 400ᵗʰ Anniversary* commemoration, October 2006 was also the month in which the 225ᵗʰ anniversary of Washington's victory over the British at Yorktown was celebrated, to great fanfare, as one of the commemoration's signature events.[59] So, while the Queen's staff was laying plans for her heroic return to Jamestown and the British Committee was welcoming the prodigal *Discovery* as its evocative emblem of Anglo-American solidarity, the Jamestown commemoration was celebrating the victory that sealed America's independence from the Mother Country. French Minister of Defense Michele Alliott-Marie, French Ambassador Jean-David Levitte, Secretary of the Interior Dirk Kempthorne, U.S. Senators John Warner and George Allen, and Congresswoman JoAnn Davis were among the speakers paying tribute to the Franco-American alliance and its triumph over the Redcoats. It was all taken with good cheer. On hand for the ceremonies at Yorktown was the venerable 3ʳᵈ Baron Cornwallis, a member of the Jamestown 2007 British Committee. "I thought it appropriate to be here at Yorktown,"

---

[59] The four-day event (October 19-22, 2006) was themed "A Salute to the Military." In addition to the usual annual fare, which featured a parade, official ceremony emceed by Colonial National Historical Park Superintendent P. Daniel Smith at the Victory Monument, and siege reenactment hosted by the Yorktown Day Association and National Park Service, the 2006 Yorktown anniversary observances included Jamestown 2007's special production titled, "We Salute You: An American Symphony 1781." The production honored America's armed forces, past and present, and included a special symphonic arrangement performed by the Williamsburg Symphonia Orchestra followed by a brilliant fireworks display.

he said with a smile to Chairman Atkinson as the ceremonies began, "because my forebear played such an important role in making all this possible."

Upon its arrival in Southampton, the *Discovery* was taken to Canary Wharf, London, adjacent to the Museum in Docklands, where a new exhibit about Jamestown ("Journey to the New World") opened on November 22. The *Discovery* remained there until the exhibition's close in May 2007, and then it commenced a four-month tour that took it to festivals and other events at Dover, Chatham, Lincoln, Bristol, Ipswich (Suffolk), and Harwich (Essex). More than 340,000 visitors came to see it, and an estimated 6.9 million saw media coverage of its visit. Among those boarding the ship at Canary Wharf were two Americans—Governor Kaine and Ambassador Tuttle—who visited the Docklands museum with other dignitaries as part of the ceremonies on December 19, 2006, marking the 400th anniversary of the three ships' departure for Jamestown.[60]

The November 15th announcement in Parliament of the Queen's plans for a visit to Jamestown had a dramatic awareness-raising effect in the United Kingdom similar to its impact in the United States. The Jamestown anniversary was an object of the Queen's attention—indeed, it not only had garnered her attention but was the focus of an American visit by the sovereign—and so it instantly seemed to merit the attention of her subjects. A variety of observances had been planned to mark the December 19th anniversary of the ships' departure for Jamestown, including a gala formal dinner at the Middle Temple hosted by the Federal Commission. Interest in the occasion soared after the Queen's announcement. The hundreds who were able to attend the sell-out event heard a stirring keynote address from Lord Chief Justice Phillips of Worth Matravers, himself a master of the Middle Temple, as well as moving remarks by Governor Kaine, toasts by Lord Watson and Virginia Delegate Vincent F. Callahan, Jr., a preview of plans for the *Royal Visit* and *Anniversary Weekend* by Virginia House Speaker William J.

---

[60] Two years later, on December 19, 2008, the *Discovery* was transferred to its new permanent home at Westenhanger Castle, near the Kent coast.

Howell, and a benediction by Chief Adkins.[61] Earlier in the day, Chairmen Atkinson and Connock led the American delegation in a private wreath-laying ceremony at Virginia Quay, near Blackwall, where a monument marks the place from which the 104 settlers departed in December 1606 bound for Virginia.[62]

While in England for the departure anniversary events, Governor Kaine was invited to Buckingham Palace for a discussion of the Queen's potential stop at the Virginia Capitol. When the details were finalized early in the new year, only a relatively short time remained before the visit. The Governor's Office and the General Assembly led preparations for the Richmond leg of the Queen's visit, while the Colonial Williamsburg Foundation lent that organization's considerable resources and experience as a primary organizer of the visit to the Historic Triangle. Both worked closely with officials from the British Embassy and the Queen's staff.

The *Royal Visit* became a centerpiece of the commemorative observances, and the Colonial Williamsburg team's attention to the logistical, protocol, security, advance, and hospitality details of the visit proved crucial to the event's success, especially since the state and federal commemoration staffs already were stretched thin by their ongoing work on the fast-approaching *Anniversary Weekend* and other major activities. Federal Commission members and staff supported Colonial Williamsburg's efforts, with Vice Chair Nancy Campbell playing a key role in the preparations, while all of the visit details were coordinated closely with the organizations responsible for the two Jamestown sites as well as the local and state commemoration

---

[61] Chairman Atkinson was emcee of the Middle Temple event, assisted by Vice Chair Dendy and Steering Committee Chairman Connock. Lord Watson and Sir Robert Worcester introduced Lord Chief Justice Phillips and Governor Kaine, respectively. Color guards from Virginia Military Institute and the London Unified Officer Training Corps presented the colors, after which both national anthems were played. Reverend Robin Griffith-Jones, Master of the Temple Church, delivered the invocation. Dinner guests received a commemorative clock as a memento, along with a copy of Lord Watson's new book, *Jamestown: The Voyage of English,* and a keepsake program that included Commissioner Gleason's manuscript, "The Beginning of Jamestown: The Royal Charter, Blackwall and the Voyage to Virginia." Executive Director Mann led the arrangements for the memorable event with the assistance of British Committee Executive Director Casson.

[62] Four wreaths were laid at the foot of the granite monument. Chief Adkins and Virginia House Speaker Howell laid a wreath on behalf of the people of the Commonwealth of Virginia, and Commissioner Flippo did so on behalf of the Jamestown commemoration planning committees. Mr. Carter Furr laid a wreath on behalf of the Order of the First Families of Virginia, and Mr. Kenneth Bass did so on behalf of The Jamestowne Society.

planning groups. Faced with the need to improvise so that another high-profile commemorative event could be staged in the heart of the anniversary year, the planning partners pulled together and accomplished the goal. It was the single event that generated the most media attention during the entire 18-month commemoration.

Members of the Jamestown 2007 British Committee and other notables from the United Kingdom and the Commonwealth attended the *Royal Visit* and *Anniversary Weekend* festivities in May 2007.[63] The Federal Commission and British Committee jointly sponsored receptions for American and British commemoration planners, British Embassy officials, and other distinguished international guests. A sizeable delegation from Bermuda attended the *Anniversary Weekend* festivities, reflecting the close connection between Bermuda and Jamestown in the 17th century. Several years after the *Sea Venture*, a large re-supply ship bound for Jamestown, wrecked on the island in 1609, the Virginia Company established a colony on Bermuda that was known for a time as "Virginiola."[64] Among the other international guests present for *Anniversary Weekend* was the Polish ambassador to the United States, Janusz Reiter. His countrymen had a significant connection to the colony because Poles with needed skill in the manufacture of glass, soap, pitch, tar, and other essentials came to Jamestown in 1608.

During the *Anniversary Weekend* ceremonies, Sir Robert Worcester and Alex King deposited several items in the commemoration time capsule, including a three-hour digital video recording of the Queen's visit and records of the July 2006 Virginia Indian festival. A month later, King and Executive Director Casson returned to the United States with a nearly four-dozen-person Kent County delegation to participate in

---

[63] British Committee participation in these commemorative events, including the important work of Executive Director Casson on preparations for the Queen's visit, is summarized in the British Committee's report at Appendix 12.

[64] Bermuda's government observed the Jamestown anniversary and celebrated the Bermuda-Virginia connection by issuing two commemorative stamps, which Bermudian officials presented to U.S. Senator John Warner, Vice Chair Dendy, and Jamestown 2007 Executive Director Jeanne Zeidler in June 2007. Among other forms of collaboration, a special exhibition commemorating Bermuda's 400th anniversary was planned for the Jamestown Settlement museum in 2009. Several Jamestown commemoration planners, including state Steering Committee Chairman Stuart W. Connock and Federal Commissioners Dendy, Flippo, and Atkinson, worked closely with Bermudian heritage tourism leaders through their service on the Honorary Council of the St. George's Foundation.

the annual Smithsonian Folklife Festival on the National Mall in Washington. The "Roots of Virginia Culture" was a featured program of the 2007 festival, and Kent County partnered with Virginia to highlight the cultural and commercial ties between the Old Dominion, Kent, and other English counties.

While the commemorative events in the United Kingdom were most impressive, any review of the impact of the Jamestown 2007 British Committee and its programs would be incomplete without looking beyond the successful individual events to the economic, educational, and cultural benefits of the program as a whole. Through this unprecedented commemorative collaboration, engaging lessons about the 400-year-old Anglo-American relationship and related topics reached school children in both countries, communities entered into cooperative relationships across the Atlantic, tourism and economic cooperation were boosted in tangible ways, cultural and historical ties were rediscovered and renewed, and the program left a legacy of ongoing cooperation.[65] Most important, the people of two nations that enjoy a cherished "special relationship" were reminded of all they share: language, culture, and history; a commitment to universal values; and an interconnected future. It was a fitting tribute to what Her Majesty, Queen Elizabeth II, aptly called "one of the most durable international collaborations anywhere in the world at any time in history."

---

[65] See the report of the Jamestown 2007 British Committee at Appendix 12.

CHAPTER 4

Understanding Jamestown's Enduring Legacies:
The National Educational Initiatives

When the "Jamestown—Journey of Democracy" website (*www.JamestownJourney.org*) went "live" in November 2005, the Federal Commission realized one of its principal goals. In its strategic plan, the Commission committed itself to the ambitious task of creating and operating the commemoration's official education curriculum website as a means of providing teachers and students across America with a user-friendly point of access for educational resources on all things Jamestown-related. The central theme of the website and curriculum was to be the 400-year-long journey of democracy from its American beginning at Jamestown to its advance in the contemporary world. Exceeding even the most optimistic expectations, the website's launch began an educational enterprise that reached millions during the commemoration and promised a continuing positive impact long after the Commission's tenure ended.

In a May 2007 commentary in *TIME*, Justice O'Connor declared that the educational mission was "the larger purpose at work [in the Jamestown] commemoration—a purpose that goes to the very heart of how we strengthen our democracy in today's world and build for the future." The 400th anniversary observances, she wrote,

> [provide] an ideal opportunity to recognize the importance of promoting civic learning: teaching our young people about our history and the responsibilities of citizenship as well as the special

significance of the rule of law in a functioning
democracy. The better we all understand
and appreciate the genesis of the American
republic and how it works, the more likely it is
that we will continue to develop the means to
live cooperatively and successfully in today's
challenging world. America persevered because
passionate, civic-minded citizens understood the
importance of this country's founding traditions
and were willing to take a stand in their defense.
But these historic lessons are not passed on to new
generations through the gene pool. They must
be taught in our schools.... Jamestown's 400th
birthday provides a platform for emphasizing
the importance of civics education taught in the
context of our nation's history. Sustaining our
democratic republic requires that we renew our
commitment to that objective.[66]

With civics education and the civic engagement of young people
as a primary objective from the start, the Federal Commission
sought the assistance of the University of Virginia Center for
Politics in developing the educational elements of its strategic
plan. Formed in 1997, the Center for Politics had a civics-
education mission, experience in deploying new technology for
instructional purposes, an emphasis on applied learning, and a
track record of partnering successfully with national educational
organizations to reach classrooms across America—all elements
that the Commission's Educational Initiatives Committee, co-
chaired by Commissioners Billings and Loomis, deemed crucial.
The Commission formally engaged the Center for Politics in
October 2004, and work began immediately on three interrelated
components: construction of the *JamestownJourney* website,
development of civics lesson plans related to Jamestown, and
formation of a curriculum review committee that would help
ensure that all of the multidisciplinary Jamestown-related
educational resources available through the website were
historically accurate, inclusive, and comprehensive. The
work was funded in part by the United States Department of
Education, which became an active partner in the program and
contributed $100,000 in grant funds to assist in website and

[66] Justice Sandra Day O'Connor, "The Anniversary Party," *TIME,* May 7, 2007, p. 68.

curriculum development and nationwide dissemination of the materials.

The *JamestownJourney* website was designed to serve as a "one-stop" venue where elementary and secondary school teachers across the country could easily obtain sound curriculum on a wide range of topics with a Jamestown nexus. With the exception of the civics-related lesson plans, which were original materials that the Center for Politics developed for the Federal Commission, partner organizations with educational expertise supplied most of the content by making their extant instructional resources accessible on or through the website. For the civics curriculum, the Center for Politics developed a series of 12 original lesson plans that illuminated Jamestown's role in the introduction of core aspects of America's republican system, including representative government, free enterprise, religious liberty, the rule of law, individual rights, and cultural diversity. The new curriculum traced the evolution, advancement, and application of these core ideas from (i) their introduction in the Jamestown (Virginia) colony, (ii) to their inclusion in the nation's charter in the founding era, (iii) through subsequent and ongoing efforts to fulfill the promise of liberty for all Americans, and (iv) to the contemporary spread of freedom and democracy to other lands around the world. Not only a better understanding of the historical background, but practical engagement of young people in the civic life of their communities, states, and nation, were the intended results.[67]

New civics lesson plans and other educational resources proffered by partner organizations were vetted by the Curriculum Advisory Committee, a panel organized and coordinated for the Federal Commission by the Center for Politics.[68] The Committee's mission was to ensure that all of the educational resources accessible through the *JamestownJourney* website met

---

[67] The Center for Politics engaged an experienced and talented social studies teacher, Meg Heubeck, to lead the civics curriculum development. She received input and assistance from a range of organizations and experts, some of which were associated with Jamestown while others were known for their expertise in civics education generally.

[68] Daman Irby of the Center for Politics ably spearheaded formation of the Curriculum Advisory Committee and its review of lesson plans, as well as development of the *JamestownJourney* website. He also was the lead organizer of the International Youth Democracy Summit at the University of Virginia, part of the democracy conference series discussed in the next chapter. Mr. Irby and Ms. Heubeck were regular participants in the Commission's meetings and, though technically not staff to the Federal Commission, played integral roles in numerous aspects of the Commission's work.

a high standard of quality, accuracy, and completeness, and were practical instructional tools that could be put to use immediately in classrooms.   The culturally diverse panel included experts on Jamestown and colonial history, experienced classroom teachers, noted scholars, and federal and state commemoration planners. Commissioners Adkins, Billings, Reid, and Trumbo served on the Committee, as did the members of Jamestown 2007's "Historical Accuracy Committee," a group previously created to review program content for various commemorative events.[69]   The dedicated volunteers who comprised the Curriculum Advisory Committee spent many hours reviewing and discussing the voluminous educational resources that were recommended for inclusion among the *JamestownJourney* offerings.

During 2006, the Federal Commission and Center for Politics focused on promoting the *JamestownJourney* website and resources to educators across the country. Flyers describing the   resources were mailed nationwide to more than 40,000 social studies teachers, curriculum coordinators,   and other educators. Representatives of the Center for Politics attended several major national education conferences and made presentations regarding the *JamestownJourney* program and instructional materials. Numerous prominent organizations were   recruited   as educational partners by the Center for Politics and/or Jamestown 2007, and these organizations spread the word to their members through newsletters, electronic messages, and special communications.[70] Visitors to the *America's 400th Anniversary* website were encouraged to access educational resources about Jamestown by clicking on a prominently placed link to the *JamestownJourney* website. These and other promotional activities not only attracted educators to the website; they also prompted contributions of

---

[69] Dr. James Horn, vice president of research for the Colonial Williamsburg Foundation and author of *A Land as God Made It: Jamestown and the Birth of America* (New York: Basic Books, 2005), chaired the Historical Accuracy Committee, and Daman Irby moderated the Curriculum Advisory Committee. For a list of the Curriculum Advisory Committee members, see Appendix 13.

[70] Among the educational partners that actively promoted use of the *JamestownJourney* website and resources were the U.S. and Virginia Departments of Education, National Park Service, History Channel, National Association of Elementary School Principals, National Association of Social Studies, National Council for History Education, National Education Association, National History Day, USA Today Education Online, Virginia Education Association, Virginia PTA, Virginia Association of Elementary School Principals, Virginia Association of Secondary School Principals, and Verizon Foundation.

valuable new educational resources for the *JamestownJourney* website by a diverse array of organizations.

By 2007, teachers, students, and other interested parties were able to access a rich variety of multidisciplinary educational resources through the website. Prominent among these were educational resources provided by key partners, such as the Jamestown-Yorktown Foundation, Colonial Williamsburg Foundation, APVA Preservation Virginia, Colonial National Historical Park, National Geographic Society, and NASA, but many other respected organizations also supplied pertinent materials.[71] Among the more than 170 lesson plans for grades K-12 available through the site were curricula that traced the cultures that converged at Jamestown and their continuing journey, illuminated the exciting archeological work currently underway at Jamestown and Werowocomoco, explored the interaction between man and nature in the unique Chesapeake estuary, and linked previous ages of discovery with contemporary space exploration. Visitors to the *JamestownJourney* website also found links to the educational websites of partner organizations and to other 400th anniversary educational programs, including the Federal Commission's International Conference Series on the Foundations and Future of Democracy, the *Jamestown Live!* educational webcast, and *America's 400th Anniversary* signature events.

The reach and impact of the Federal Commission's *JamestownJourney* educational initiatives were expanded significantly through collaboration with the state's Jamestown 2007 organization on its November 9, 2006 educational webcast, titled *Jamestown Live! Experience the Journey that Changed the World.* One of the commemoration's signature events, the hour-long webcast was accessible free through the History Channel's educational website and by satellite downlink, and it reached more than a million elementary, middle, and home-

---

[71] Other entities contributing educational resources included Virtual Jamestown, Foundation for Teaching Economics, National Endowment for Humanities (Edsitement), Smithsonian Institution's National Museum of Natural History, United States Slavery Museum, National Women's History Museum, Powhatan Museum of Indigenous Arts and Culture, Sultana Projects, Dan Roberts' "A Moment in Time," University of Virginia Center for Politics, ThanksUSA, The Road to Jamestown, NASA Connect, James River Association, Charles City County, Virginia, and Virginia Department of Conservation and Recreation.

schooled students throughout the United States.[72] The Federal Commission's contributions to the webcast were substantial: the program's educational content was based on *JamestownJourney* curricula; teachers registered their classes to participate via the *JamestownJourney* website; Center for Politics staff assisted in script development and review; the webcast was featured prominently in the Center's mailings, electronic messages, conference presentations, and other activities promoting the *JamestownJourney* educational resources; and Chief Adkins played an important role in the program itself as one of several notable figures interviewed by the show's student reporters.

The *Jamestown Live!* program stressed the colony's legacies related to democracy, cultural diversity, and exploration. Hosted by well-known national correspondent Gwen Ifill,[73] the fast-paced program resembled a television news magazine with student reporters interviewing experts live at the Jamestown Settlement and in pre-recorded conversations from Historic Jamestowne.[74] Student viewers also submitted questions online, and musical segments enlivened the show while highlighting historical facts and commemoration themes. In addition to the online live audience, which included young people from every American state, the nation's capital, Guam, Puerto Rico, and 16 other countries,[75] "student ambassadors" from 49 states attended in person, hundreds of Virginia school children were in the on-site audience, and viewership was greatly extended in ensuing months through online downloads, cable broadcasts, and digital video (DVD) distributions. The program remained available

---

[72] A 2001 educational webcast led by Virginia First Lady Roxane Gilmore had reached 25,000 school children, mostly in Virginia, and had demonstrated the strong classroom appeal of the Jamestown story.

[73] Ifill was senior correspondent of *The NewsHour with Jim Lehrer* and moderator of *Washington Week*, two popular public affairs programs aired by the Public Broadcasting System (PBS).

[74] In addition to Chief Adkins, the expert interviewees included an astronaut (Kathryn Thornton of NASA), an archaeologist (Dr. William Kelso, director of the Jamestown Rediscovery Project at Historic Jamestowne), a noted historian and author (Dr. James Horn, vice president of research at Colonial Williamsburg), a sea captain (Captain Eric Speth, maritime program manager for the Jamestown-Yorktown Foundation), and the co-chair of the commemoration's African American Advisory Council (Dr. Rex Ellis, vice president of the Colonial Williamsburg Foundation). Chief Adkins was interviewed by student reporter Will Mann.

[75] Live viewership of the webcast was conservatively estimated at a million students but likely reached a much larger audience. More than 9,800 educators registered via the *JamestownJourney* website to have their classes participate, and those classes represented nearly a million students. Whole school districts could access the program via a single registration and satellite feed, however, and then disseminate the program to students throughout the district via its cable channels.

throughout the 2006-2007 school year via the *JamestownJourney* and partner websites; the History Channel aired the program several times on its educational access channel; and Jamestown 2007 produced and disseminated DVDs containing topical segments from the show.

Jamestown 2007's partnerships with the History Channel and with *TIME* magazine's popular educational arm, *TIME for Kids*, were instrumental not only in the success of the *Jamestown Live!* webcast, but also in broadly promoting the educational resources available on the Federal Commission's curriculum website. The History Channel highlighted the Jamestown-related website and educational resources in the fall 2006 back-to-school issue of its *The Idea Book* publication, which had a circulation of 220,000 educators, and repeatedly in its electronic newsletter that regularly reached 125,000 educators and parents. Like other educational partners of Jamestown 2007 and the Federal Commission, *TIME for Kids* sent a series of electronic messages to its readers urging them to visit the *JamestownJourney* site to register for the webcast and to access curriculum materials. For classroom use, *TIME for Kids* also produced and supplied 85,000 American educators with poster-size teacher's guides that contained Jamestown-related visuals, lesson plans, and *JamestownJourney*'s website address. In addition, pertinent lesson plans available on the *JamestownJourney* website were highlighted graphically on screen throughout the *Jamestown Live!* webcast itself, providing continuing promotional value as the program was replayed on the History Channel's educational access channel and via online downloads and DVDs.

The far-reaching impact of these interrelated educational partnerships and collaborations is partly evidenced by the impressive number of educators who have signed on to use the *JamestownJourney* educational resources since the website was launched three years ago. As of the date of this report, more than 18,000 people from all 50 states, the District of Columbia and 55 countries have registered as users. Since many of the users are educators who teach multiple classes and likely reuse the materials year after year and share them with others, the Center for Politics estimates that Jamestown-related resources have reached millions of students since the website went "live" in November 2005. The Federal Commission has taken steps to extend this impact well beyond the commemoration by making a legacy grant to the Center for Politics for the continued operation, content management, and promotion of the website and educational materials. The Center's plans include a partnership with the Verizon Foundation that will include the *JamestownJourney* resources among the large volume of high-quality lesson plans and curricular resources that teachers across the country and around the world regularly access through that foundation's *Thinkfinity* educational portal. In addition to broadly disseminating materials that tell the true story of Jamestown's importance, the Center for Politics will continue the efforts of the Federal Commission to improve the accuracy of the states' educational content standards related to colonial history in general and Jamestown's role in particular.

The impact of the Commission's anniversary-related educational initiatives also will be extended through grants that the Commission made during 2008 to the key educational organizations in the Historic Triangle and surrounding area whose ongoing mission includes teaching young people about the legacies of Jamestown and the Virginia colony. These include the Jamestown-Yorktown Foundation, Historic Jamestowne (through APVA Preservation Virginia), the Colonial Williamsburg Foundation, and the Friends of the Captain John Smith Chesapeake National Historic Trail. In addition, the Commission made legacy grants to the APVA's Jamestown Rediscovery Project and to the Department of Archaeology at the College of William and Mary to support ongoing investigation, education, and interpretation at the James Fort and Werowocomoco archaeological sites, respectively.

A key theme of the Jamestown 400th commemoration, and thus an important element running through all of the Federal Commission's educational initiatives, was the importance of the cross-cultural encounters, conflicts, and collaborations that occurred in early Virginia, presaging the cultural diversity that would become such a vital aspect of the American story. Rather than the product of a single source or event, Jamestown's enduring legacies evolved out of a rich confluence of ideas, experiences, and cultures. From the early interaction of Virginia Indian, English, and African cultures at Jamestown and throughout colonial America grew an increasingly diverse and democratic society that kept striving to fulfill its own ideals even as it inspired and assisted champions of self-government in other lands. This uplifting story was woven throughout the educational resources developed for and through the Jamestown commemoration. In addition, state and federal commemoration planners made a concerted effort to remedy the omissions of past commemorations by providing opportunities for the heirs of two of the three cultures that converged at Jamestown— Native Americans and African Americans—to tell their stories in their own voices.

While educational content illuminating the culture and contributions of Virginia's Indian tribes ran throughout the commemoration's federal, state, and community-based initiatives, two specific educational programs focused on Native Americans were signature events of *America's 400th Anniversary.* The first was a symposium on October 5-7, 2006, entitled "Virginia Indians: 400 Years of Survival," which drew several hundred participants for seminars at the newly renovated Williamsburg Lodge followed by a two-day tour of Indian tribal centers around the state. Organized by the Virginia Indian Advisory Council, with content agreed upon by Chief Adkins and his fellow tribal chiefs, the program included panels on legal issues facing Native Americans, the challenges involved in preserving Indian history and culture, and the ongoing archaeological investigation of Werowocomoco, the recently confirmed site of Chief Powhatan's headquarters on the banks of the York River in Gloucester Country. A primary organizer of Indian programming for the commemoration, Chief Kenneth Adams of the Upper Mattaponi tribe, viewed the symposium as groundbreaking. "We have never before had an opportunity to tell our own story in our own words on such a comprehensive level," he observed.

Nine months later, the Virginia tribes welcomed tribal representatives from around the country for a cultural festival at the Hampton Coliseum. The two-day American Indian Intertribal Cultural Festival was the largest Native-American event ever held in Virginia, attracting an audience that Jamestown 2007 planners estimated at 18,000. The festival featured a grand entry procession, lively lectures, cultural demonstrations, children's programming, historical exhibitions, Native crafts, and other educational elements. Addressing tribal representatives at the festival's July 20 welcoming reception, Chief Adkins and Chairman Atkinson recalled the early commitment of commemoration planners to an accurate and inclusive telling of the Jamestown story, and noted the commemoration's contribution to broad-based awareness of the Virginia Indian tribes' contributions over the four centuries since Jamestown's founding. The presence of tribal representatives from around the country, they noted, was a tribute to the Virginia tribes and affirmed that the indigenous peoples who first encountered English settlers on the American shores are still present and still contributing to American society and culture.

To increase understanding of the African-American experience at Jamestown and the culture and contributions of African Americans during the nation's four-century-long journey, the commemoration's African American Advisory Council adopted "The African American Imprint on America" as its overall theme, and planned a national symposium in February 2007 as well as programs at Virginia's historically black colleges and universities that focused on particular areas of contribution, or "imprints." Jamestown 2007 also sponsored an educational, cultural, and commercial exposition as part of the commemoration's celebration of African-American contributions. The summer 2007 Virginia Black Commerce and Cultural Expo held at the Hampton Roads Convention Center featured exhibits on African-American history supplied by cultural organizations around Virginia and attracted 8,500 attendees.

For the national symposium, the African American Advisory Council recommended a partnership with well-known media personality Tavis Smiley, whose annual "State of the Black Union" forum featured a discussion of issues affecting the African-American community and regularly attracted high-profile African-American panelists, a live audience of several thousand, and national cable television coverage. Commissioner Reid, a member of the Council, initiated the discussions with Smiley, and the state's Jamestown 2007 organization ultimately secured an agreement by which the 2007 State of the Black Union symposium was held at Hampton University's convocation center on February 9, 2007. The day-long program, which filled the 10,000-person arena and was covered in its entirety by the cable television network C-SPAN, focused on the "African American Imprint on America" theme and featured panels comprised of state and national political figures, commentators, educators, and cultural leaders, among whose number were

Commissioner Reid and her husband, actor Tim Reid. The preceding day, a smaller forum held in Phi Beta Kappa Memorial Hall at the College of William and Mary brought together nine noted scholars to examine the role of African Americans at Jamestown and the long-term implications of those early cross-cultural interactions.

Commemoration planners' educational objectives also were reflected in new museum exhibits and educational programs offered at Historic Jamestowne and Jamestown Settlement. At Historic Jamestowne, visitors to the new Archaearium were able to view recently unearthed artifacts from the James Fort that evidenced much greater interaction between the English settlers and Indians within the fort than was previously thought to have occurred. At Jamestown Settlement, pre-commemoration improvements markedly expanded the size of the museum, enabling the Jamestown-Yorktown Foundation to dedicate significant space to exhibits highlighting each of the three cultures that converged at Jamestown.[76] The new changing gallery at Jamestown Settlement housed the commemoration's signature exhibition, *World of 1607*, which included nearly 400 iconic objects of the early 17th century loaned from national institutions, personal collections, and public and private museums in 10 countries on three continents.[77] The exhibition impressed visitors throughout 2007, and provided a dramatic global context for the transformational events that took place at Jamestown beginning in 1607.

Many new educational and cultural attractions, exhibits, and programs were launched in Virginia during the 400th anniversary commemoration, and the organizations responsible for these initiatives often engaged in outreach and supplied content that reinforced and extended the commemoration's key messages and educational themes. Commissioner Flippo played a pivotal role in many of these statewide and community-based efforts in her dual capacity as chair of the Jamestown 2007 Programs and

---

[76] The new African exhibits in the expanded museum at Jamestown Settlement were previewed at a gala event in October 2006 attended by representatives of the Angolan Embassy and other dignitaries. The African-American imprint on America was the theme of the gala's keynote speech by Dr. Cassandra Newby-Alexander, associate professor of history at Norfolk State University and a member of the Federal Commission's Democracy Program Planning Council.

[77] Among the objects was a 15th century copy of the Magna Carta, owned by Viscount Coke and the trustees of the Holkham Estate (the Earl of Leicester).

Events Committee. Under that panel's auspices, representatives of Virginia's leading museums and historical and cultural organizations comprised a "Virginia Cultural Network" that worked jointly to plan and execute a wide array of anniversary-related initiatives, and communities throughout Virginia engaged in educational and cultural activities highlighting aspects of their history. In addition, some of the state's most venerated historical sites and tourist attractions, including the presidential homes at Mount Vernon and Montpelier, accomplished major facility improvements before or during the commemoration. A significant new attraction, one of the world's most impressive military museums—the National Museum of the United States Marine Corps—opened its doors for the first time in November 2006 near Quantico, Virginia, with President Bush leading the ceremonies.

Two other influential organizations—the National Geographic Society and NASA—merit special reference in connection with the Federal Commission's national education initiatives. In addition to providing valuable educational resources for access via the *JamestownJourney* website, both organizations contributed in vital ways to achievement of the commemoration's broad educational mission.

In November 2005, the National Geographic Society hosted a Chesapeake Education Summit at its Washington, D.C., offices in conjunction with the annual meeting of the Chesapeake Bay Executive Council. Commissioners Loomis, Rives, and Atkinson attended the Summit, and Chairman Atkinson made a presentation on the *JamestownJourney* educational initiatives. He invited the represented organizations to make their educational resources available through the Commission's website and stressed the opportunity afforded by the Jamestown 400th commemoration to advance goals related to restoration of the Chesapeake Bay. Various organizational contacts and collaborations followed, but none was more consequential than the active dialogue that ensued with the leadership and staff of the National Geographic Society. In November 2006, the Federal Commission and National Geographic Society executed an "alliance" agreement providing for joint educational activities related to the commemoration, including the Society's active promotion of the *JamestownJourney* website and its publication of various print and electronic materials related to Jamestown.[78] During the same time, the Federal Commission worked closely with the Society to build support for the proposed Captain John Smith Chesapeake National Historic Trail. As discussed more fully in Chapter 6, the Federal Commission was among the first groups to lend its imprimatur and active backing to creation of the all-water pathway, which became a major educational legacy of the commemoration.

Collaboration with NASA on educational matters was similarly significant. With the space agency's active participation in the commemoration, the Commission gained access to exciting and informative educational resources on contemporary space exploration, including plans to establish a permanent outpost on the Moon. The educational materials, together with exhibits and prominent participation by astronauts in commemorative programs and events, connected the 17th century voyages of discovery with modern exploratory missions, enabling students to better appreciate how rapidly the world of their day can change as vast new horizons are opened. "The same courage and conviction that brought the Jamestown settlers to America in 1607 continues to drive today's explorers," said Astronaut Sunita Williams, speaking from the International Space Station to those attending Jamestown's anniversary ceremonies on May 13, 2007. "We salute those who blazed those early trails in Jamestown, and we are proud to serve as a stepping stone on our nation's journey back to the Moon, on to Mars and to points beyond." Two months later, a metal cargo tag recently unearthed at Historic Jamestowne and gold and silver coins commemorating the Jamestown anniversary traveled to the International Space Station aboard the space shuttle *Atlantis* and then returned to assume honored showplaces in the Jamestown museums. There, they would remind visitors young and old of the spirit of discovery that brought brave travelers to the New World four centuries ago and is opening up new worlds

---

[78] Among the Jamestown-related works produced by the National Geographic Society were magazine articles, books, and children's books on Captain John Smith and his exploration of the Chesapeake Bay, a documentary entitled "Nightmare in Jamestown," an educational video entitled "John Smith's Voyage of Discovery," lessons plans for grades K-12, large maps (in adult and children's versions) depicting the Chesapeake region in the early 1600s (including natural habitats and Indian communities) compared to today, and a May 2007 magazine cover story and multiple articles on the history and impact of the Jamestown settlement.

in our time.[79]

While the *JamestownJourney* educational initiatives were targeted toward young people in elementary, middle, and high schools, the Federal Commission also engaged the higher education community and noted scholars from around the country and across the seas. The principal vehicle for that engagement was the International Conference Series on the Foundations and Future of Democracy, a year-long program that involved 10 Virginia colleges and universities and scholars from many other institutions. That educational initiative is the subject of Chapter 5.

----

[79] NASA Administrator Michael Griffin participated in the *Anniversary Weekend* ceremonies, and, like Astronaut Williams, he stressed the connection between exploration in Jamestown's day and the planned missions outlined in NASA's "Vision for Space Exploration." NASA astronauts also participated in the *Godspeed Sail* portside festivals in summer 2006, the *Jamestown Live!* educational webcast in November 2006, and Cape Henry observances on April 26, 2007, marking the 400th anniversary of the settlers' first landing on American shores. NASA's popular exhibits were prominently featured at Anniversary Park during the *Anniversary Weekend* celebration and at the *Godspeed Sail*'s Landing Party festivals at major East Coast seaports.

CHAPTER 5

Cradle of Democracy in the Modern World:
The International Conference Series and World Forum

The seeds of representative government in America were first planted at Jamestown, and many of our nation's democratic ideals and institutions trace their roots to that crucial beginning.[80] Those ideals and institutions in turn have guided the people of many other nations in creating their own republican forms of government. Recent generations of Americans have witnessed freedom's dramatic gains abroad—a *tripling* of the number of democracies in the world—while closer to home progress has continued in the centuries-old pursuit of a more perfect American union.

If anyone doubted the validity of the asserted connection between the settlement at Jamestown 400 years ago and the remarkable contemporary advance of democratic principles, there were commemoration-year addresses by the President, Vice President, and Chief Justice of the United States, and the Queen of England to attest to the proposition. Were an

---

[80] Commissioner Billings chronicled the beginnings of representative government in early Jamestown in *A Little Parliament: The Virginia General Assembly in the Seventeenth Century* (Richmond: Library of Virginia, 2004). The important volume was one of three items that Federal Commission Vice Chair Dendy deposited in the Jamestown 2007 time capsule on the Commission's behalf during *Anniversary Weekend*. The others were a framed copy of President Bush's proclamation on *America's 400th Anniversary* and a DVD containing more than 100 Jamestown-related lesson plans distributed via the Commission's *JamestownJourney* educational website. The Commission contributed various other records and mementos to the time capsule in late 2007 before it was finally sealed and buried at Jamestown, where it was to remain unopened until preparations for the 450th anniversary commemoration.

incorrigible skeptic still to suggest that such claims by Americans were self-serving and that a monarch's *bona fides* in matters democratic were suspect, a definitive answer could be found in the words of two British prime ministers, themselves stalwart advocates of democratic ideals and peerless practitioners of the art, having won a combined six national elections at the helms of different parties in a country that traces its constitutional lineage to Magna Carta.

"It is fitting that men and women from around the world—many of them leading advocates for democratic reform in their own countries—would gather there in Williamsburg, just a few miles from Jamestown, to discuss democracy's future," commented former Prime Minister Tony Blair in pre-recorded remarks to delegates assembled for the *World Forum on the Future of Democracy* in September 2007,

> The journey that began .... at Jamestown 400 years ago has seen America become a great nation and force for freedom around the world. Together, Britain, the United States, and other nations that share our values have faced down tyrants and fought and given their lives to defend freedom from fascism, communism, and today from those who use terror to achieve what they cannot achieve by persuasion. We have stood up for the basic rights of all people to live in peace, with justice, and to govern themselves. This journey to Jamestown truly has changed the world, and is changing it still.

"In the long history of mankind, democratic societies occupy only a brief part," observed Baroness Margaret Thatcher in a videotaped message. "[F]reedom requires sacrifice. The courageous seafarers and settlers who came to Jamestown four centuries ago had no idea of the hardships they would face. But they persevered, and a tiny settlement became a great nation, a great democracy, and a great partner and defender of free peoples around the world."

Former Presidents George H.W. Bush and William J. Clinton served with former Prime Ministers Thatcher and Blair as honorary chairs of the International Conference Series on the Foundations and Future of Democracy, and they likewise drew a straight line between the events at Jamestown and democracy's dramatic extension in the modern era. "Representative government in America began at Jamestown, and many of the world's great ideas about liberty were worked out by the giants of the founding generation here in colonial Williamsburg and in other colonial capitals," said former President Bush in pre-recorded remarks to the *World Forum* delegates,

> In the twentieth century, our country—along with strong partners and friends such as the United Kingdom—sacrificed blood and treasure to defeat a series of totalitarian threats. In doing so, we preserved the chance for the world's people to live in peace and freedom. One needs only to look at Europe's outstanding progress since the Iron Curtain came down to see the power and potential of people, once freed, to chart their own course. Yet we know that the business of democracy is hard, hard work. New challenges and new opportunities arise every day, and they demand the best each generation has to contribute.... The journey launched at Jamestown continues, and even 400 years later there is still much to be done!

"After four centuries, the unprecedented American experiment in enlightened self-government is alive and well, and its impact on the global community remains profound," noted former President Clinton in a letter highlighting the value of the democracy conference series. "As in the times of Jamestown's founding, democracy still has its enemies, but we can be proud that today, for the first time in all of human history, more than half the world's people now live under governments of their own choosing, and America continues to stand as a shining example of democracy and freedom."

While much of the *America's 400th Anniversary* commemoration necessarily looked backward at the four-century journey begun at Jamestown, the democracy conference series provided an opportunity for a mix of scholars and commentators, politicians and government officials, teachers and students to look forward and to consider how best to advance democratic ideals in the years ahead. As the commemoration approached, the progress of democratic principles unquestionably had been dramatic, but equally clear was the imposing magnitude of the challenges that loomed—challenges not only to democracy's introduction in lands not then free, but to the survival and stabilization of the world's many fragile new democracies and to the health and vitality of mature democracies, such as America's, where political participation and civic engagement had waned. A series of illuminating discussions on these timely topics not only would call attention to the journey from Jamestown that already had changed the world; it would also help chart the course for the journey ahead. From the four-century-old cradle of democracy would come useful new thinking about how to fulfill the promise of freedom. And that is how the commemoration would end—with the final signature event, the *World Forum on the Future of Democracy*, focusing everyone's sights *forward*.

The idea of convening such a forum emerged early in the planning for the Jamestown 400th commemoration. It was included prominently in the "Critical Pathways" report that the Jamestown 2007 Steering Committee adopted in 2001, following a year-long strategic planning process led by Chairman Atkinson in his then-capacity as vice chair of the state Steering Committee.[81] The earliest iterations of the idea involved making Jamestown the locus for a commemoration-year gathering of heads of state, along the lines of a NATO conference or "G-8" summit of industrialized nations. The concept soon evolved away from a summit of world leaders, however, partly because of post-September 11, 2001 security concerns and partly because of plans for an *America's Anniversary Weekend* signature event to which the American president and British sovereign would be invited. Not only were the prospects for attracting multiple world leaders uncertain given the volatile state of international affairs, but commemoration planners also felt that a democracy forum could make a greater contribution if it were successful in bringing together scholars, commentators, political activists, and governmental practitioners from mature and emerging democracies for a highly substantive dialogue on the factors that determine the success or failure of democratic institutions. While the participation of some high-level government officials was deemed important for the profile and content of such a program, the goals of diverse participation and substantive dialogue among scholars and practitioners would be difficult to accomplish in a setting dominated by the presence of

---

[81] At the time, the state Steering Committee often acted through a leadership committee known as the Jamestown 2007 Executive Committee, and the Critical Pathways report was prepared under the Executive Committee's auspices.

multiple heads of state, with the inevitable media, security, and logistical frenzy that attends such events.

When the Federal Commission developed its strategic plan in 2003 and 2004, the idea of a "democracy forum" was listed prominently among the planned signature events then being marketed to potential corporate sponsors by Jamestown 2007, but it remained little more than a general concept and fervent hope. Representatives of the Federal Commission, the state Steering Committee, and several noted scholars and community leaders held a productive brainstorming session on the subject in August 2003. Then, in spring 2004, with the enthusiastic concurrence of the Jamestown 2007 leadership, the Federal Commission assumed leadership of the project and expanded the program to encompass a year-long series of university-based conferences rather than a single gathering. The University of Virginia Center for Politics proposed convening young people from around the world in summer 2006 for an "International Youth Democracy Summit," an idea the Federal Commission embraced as the kick-off event in the series. Other higher education institutions were invited to hold conferences on particular topics relevant to democratic development, and, by December 2005, the Commission had accepted proposals from nine colleges and universities in Virginia to host such topical conferences. The Commission itself would host the concluding *World Forum on the Future of Democracy* in association with three primary partners—the Colonial Williamsburg Foundation, the College of William and Mary, and Jamestown 2007.[82]

With organizational responsibility shared by multiple colleges, universities, and other institutional partners, the managerial challenge was daunting. The Federal Commission's Democracy Conference Committee, co-chaired by Commissioners Dendy and Nau, assumed the lead oversight role, and its members also served on a larger Democracy Program Planning Council that included representatives of the higher education institutions hosting topical conferences, the major planning partners for the

---

[82] One of the earliest proponents of a democracy-related conference as a Jamestown 2007 signature event was Dr. James H. Poissant, a consultant who met with Virginia's commemoration organizers in the first years of the planning effort. His consulting firm, Poissant International LLC, had experience in successfully organizing such large assemblages, and was engaged by the Federal Commission in 2003-2004 to provide guidance on the probable scope and cost of such an undertaking.

culminating *World Forum*, and others with pertinent expertise.[83] At the instigation of Chairman Atkinson and Colonial Williamsburg President Colin Campbell, the outgoing president of the College of William and Mary, Timothy J. Sullivan, agreed in November 2004 to chair the Planning Council, and he also led a smaller task force that coordinated intensive planning for the *World Forum*.

While the managerial task could not have been accomplished without an enormous commitment of time and effort by the commemoration's volunteer leaders, the glue that held the disparate elements together was the Commission's able democracy conference project director, Drema L. Johnson, who joined the staff in June 2005. Ms. Johnson in turn was assisted by the staff of key partners and vendors, most notably the following: Eliza Eversole, Mark Duncan, and the exceptional team at Colonial Williamsburg; Stewart Gamage, vice president for public affairs at the College of William and Mary, and her dedicated colleagues; and Ken Ashby, Maris Segal, and the accomplished professionals at Prosody Creative Services, which the Commission engaged to provide production and related services. Brent Beemer, program director for the Bureau of Educational and Cultural Affairs in the Department of State, and other Bureau officials provided crucial assistance with the identification, invitation, and arrangements for participation in the *World Forum* by international delegates. Other staff members of the Federal Commission and the state's Jamestown 2007 office provided vital support. Funding was provided by the Bureau of Educational and Cultural Affairs of the Department of State, the Department of the Interior, the Commonwealth of Virginia, Jamestown 2007, Inc., the College of William and Mary, the Colonial Williamsburg Foundation, and private sponsors. In addition, the institutions hosting topical conferences on campuses across the Commonwealth assembled their own management teams and assumed full responsibility for conference logistics, funding, and administration.

Responsibility for raising public awareness of the democracy conference series fell primarily to the Federal Commission. Jamestown 2007's ongoing promotion of *America's 400th*

---

[83] The membership of the Democracy Program Planning Council and a list of conferences and sponsors are found in Appendix 14.

Anniversary helped the cause by identifying the *World Forum on the Future of Democracy* as the commemoration's signature-event finale, and the Federal Commission promoted the year-long conference series through its *JamestownJourney* website. Justice O'Connor was an especially enthusiastic booster of the democracy conference program, mentioning it frequently in commemoration and non-commemoration settings, and Vice President Cheney emphasized the *World Forum*, along with *Anniversary Weekend* and the *Royal Visit*, as the anniversary year's main events when he visited Jamestown at the start of 2007. Beginning in August 2006, the topical conferences themselves generated news coverage that spurred mounting interest in the series. As the *World Forum* approached, the Commission in summer 2007 launched a second website (*www.JamestownDemocracy.org*) to display highlights from the preceding conferences and provide information about the upcoming series finale.[84]

Mindful of the scholarly character of the program, the Commission concluded that its primary target audience for promotional purposes consisted of national opinion leaders with an interest in history, government, and public affairs. Accordingly, it contracted in 2006 with Dr. Dan Roberts, an accomplished University of Richmond history professor, for a year-long series of historical vignettes about Jamestown and the "Journey of Democracy" begun there.[85] Taking advantage of the existing audience for Dr. Roberts' popular *A Moment in Time* radio program—it was heard daily by more than two million public and satellite radio listeners in 3,000 American communities and worldwide over 400 stations of the Armed Forces Radio Network—the Federal Commission was able to reach millions of Americans each week with an entertaining, two-minute educational lesson about democracy's roots at Jamestown combined with a brief promotional message

---

[84] Media relations were coordinated for the Federal Commission by its communications director, William Allcott, and consultants Siddall, Inc., The Hodges Partnership, and Greystone Partners.

[85] The Commission contracted with Broadcast Partners LLC, a media partnership formed by Dr. Roberts and the University of Richmond.

concerning the democracy conference series.[86] The informative broadcasts were then made available in both print and audio format through a link on the *JamestownJourney* website.

The International Conference Series on the Foundations and Future of Democracy commenced on August 7, 2006, at the University of Virginia, as high school students from across the United States and 20 countries assembled for the International Youth Democracy Summit. Federal Commissioners, University leaders, Planning Council members, and other commemoration VIPs joined the 300 exuberant young people for an inspiring opening ceremony that included original music and dance by Jamestown 2007's *Anniversary Voices* and other performers, reflections by "Thomas Jefferson" (played by Bill Barker of Colonial Williamsburg), remarks by American and international youth delegates, and a keynote address by Undersecretary of State for Public Diplomacy and Public Affairs Karen Hughes. The event also served as the public roll-out for the conference series and its honorary leadership. Planning Council Chairman Sullivan unveiled the schedule for the year-long program of topical conferences and announced that former Presidents Bush and Clinton and former Prime Minister Thatcher would be the honorary chairs of the conference series, with former House of Representatives Speaker Thomas S. Foley and former Attorney General William Barr serving as the honorary vice chairs. (The fourth honorary chair, former Prime Minister Blair, joined the group in June 2007 upon the conclusion of his tenure in office.)

Sponsored by the University of Virginia, its Center for Politics, and Presidential Classroom, the International Youth Democracy Summit was distinctive in that the student attendees were high-school age, not college students. The conference thus was held in the summertime and took place six months before the rest of the programs in the conference series. The youth summit also represented something of a bridge between the elementary- and secondary-school focus of the *JamestownJourney* educational

---

[86] Each radio broadcast began with the introduction, "Dan Roberts and *A Moment in Time* with 'Jamestown—Journey of Democracy,' tracing the global advance of democratic ideals since the founding of Jamestown, Virginia, in 1607..." After the historical vignette, Roberts concluded the broadcast: "This series is supported by the Jamestown 400th Federal Commission with its International Conference Series on the Foundations and Future of Democracy—see *JamestownJourney.org*. At the University of Richmond, this is Dan Roberts." In the run-up to the *World Forum*, the tag line referenced that upcoming event and encouraged listeners to go to *www.JamestownDemocracy.org*.

initiatives and the university-level audience for the democracy conference series. A remarkable success, the gathering brought together students from around the nation and the world for four days of impressive lectures and presentations, inspiring dialogues, and informative visits to venues associated with democracy's American journey—Monticello, Jamestown, Williamsburg, and Capitol Hill in Washington. While the students heard from knowledgeable leaders and scholars, they also listened to each other, beginning a dialogue that would continue over the Internet long after the summit had ended.

After an autumn respite, the democracy conference series resumed in late January 2007 on the southern Virginia campuses of Longwood University and Hampden-Sydney College with sessions addressing the theme, "Sustaining Democracy in the Global Age." Hundreds of scholars from around the country converged to discuss democratic development from a contemporary geopolitical perspective, focusing on regional issues, identity politics, national security, economic globalization, and a broad range of other national and multinational concerns. Former Ambassador to the United Nations Richard Holbrooke delivered the keynote address and canvassed the historic progression of American policy on the global promotion of democracy. With the conflict in Iraq among the most salient topics of the day, former Congressman Lee Hamilton, co-chairman of the bipartisan advisory panel known as the "Iraq Study Group," provided timely remarks on the conflict and the limits of American power in promoting democratization.

A month later, the scene shifted to Hampton Roads, only miles from Cape Henry past which English settlers and then Angolan slaves sailed four centuries earlier, for a conference hosted by Norfolk State University, one of Virginia's historically black colleges and universities. Entitled "America's 400th Anniversary: Voices from Within the Veil," the forum convened noted scholars, community leaders, and political practitioners for a two-day reflection on the contrasting democratic images and oligarchic realities of early Jamestown and the larger subject of evolving concepts of democracy, political participation, and civil rights. Virginia Governor Timothy M. Kaine, noted author and political commentator Juan Williams, and Dr. Mary Frances Berry, former chairman of the United States Civil Rights Commission, were among the leading presenters. The program also featured reflections on politics and faith and a stirring joint performance by the Virginia Symphony Orchestra and Norfolk State University Choir narrated by Commissioner Reid and television actor James Avery.

Meanwhile, at Jamestown and Williamsburg, the Mercatus Center of George Mason University convened a bipartisan group of congressional chiefs of staff for a two-day retreat focusing on the historic interrelation of political and economic freedoms and the importance of competitive markets and private property in successful democratic systems. A popular gathering annually among congressional staffers, the Center's retreat in 2007 was entitled, "Markets and Democracy," and it provided opportunities for leading economists and other scholars to engage in a robust dialogue with governmental practitioners at the federal level. The keynote speech was delivered by Dr. Gordon Wood, the noted author on America's founding and professor of history at Brown University, who used the occasion to trace the legal and political origins of corporations as vehicles for pursuing public purposes and private ventures.

A multi-day forum on the "Democracy and the Rule of Law" was the first of three democracy conferences held in April 2007. Hosted by the University of Richmond School of Law in association with the American and English Inns of Court, American Arbitration Association, English Commercial Bar Association, and John Marshall Foundation, the conference included presentations and panel discussions featuring the Chief Justice of the United States, the Lord Chief Justice of England and Wales, Justice O'Connor, and other leading jurists and lawyers from the United States, the United Kingdom, and other countries. The spirited discussions touched on constitutionalism, doctrines of religious and political liberty, the role of the judiciary, separation of powers, and other timely topics. As described in Chapter 3, the conference concluded at Historic Jamestowne, where a plaque honoring the Jamestown colonists' contributions to the rule of law was presented on behalf of the English Inns of Court.

The next conference took place back in Norfolk, where American and British military planners, diplomats, and scholars assembled to discuss "Democracies in Partnership: 400 Years of Transatlantic Engagement." Sponsored by Old Dominion University and NATO's Allied Command Transformation, the conference addressed the historic and continuing role of international partnerships and collective security in preserving the opportunity for democratic success around the world. The topics included contemporary issues facing the NATO alliance, differing strategic cultures, shifts in the balance of power, the impact of commercial globalization and technological advances, and modern democracy movements.   The British Ambassador, Sir David Manning, and the NATO Supreme Allied Commander, General Lance Smith, were among the leading figures to address the gathering.

While issues of international import were being dissected at the conference in Norfolk, local government and community leaders were joining scholars and students in Virginia's capital city for a dynamic, day-long dialogue on cultural diversity and community engagement under the heading, "We Are the Change! Democracy and Inclusion in the 21st Century." Hosted by Virginia Commonwealth University, Richmond Region 2007, and other regional partners, the conference included remarks by Mayor Cory Booker of Newark, New Jersey, and Richmond Mayor (and former Virginia Governor) L. Douglas Wilder. The two mayors and other speakers highlighted the importance of a broad-based and inclusive approach to self-government—one that bridges social, cultural, and other divides—as a key to the reinvigoration of democratic participation and to successful governance in the years ahead.

The final topical conference—"Foundations of Democracy"— took place at Virginia Polytechnic Institute and State University (Virginia Tech) in early September and set the historical context for the discussion that would follow two weeks later at the *World Forum*. Leading scholars on classical democracy and Enlightenment-era thought assembled in Blacksburg to explore the philosophical foundations of democracy and to canvass the political ideas that facilitated the establishment and subsequent evolution of the American system of government as well as the emergence of democratic institutions elsewhere.   The assembled scholars also reflected on ways that democracy might be expected to evolve in the 21st century.

At each topical conference, representatives of the Federal Commission, variously including Chairman Atkinson, Vice Chair Dendy, Executive Director Mann, and Planning Council Chairman Sullivan, offered context-setting remarks that connected the individual conference's deliberations to the larger picture being painted by the year-long conference series. The Commission also arranged for a complete, gavel-to-gavel electronic record of the proceedings to be captured for later use by scholars and practitioners. As a legacy project, the Commission provided for subsequent publication of conference-series excerpts under the title, *Jamestown Commentaries on the Foundations and Future of Democracy*, and made a grant to the University of Virginia Center for Politics for the ongoing operation of the *www.JamestownDemocracy.org* website, where conference highlights could be viewed, electronic and print records of the proceedings could be ordered, and other efforts related to democratic development could be facilitated.

The culminating *World Forum on the Future of Democracy* attracted 600 delegates from around the United States and 85 more from 16 countries[87] for a lively three-day program of speeches and presentations, panel discussions, and dialogues with leading scholars, journalists, activists, and public officials.[88] The activities commenced on the afternoon of Sunday, September 16, as delegates visited the Jamestown sites and Colonial Williamsburg, traversing the ground rightly considered "ground zero" for the democratic explosion that

---

[87] The countries represented were: Bahrain, Bangladesh, Bolivia, Egypt, Georgia, India, Indonesia, Kyrgyzstan, Pakistan, Peru, Philippines, Russia, South Africa, Tunisia, Turkey, and Ukraine.

[88] Conference sessions were hosted in succession by Chairman Atkinson, President Campbell of Colonial Williamsburg, Senator Norment, President Gene R. Nichol of the College of William and Mary, Federal Commission Vice Chairs Campbell and Dendy, and Planning Council Chairman Sullivan. In preparing for the *World Forum*, members of the planning task force divided responsibility for major functions under the leadership of Planning Council Chairman Sullivan and Project Director Drema Johnson. President Campbell recruited the impressive array of scholarly speakers and journalists, with assistance from former Ambassador Mitchell B. Reiss, vice provost for international affairs at the College of William and Mary. President Campbell and Chairman Atkinson guided program content decisions and supervised the production work by Prosody Creative Services. William and Mary Vice President Stewart Gamage led preparations for the evening forum on the William and Mary campus and arrangements for student participation in the conference and, with Chairman Atkinson, coordinated conference communications. Vice Chair Nancy Campbell directed efforts by the Colonial Williamsburg staff and others related to delegate and VIP hospitality, set development, conference materials, gifts, and special events. Vice Chair Dendy led donor outreach efforts (except as to foundations, for which President Campbell was the liaison) and oversaw conference budgeting and contracting. Executive Directors Mann and Zeidler provided administrative and logistical support.

has transformed the modern world. Assembling for opening ceremonies at the Williamsburg Lodge and Conference Center that evening, they heard welcoming remarks from Colonial Williamsburg President Colin Campbell, Chairman Atkinson, Chief Adkins, Congressman Robert C. Scott, Planning Council Chairman Timothy Sullivan, U.S. Senator John Warner, and Governor Timothy Kaine. Justice O'Connor delivered an opening address on democracy and the rule of law, and two of the conference series' honorary chairs—former Prime Minister Margaret Thatcher and former President George H. W. Bush—offered pre-recorded reflections on the journey of democracy since Jamestown and the value of the democracy conference series.

The forum's plenary sessions began the next morning with a series of panels that focused on the "Architecture of Liberty." Moderated in turn by James Lehrer, anchor of PBS's *The NewsHour*, and Walter Isaacson, president of the Aspen Institute, the panels addressed the topics, "Developing a Structure for Deliberative Democracy—the Framers' Debate," "Has America Kept the Founders' Faith?" and "Are America's Founding Principles Relevant in a Global Age?" Among the panelists were noted scholars of the founding era Joseph Ellis, Gordon Wood, and Hunter Rawlings, *New York Times* columnist David Brooks, former Attorney General William Barr, Robert Hormats of Goldman Sachs, Rockefeller Brothers Fund President Stephen Heintz, Kumi Naidoo (secretary general of CIVICUS), Joan Brown Campbell (director of the department of religion at Chautauqua Institution), and Ambassador Choi Young-Jin, the permanent representative of the Republic of Korea to the United Nations.

During lunch the delegates took a break from the panel discussions to hear a major address by Secretary of Defense Robert M. Gates, who was presented by Senator Warner. Addressing the topic, "Promoting Democracy Abroad: A Realist's View," Secretary Gates canvassed the history of American efforts to facilitate democratic development around the world. "From time to time," he declared, "we have strayed from our ideals and have been arrogant in dealing with others. Yet what has brought us together with our democratic allies is a shared belief that the future of democracy and its spread is worth our enduring labors and sacrifices, reflecting both our interests and our ideals."

In mid-afternoon the proceedings at the Williamsburg Lodge recessed, and delegates reassembled in the evening at nearby William and Mary Hall, where more than 3,000 college students, community leaders, and local citizens joined the conference attendees for a panel discussion titled, "The Future of Democracy: Why Does It Matter? An International Dialogue Hosted by Jim Lehrer." Recorded for later broadcast on Lehrer's *The NewsHour,* the lively panel featured Justice O'Connor, former Secretary of State Lawrence Eagleburger, and Dr. Ali Ansari, director of the Institute for Iranian Studies at Scotland's University of St. Andrews. The trio not only addressed issues raised by Lehrer, but also fielded videotaped questions from the international delegates and from William and Mary college students on issues ranging from religious liberty and regional conflicts to government surveillance and civil liberties. Prior to the panel discussion, attendees heard remarks by Virginia Attorney General Robert F. McDonnell and by William and Mary student Kaitlyn Adkins, a delegate to the International Youth Democracy Summit, who introduced a video with highlights from the youth summit held a year earlier in Charlottesville. After the program, delegates returned to the Williamsburg Lodge, where they were guests at the *World Forum*'s main reception hosted by Jamestown 2007.

The final day of the conference was devoted to panel discussions on "Global Issues and Challenges to Democracy," a luncheon featuring an open forum for international delegates, remarks by Virginia Lieutenant Governor William T. Bolling, and a gala dinner and closing ceremony. Panel sessions addressed "Terrorism and Security," "Protecting Religious Freedom and Minority Rights," "World Markets and Democracy," and "Sustainable Development," and included Admiral James M. Loy (former deputy secretary of homeland security), Ambassador Chan Heng Chee of the Republic of Singapore, NAACP Legal Defense Fund President Theodore M. Shaw, Martha Crenshaw (senior fellow, Center for International Security and Cooperation, Stanford University), Mitchell B. Reiss (vice provost for international affairs, College of William and Mary), Mokhtar Lamani (senior visiting fellow, Center for International Governance Innovation), former U.S. Senator Charles S. Robb, Jessica P. Einhorn (dean of the Paul S. Nitze School of Advanced International Studies, John Hopkins University), Ingrid Mattson (president of the Islamic Society of North America), Rodney Smolla (dean of the Washington and Lee University Law School), Virginia Justice Donald W. Lemons, Carol J. Lancaster (director of the Mortara Center for International Studies, Georgetown University), and John Hewko (director of the Millennium Challenge Corporation).[89]

At the concluding dinner, delegates and guests heard moving remarks from two international delegates—Lyubov Palyvoda from Ukraine and Pablo Canedo of Bolivia—who spoke of efforts to promote democracy in their own countries. Unable to attend the *World Forum* in person due to diplomatic responsibilities in the Middle East, former British Prime Minister Tony Blair addressed the gathering electronically and commended the delegates:

> Many of you have come a great distance to lend your experiences and ideas to the vitally important dialogue that has taken place at this World Forum on the Future of Democracy. I congratulate you on your commitment and wish you well in your work as you return to your homelands. The international discussions that have taken place throughout this year-long Conference Series on the Foundations and Future of Democracy have made a really valuable contribution to our understanding of each other and of the opportunities before us. Let us now resolve to build on these and other fruitful discussions to bring positive change throughout our world. Others may seek to tear down. Let us seek to build up. Let us build on a foundation of freedom whose cornerstone was put in place not far from your present site, now four centuries ago. And let us continue on a journey that has brought hope to millions and is still changing the world for the better.

The event concluded with a video presentation that traced the progress of democracy over the four centuries since Jamestown and included highlights of the year-long conference series. The final live words of the evening belonged to "Thomas Jefferson," appearing, as he had at the Youth Summit, through the gifted

---

[89] A complete list of *World Forum* speakers and excerpts of remarks may be found at *www.JamestownDemocracy.org.*

performance of Colonial Williamsburg's Bill Barker. "In our day, and in the centuries since," he said, "bold and imaginative people have written, thought, studied, discoursed, searched, and sacrificed to nourish the tree of liberty. You came here to do the same. I and future generations thank you."

Many of the salutary legacies of the democracy conference series will never be known. They will reflect the inspired labors of champions of democracy, scholars and activists, practitioners and theorists, the young and the not-so-young, Americans and people from other lands, who traveled across-country or around the world to attend the conferences, who viewed parts of them online via the Commission's *JamestownDemocracy* website or partner websites, or who will read of them in the *Jamestown Commentaries on the Foundations and Future of Democracy*. They will come from people who drew ideas and inspiration from hearing the experiences of others engaged in democracy's struggles, or who will attend other conferences encouraged by the success of this series, or who will publish their own insightful works illuminating the elements that make democracies successful, or who will listen, learn, read, and study any of the hundreds of scholarly papers and practical presentations for which this year-long series served as a forum or catalyst. Punctuating 18 months of enthusiastic celebrations, solemn remembrances, and entertaining and educational programs, the *World Forum on the Future of Democracy* and democracy conference series looked forward, and in so doing honored the tradition of giving back that is a foremost attribute of the nation born 400 years earlier in the cradle that was Jamestown.[90]

"Never in human history has freedom made such an advance," declared former Prime Minister Thatcher in her remarks to the *World Forum* delegates,

> Yet, it is only a beginning. These conferences held over the past year here in Virginia have highlighted the enormity of the challenges ahead. Yet, they have also shown the resilience of the human spirit and the creative power of free people. I applaud

---

[90] To continue and build on the legacy of the democracy conference series, the Commission in 2008 provided legacy grants to the University of Virginia Center for Politics for publication and distribution of the *Jamestown Commentaries on the Foundations and Future of Democracy,* ongoing operation of the Commission's democracy-related website, and development of opportunities for further international dialogue and exchange related to democratic development.

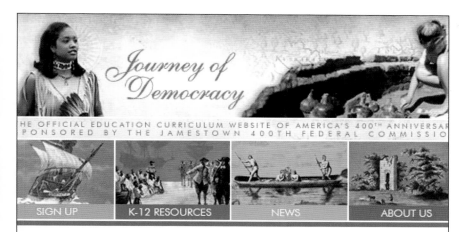

HE OFFICIAL EDUCATION CURRICULUM WEBSITE OF AMERICA'S 400ᵀᴴ ANNIVERSAR
PONSORED BY THE JAMESTOWN 400TH FEDERAL COMMISSIO

SIGN UP   K-12 RESOURCES   NEWS   ABOUT US

Welcome to the official education curriculum website of "America's 400th Anniversary"   LESSON PLANS

Home page from the Federal Commission's "Jamestown—Journey of Democracy" website, the official education curriculum website of America's 400th Anniversary

Journalist Gwen Ifill interviews Chief Stephen R. Adkins of the Chickahominy Indian Tribe, member of the Federal Commission, for the Jamestown Live! *educational webcast*

Commissioner Flippo (right), chair of the Jamestown 2007 Programs and Events Subcommittee, and Vice Chair Dendy display the Virginia 2007 Community Program banner before depositing it in the time capsule during Anniversary Weekend *(Historic Jamestowne, May 11, 2007)*

Thomas Jefferson (Bill Barker of Colonial Williamsburg) addresses delegates to the International Youth Democracy Summit *in the University of Virginia's Old Cabell Hall during the August 8, 2006 opening ceremony of the Democracy Conference Series*

Leaders assemble in Old Cabell Hall following the Democracy Conference Series opening ceremony and kickoff of the International Youth Democracy Summit (from left to right: Virginia Secretary of Education Thomas R. Morris; Chairman Connock; University of Virginia Executive Vice President and Chief Operating Officer Leonard W. Sandridge; Chairman Atkinson; Thomas Jefferson (Bill Barker); Planning Council Chairman Chairman Sullivan; University of Virginia Center for Politics Director Larry J. Sabato)

Karen Hughes, Undersecretary of State for Public Diplomacy and Public Affairs, delivers the keynote address at the opening session of the International Youth Democracy Summit *(University of Virginia, August 8, 2006)*

Richard Holbrooke, former Ambassador to the United Nations, describes America's historical approach to democratic development during a January 25, 2007 conference at Longwood University (at right: Dr. Patricia Cormier, president of Longwood University)

Former Congressman Lee Hamilton responds to questions from delegates attending the Longwood University conference on "Sustaining Democracy in the Global Age"

Author Juan Williams delivers remarks at the Norfolk State University conference, "Voices from Within the Veil," on February 22, 2007

Associate Justice Stephen Breyer is interviewed on development of the rule of law in England and America during a "Democracy and the Rule of Law" conference break at the University of Richmond on April 12, 2007

Newark Mayor Cory Booker addresses the Virginia Commonwealth University conference on "Democracy and Inclusion in the 21st Century"

Former Virginia Governor L. Douglas Wilder, Mayor of Richmond, shares insights with conference participants at Virginia Commonwealth University on April 19, 2007

General Lance Smith, NATO Supreme Allied Commander, discusses the transatlantic alliance and its implications for democratic development at Old Dominion University on April 19, 2007

Participants in the opening ceremony of the World Forum on the Future of Democracy gather on stage after the program (Colonial Williamsburg, September 16, 2007) (front row, from left to right: U.S. Representative Robert C. Scott (VA-3); Governor Kaine; Commissioner Adkins; Planning Council Chairman Sullivan; College of William and Mary President Nichol; back row, from left to right: Vice Chair Dendy; Vice Chair Nancy Campbell; Vice Chair Colin Campbell; Justice O'Connor; Senator Warner; Chairman Atkinson)

Former British Prime Minister Tony Blair, Honorary Chair of the Democracy Conference Series, addresses the concluding session of the World Forum on the Future of Democracy *on September 18, 2007*

At the World Forum on the Future of Democracy *in Williamsburg on September 17, 2007, moderator Jim Lehrer of PBS' NewsHour (right) leads noted historians (from left to right) Gordon S. Wood, Hunter R. Rawlings III, and Joseph J. Ellis in discussing the structure for deliberative democracy designed by the American framers*

Defense Secretary Robert M. Gates delivers a major address on U.S. policy on democratization at the World Forum *on September 17, 2007*

Commissioner Trumbo (left) and Vice Chair Campbell (center) share a moment with Justice O'Connor as delegates gather at Colonial Williamsburg for the World Forum

Ukrainian delegate Lyubov Palyvoda describes the democracy movement in her country during the closing session of the World Forum

Moderator Jim Lehrer poses a question during a World Forum *session considering whether America has kept faith with its founders (from left to right: Robert Hormats of Goldman Sachs; Joan Brown Campbell of Chautauqua Institution; columnist David Brooks; former Attorney General William P. Barr; Jim Lehrer)*

Pablo Canedo, delegate from Bolivia, offers reflections on the major conclusions of the World Forum *during its final session*

Senator Charles S. Robb, a sponsor of legislation creating the Federal Commission, participates in a World Forum panel on terrorism and security moderated by Admiral James M. Loy (from left to right: Senator Robb; College of William and Mary Vice Provost Mitchell B. Reiss; Dr. Martha Crenshaw of Stanford University; Dr. Ali Ansari of the University of St. Andrews; Admiral Loy)

Timothy J. Sullivan (left), Democracy Program Planning Council chair, receives a gift from Chairman Atkinson in recognition of his leadership role in the Democracy Conference Series

Virginia Supreme Court Justice Donald W. Lemons (left) discusses the Democracy Conference Series with Justice O'Connor during the series finale in Williamsburg

World Forum delegates and guests enjoy the conference's concluding banquet in the Virginia Room of the newly renovated Williamsburg Lodge on September 18, 2007

Former Secretary of State Lawrence Eagleburger makes a point about the future of democracy during a forum at William and Mary Hall on September 17, 2007 (from left to right: moderator Jim Lehrer; Secretary Eagleburger; Dr. Ansari; Justice O'Connor)

Mrs. Lynda Robb (left) enjoys a moment with World Forum *planners (from center left to right: College of William and Mary Vice President Stewart Gamage; Planning Council Chairman Sullivan; Project Director Johnson)*

CIVICUS Secretary General Kumi Naidoo comments during a World Forum *panel addressing the global relevance of America's founding principles (from left to right: Ambassador Choi Young-Jin of the Republic of Korea; Dr. Naidoo; Stephen Heinz of the Rockefeller Brothers Fund; moderator Walter Isaacson of the Aspen Institute)*

An international delegate to the World Forum *participates in dialogue about conditions conducive to democracy around the world*

all those who have taken part in this noble endeavor. To preserve and advance democracy is our greatest challenge. So have courage, hold to your principles, and we will prevail.

———————

CHAPTER 6

In the Bosom of the Bay:
New Discoveries and Ancient Lessons from the Chesapeake

Without the Chesapeake Bay, there would have been no Jamestown. Without the Bay, Virginia would not have been the cradle of the American nation and of modern democracy. Perhaps some other place would have played that vital role, or perhaps our history would have been profoundly different. But we can be reasonably certain that, without the abundance of the Chesapeake estuary, the highly developed Powhatan society would not have been on the scene to provide essential succor to the early Jamestown settlers. Were if not for the protection offered by the Bay and its tributaries, those settlers likely would have planted their hopes—and ours—elsewhere, with uncertain results. Williamsburg would not have been the intellectual font for the American Revolution and founding. Yorktown would not have been the place where the Bay, the French, and George Washington conspired to trap Lord Cornwallis's army and finally win independence. And Virginia likely would not be, as contemporary commentators have called it, "the indispensable creator of the Republic and the Constitution that has held together the world's greatest democracy."[91]

The Chesapeake estuary is to the modern world what Mesopotamia was to the ancient—a point of origin, a source of sustenance, an incubator for ideas, and, even today, a place where

---

[91] Michael Barone and Richard E. Cohen, *The Almanac of American Politics 2006* (Washington, D.C.: The National Journal Group, 2005), p. 1705.

matters of great moment still occur, and where the pressing business of the present tends to obscure the crucial lessons of the past. Four centuries after Jamestown, Virginians and Americans are still trying to understand the life-giving secrets of the Chesapeake, the richest estuary in the world, so as to be better stewards of its incomparable gifts. But, as if to draw us in and spur us on to greater efforts to understand and preserve, the Bay chose the run-up to Jamestown's 400th anniversary as the time to give up some of its most fascinating secrets.

We learned in the two decades before the Jamestown commemoration that a celestial event—the impact of the sixth largest meteor ever to strike the planet—occurred 35 million years ago near the site of present-day Cape Charles, Virginia, setting in motion events that many years later helped form the incomparably intricate and abundant Chesapeake estuary. We learned—from the rings in ancient cypress trees—that the first Jamestown settlers arrived amid a drought of historic dimension, a circumstance that significantly affected the interactions of the indigenous people and English settlers in the early years of the Jamestown undertaking. Perhaps most dramatically, we learned the actual location of the two seats of power—the original fort at Jamestown and the headquarters of Chief Powhatan at Werowocomoco—and began to probe beneath the surface for the lessons those sites could teach.

When Dr. William M. Kelso, lead archaeologist of the APVA's Jamestown Rediscovery Project, announced in September 1996 that the James Fort had been found after two years of research, the longstanding supposition about its loss to the James River was instantly refuted, and the painstakingly slow process of unearthing its illuminating treasures commenced. It would yield, by the time of the commemoration, more than 1,100,000 artifacts that transformed understanding of what happened at Jamestown, what the place looked like, what people did there, and how the suffering there led on to survival and eventually to success.[92] For the 400th anniversary commemoration it yielded something else of enormous value: a newsworthy new angle to the Jamestown saga and a stunning story of discovery that triggered nationwide and worldwide interest in the place where

---

[92] See William M. Kelso, *Jamestown: The Buried Truth* (Charlottesville and London: University of Virginia Press, 2006).

America began. The archaeological research and revelations at Historic Jamestowne alone were the subject of more than seven billion news impressions worldwide in the decade between the discovery of the fort and the anniversary observances.

Meanwhile, 12 miles due north of Jamestown on the north bank of the York River at Purtan Bay, a less heralded but no less important discovery was taking place. Digging on a Gloucester County farm owned by Robert and Lynn Ripley, a team of archaeologists led by Dr. Martin Gallivan of the College of William and Mary and Dr. E. Randolph Turner III of the Virginia Department of Historic Resources in 2003 and 2004 unearthed compelling evidence that the farm is the site of Werowocomoco, a center of Native civilization for thousands of years and the headquarters of the paramount chief, Wahunsonacock (known to history as "Powhatan"), at the time of Jamestown's founding. There, Captain John Smith negotiated for life-saving supplies of corn for the Jamestown settlers and nearly lost his own life in 1609, saved only by a warning from the Chief's daughter, Pocahontas. Those and other momentous decisions made at the site helped determine the fate of the first English settlement. Indeed, the early Virginia story is a tale of two capitals— Jamestown and Werowocomoco—and their "discovery" just before the 2007 commemoration has opened the way for decades of productive new investigation and education about the cultures and conditions, people and places that were pivotal in the birth of our nation.

Spurred by the immensely important archaeological find at James Fort as well as the approaching quadricentennial observances, the federal government and private donors rallied to provide $54 million in funding for the expedited development of new research, educational, and interpretive facilities at Historic Jamestowne. At the center of this remarkable effort was Commissioner Rives, who guided the ambitious program through its planning and construction phases in his capacities as the National Park Service's Jamestown 400th project director and acting superintendent of the Colonial National Historical

Park.[93] His vital partner in the effort was the executive director of APVA Preservation Virginia, Elizabeth S. Kostelny, who ably led the preservation organization as it worked out newly invigorated collaborative relationships with the National Park Service, the Jamestown-Yorktown Foundation, and other key organizations. Crucial also was the support provided by the Federal Commission, especially the efforts of Commissioners Griles, Mainella, Bomar, Smith, Loomis, and Billings.

The significant capital investment and expedited development of state-of-the-art facilities at Historic Jamestowne were matched by the transformative changes that took place at Jamestown Settlement in the decade prior to 2007. New educational facilities, visitor amenities, interpretive areas, and a dramatically expanded museum were fruits of a $70-million investment by the Commonwealth of Virginia and private benefactors. Few heritage tourism attractions in the world of 2007 could boast combined capital investments approaching $125 million, and the best news was that the two adjacent Jamestown sites were improved in ways that made them more complementary to each other than competitive with each other.[94]

During the commemoration planning process, as the site plans were being refined and then implemented, leaders of the state Steering Committee and Federal Commission used their influence to foster an atmosphere of cooperation and collaboration, encouraging the able staffs at Jamestown Settlement and Historic Jamestowne and their governing boards to work together to provide visitors not only an enhanced

---

[93] Commissioner Rives is quick to share credit, and the effort did indeed receive crucial support from varied quarters, including Interior Secretaries Norton and Kempthorne, Deputy Secretary Griles, Park Service Directors Mainella and Bomar, Park Superintendents Alec Gould and P. Daniel Smith, and, on Capitol Hill, U.S. Senator John Warner, other members of the Virginia congressional delegation, and Warner's legislative assistant and chief of staff, Commissioner Loomis.

[94] In addition to the improvements on the two Jamestown sites, 198 acres of land with riverfront access, located to the west across Route 31 from Jamestown Settlement, were acquired by James City County and the Commonwealth of Virginia through the efforts of the Trust for Public Land, James City County, the Jamestown-Yorktown Foundation, the Virginia Department of Transportation, the National Oceanic and Atmospheric Administration, Dominion Foundation, and the Virginia Land Conservation Foundation. The important tract, located adjacent to and visible from the Jamestown sites, provided the temporary site for Anniversary Park on *America's Anniversary Weekend* in May 2007 and was secured for appropriate public uses rather than commercial development as a result of the acquisition. Commissioners Loomis, Rives, Atkinson, and Dendy were among the federal, state, local, and private actors who assisted in the extended effort to fund acquisition of the tract.

experience at each individual site, but a more seamless experience involving both sites.[95]   Commemoration-year joint ticketing and transportation arrangements were deemed especially important to this effort, and Commissioners Loomis and Rives were instrumental in arranging federal funding for a fleet of natural-gas-powered buses that were used to connect both Jamestown sites with a new regional visitor center established by Colonial Williamsburg beginning in 2005. By 2007, Historic Jamestowne and Jamestown Settlement were both experiencing visitation increases in the range of 40-50 percent during a time when heritage tourism was waning in many other places. The appeal of the new facilities, effective marketing by the organizations responsible for the sites, and the bonanza of commemoration-related media attention were obvious factors in the growth, but so were the complementary character of the activities and attractions at the two sites and the increased ease with which visitors could access them.

While the dramatic unearthing of the James Fort spurred new research and interpretive initiatives at Historic Jamestowne, the archaeological discovery at Werowocomoco came almost a decade later—just before the commemoration—and under conditions that limited immediate news coverage. Dr. Kelso's discoveries at James Fort produced sudden, definitive confirmation that the original fort had been found, but the revelations on the Ripley farm were more gradual and less widely publicized. As the evidence mounted, the Ripleys took seriously their stewardship of the immensely significant archaeological find and engaged the Virginia Indian tribes as well as the archaeological team and educational institutions in discussions about how the site could best be preserved, investigated, and interpreted. Those discussions were ongoing as the commemoration drew to a close, with Chief Adkins participating prominently among the discussants, but as of that

---

[95] Focused efforts to harmonize the planning and operations at the two Jamestown sites began shortly after formation of the Jamestown 2007 Steering Committee 10 years before the anniversary. Virginia First Lady Roxane Gilmore and Lieutenant Governor John Hager led successive efforts in 2000-2001 to create more of a "one Jamestown" experience. Work on joint ticketing, integrated transportation systems, and other coordinated measures continued thereafter with the encouragement of the Steering Committee, the Management Committee, and the Federal Commission. Much good work was done along the way by the professional staffs of Jamestown Settlement and Historic Jamestowne. Ultimately, it was the completion of the dramatic facility improvements envisioned in the two sites' master plans, as well as successful collaboration on commemorative events, that seemed to produce a cooperative spirit and better-integrated visitor experience.

time no foundation or other organization had been established to provide for the long-term preservation of the site. The Federal Commission considered such permanent arrangements to be among its "legacy" objectives, but it ultimately concluded that the Commission's best means of helping to secure Werowocomoco's future lay in calling attention to its importance by, among other things, highlighting the discovery in the *JamestownJourney* educational curriculum, providing grant support for ongoing archeological research, and backing broader educational efforts encompassing the site and the region, such as the development of the Captain John Smith Chesapeake National Historic Trail.

The first such historic pathway entirely on water, the Captain John Smith Chesapeake National Historic Trail was created by legislation signed into law by President Bush on December 19, 2006, the 400th anniversary of the day that Smith and his fellow settlers first set sail for Virginia.[96] The President's action capped a whirlwind effort that saw the historic water trail proceed from novel concept to statutory reality in less than two years. The project was spearheaded by Patrick Noonan, chairman emeritus of The Conservation Fund and a member of the board of trustees of the National Geographic Society.[97] Appearing before the Federal Commission in June 2005, Noonan described Smith's remarkable voyages of discovery in 1608, during which the intrepid captain and his small crew explored and mapped almost 3,000 miles of Chesapeake shoreline, visited scores of Indian villages, and kept detailed journals. The addition of the proposed water trail to the National Trails System would commemorate Smith's achievement and provide innovative educational opportunities related to Native American history, early English settlement, and the Chesapeake's Bay's natural resources. Trail maps, guide books, classroom and field experiences, museum and website exhibits, and interpretive buoys were among the educational activities envisioned.

The plans outlined by Noonan immediately impressed the members of the Federal Commission, who saw significant

---

[96] Chairman Atkinson announced the President's action to the hundreds of Britons and Americans who assembled at the Middle Temple in London on December 19, 2006, for a gala dinner marking the 400th anniversary of the three ships' launch.

[97] Together with Gilbert Grosvenor, chairman of the National Geographic Society, and William Baker, president of the Chesapeake Bay Foundation, Noonan founded an advocacy organization known as the "Friends of the Captain John Smith Chesapeake National Historic Water Trail."

synergy in the educational components of the John Smith Trail project and the Commission's *JamestownJourney* educational initiatives.   Commissioners also perceived the water trail as a high-profile program that could help focus attention on other important but less well-known historical sites in the Chesapeake region, including Werowocomoco. The Federal Commission, therefore, became the first public body to endorse creation of the water trail, and members of the Commission lent both valuable expertise and influential support to the effort. Thanking the Federal Commission later for its crucial backing, Patrick Noonan observed that "the Commission's early, strong endorsement gave the trail credibility essential to its establishment. In helping to achieve National Historic Trail status for the John Smith Trail, the Commission left a legacy for future generations of Americans to celebrate John Smith's historic voyages across the Chesapeake." As a further contribution to that legacy, the Commission provided grant funding for development of an interpretive kiosk at Historic Jamestowne. A replica of the "smart buoys" found along the water trail route, the kiosk would feature a touchscreen that visitors could use to access live environmental and meteorological data, stories about Jamestown and the 400th-anniversary commemoration, and information about the John Smith Trail.

In May-September 2007, a crew of modern explorers retraced Smith's 1608 expedition aboard a 28-foot open boat, or "shallop," like the one Smith and his men used four centuries earlier. Sponsored by Sultana Projects, an education and preservation group active in the Chesapeake region, the shallop's hearty crew departed from Historic Jamestowne on *Anniversary Weekend* and journeyed by oar and sail to dozens of sites along the Chesapeake and its tributaries.   At its stops the crew entertained and educated hundreds of students and adults, introducing them not only to the story of Smith's remarkable feat but also to the water trail and the exciting new opportunities it presented for exploration and education.

Meanwhile, the Commonwealth's fleet was also on the move in the Chesapeake. On April 24, 2007, the *Susan Constant, Godspeed,* and *Discovery* set sail from Jamestown en route to the mouth of the Bay, just off Cape Henry, where they provided the backdrop for a series of ceremonies, reenactments, and other events marking the 400th anniversary of the settlers' "first landing" there on April 26, 1607. Rough seas and heavy fog made the mission treacherous at times, but the sight of the three ships under sail provided one of the commemoration's most evocative images. The ships were back at Jamestown for *Anniversary Weekend* in mid-May, but the *Godspeed's* "Journey up the James"—a Jamestown 2007 signature event—took it to several riverside venues and eventually all the way upriver to the falls of the James River at Richmond.[98] As with its East Coast sail a year earlier, the *Godspeed* attracted dignitaries, tourists, and members of the news media to local festivals and anniversary events. The keynote speaker for the festivities in Richmond was Lord Watson, co-chair of the Jamestown 2007 British Committee.[99]

The Federal Commission viewed the Jamestown 400th anniversary as a once-in-a-lifetime opportunity to call attention to the singular importance of the Chesapeake and its tributaries. By highlighting the region's storied past, the Commission hoped to inspire a new generation to take seriously its own obligation as stewards of a unique natural and historical treasure. This goal guided the Commission's productive collaborations with the National Geographic Society, the Conservation Fund, and numerous other partners engaged in preservation and education activities in the Chesapeake region. Before concluding its work, the Commission took an additional step to foster ongoing investigation, education, and interpretation at the sites that served as headquarters for the two cultures that encountered and interacted with each other in Tidewater Virginia beginning in 1607. Through legacy grants to the APVA's Jamestown Rediscovery Project and the College of William and Mary's Department of Archaeology, the Federal Commission provided support for the next exciting

---

[98] The distinctive role of the James River in American history is discussed in *The River Where America Began: A Journey Along the James* (Lanham: Rowman & Littlefield Publishers, Inc., 2007) by Bob Deans.

[99] As the *Godspeed* visited Richmond, Chief Adkins and other tribal leaders gathered along the James River southeast of the city at Tree Hill Farm, believed to be the birthplace of Chief Powhatan. Officials with Gray Land and Development Company, Tree Hill Farm's owner, announced the company's plan to convey—by gift—7.5 acres of the farmland to Virginia's eight state-recognized tribes. Plans call for the site—to be known as "Machicomico," which is Algonquian for "meeting place or house"—to be developed into a meditation garden, meeting place, and educational facility. The property will be used for tribal activities and as a venue for educating the public about Virginia's indigenous peoples. The Commission provided a legacy grant in 2008 to aid in realization of those plans for the site.

phase of archaeological investigation at the James Fort and Werowocomoco sites, respectively.

ACKNOWLEDGEMENTS

This report was prepared under the direction of Commissioners Atkinson and Billings, co-chairs of the Editorial Review Committee, and Commissioners Adkins, Campbell, Dendy, Gleason, Smith, and Trumbo, who comprised the Committee. Executive Director Mann compiled the detailed information from which the report was drafted. The full Federal Commission participated in editing and finalizing the document, and approved it at the Commission's final meeting on December 12, 2008.

The Commission wishes to acknowledge the many people and organizations who have contributed to the success of the commemorative program and thus to the content of this report. Throughout these pages, we have endeavored to recognize those individuals and entities most directly involved, and to note their particular contributions. Inevitably, however, some have been omitted. For every Federal Commission endeavor and accomplishment chronicled here, there were important state and local contributions, the intensive labors of dedicated staff members, the vital aid of generous sponsors and partners, and the canny and creative services rendered by consultants and vendors.

While not diminishing the many other crucial contributions, we wish to express particular appreciation here to those with whom we have collaborated most closely throughout this worthwhile effort: the Jamestown 2007 Management and Steering Committees, Jamestown 2007, Inc., and the Jamestown 2007 office; the National Park Service and Colonial National Historical Park; APVA Preservation Virginia; the Jamestown-Yorktown Foundation and Jamestown-Yorktown Foundation, Inc.; the Jamestown 2007 British Committee; Prosody Creative Services; the University of Virginia Center for Politics; the Colonial Williamsburg Foundation; and the College of William and Mary.

We acknowledge with special gratitude the efforts of the federal and state officials who aided in the provision of financial and other crucial support by the United States Congress, the United States Departments of the Interior, State, and Education and other federal agencies, and the Commonwealth of Virginia, as well as the public-spirited organizations that provided resources for commemorative programs through donations to the Federal Commission or Jamestown 2007: Norfolk Southern Corporation; Colonial Williamsburg Foundation, Inc.; Verizon Communications, Inc.; Anheuser-Busch Companies, Inc.; Philip Morris USA; James City County; AirTran Airways; SunTrust Bank, PLC; Dominion; Ferguson Enterprises, Inc./Wolseley PLC; TowneBank; City of Poquoson; Rutherfoord Insurance; Target Corporation; Lockheed-Martin Corporation; CONSOL Energy/CNX Gas Corporation; McGuireWoods LLP; Carnegie Corporation of New York; and the Rockefeller Brothers Fund.

We also wish to acknowledge the important roles played by the following organizations: Kent County Council; National Geographic Society; NASA; Friends of the Captain John Smith Chesapeake National Historic Trail; Broadcast Partners LLC (Dr. Dan Roberts' *A Moment in Time*); Bureau of Educational and Cultural Affairs of the Department of State; Hampden-Sydney College; George Mason University; Longwood University; Norfolk State University; Old Dominion University; University of Richmond; University of Virginia; Virginia Commonwealth University; Virginia Tech; Historic Triangle Host Committee; Virginia Tourism Corporation; City of Williamsburg; New Kent, James City, and York Counties; Presidential Classroom; The Mercatus Center; Richmond Region 2007; American and English Inns of Court; John Marshall Foundation; and NATO.

This report includes more than seven dozen photos of key people and events during the commemoration, and the Commission expresses its appreciation to the following individuals and organizations who made this possible by authorizing use of their photos in this volume: Colonial National Historical Park and National Park Service; Tami Heilemann, U.S. Department of the Interior; Colonial Williamsburg Foundation; Mike Cell and the Jamestown 2007 British Committee; Jamestown-Yorktown Foundation; Jamestown 2007; Prosody Creative Services; University of Virginia Center for Politics; White House Photo Office; Bob Brown, Richmond Times-Dispatch; and Susan M. Trumbo.

Among the many forms of assistance provided to the Federal Commission by Commissioner Smith and his colleagues at the Colonial National Historical Park, the Park has agreed to serve as the repository of the Federal Commission's archives and memorabilia of interest from the commemoration. Those archives include the detailed minutes of the Commission's 16 meetings as well as other materials, which have been arranged topically to assist researchers. Persons interested in learning more about the Commission's work are encouraged to contact Superintendent Smith or the staff at the Colonial National Historical Park for access to these records.

The Federal Commission concluded it final meeting at Jamestown Island on December 12, 2008. At the Chairman's request, the Commission adjourned "in memory of the English settlers who founded the Jamestown settlement, the people they encountered and those who followed, and all who sacrificed during the next four centuries to fulfill America's founding promise and to secure for future generations the many blessings that God has bestowed on the United States of America." It is to those pioneers we acknowledge our greatest debt.

Federal Commissioner Mary A. Bomar, Director of the National Park Service, cuts the ribbon to open the new Visitor Center at Historic Jamestowne on May 12, 2007 (from left to right along the ribbon: architect Carlton Abbott; APVA Preservation Virginia Executive Director Elizabeth Kostelny; National Park Service Acting Regional Director Sandy Walter; Commissioner Bomar; Commissioner Rives; Commissioner P. Daniel Smith, Director of the Colonial National Historical Park)

Virginia Attorney General Robert F. McDonnell and other dignitaries gather in front of the monument to the original Jamestown voyagers at Cape Henry in Virginia Beach following ceremonies on April 26, 2007, marking the 400th anniversary of the first landing (from left to right: singer Cindy Warner; APVA Executive Director Kostelny; Commissioner Rives; NASA Astronaut Charles J. Camarda; Attorney General McDonnell; Commissioner Billings; Chairman Atkinson; Lt. Colonel Joel Clark (Fort Story Commander); Executive Director Mann; Vice Chair Dendy; Commissioner Smith)

Justice O'Connor welcomes Her Majesty, Queen Elizabeth II, during May 4, 2007 ceremonies in the re-created James Fort at Jamestown Settlement

Virginia Indians visiting England in July 2006 gather in front of the monument to Pocahontas on the grounds of St. Georges's Church at Gravesend, where the revered princess was buried in 1617

Vice President Cheney and Mrs. Lynne Cheney, accompanied by Commissioner Smith (right), tour Historic Jamestowne during the Royal Visit on May 4, 2007

Patrick Noonan (left), Conservation Fund Chairman Emeritus and proponent of the Captain John Smith Chesapeake National Historic Trail, stands in front of the replica of Smith's shallop with (from left to right) Commissioner Bomar, Chairman Atkinson, and National Geographic Society Chairman Gilbert Grosvenor

The Sultana Projects' crew takes the replica of Smith's shallop down the James River following its launch from Historic Jamestowne on Anniversary Weekend

During remarks at the Middle Temple gala dinner on December 19, 2006, Chairman Atkinson announces that President Bush earlier that day signed legislation creating the Captain John Smith Chesapeake National Historic Trail (at left: Lord Chief Justice Phillips of Worth Matravers)

Chief Justice John G. Roberts, Virginia Supreme Court Justice Donald W. Lemons, and Federal Commission members pause following dedication of the "rule of law" plaque at Historic Jamestowne on April 14, 2007 (from left to right: Justice Lemons; Chairman Atkinson; Chief Justice Roberts; Executive Director Mann; Commissioner Rives; Commissioner Flippo; Virginia Circuit Judge (and Commissioner) Malfourd W. (Bo) Trumbo; Vice Chair Dendy)

Senator John Warner (left), Interior Secretary Dirk Kempthorne (second from left), and French Defense Minister Michele Alliott-Marie (center) pay tribute to fallen soldiers at the Yorktown battlefield monument on October 19, 2006, the 225th anniversary of the decisive Revolutionary War victory

Chief Adkins invokes the Great Spirit in his Native tongue as he delivers the invocation during the opening ceremony of the World Forum on the Future of Democracy

Thomas Jefferson (Bill Barker of Colonial Williamsburg) reads from the Declaration of Independence during the commemoration's final signature event on September 18, 2007

From the rediscovered James Fort, the monumental Captain John Smith peers over the palisade and into the James River, where ships bearing English settlers and supplies arrived four centuries earlier

The Commonwealth of Virginia's fleet—replicas of the Discovery, Susan Constant, and Godspeed—sail down the James River and into the Chesapeake Bay to participate in events marking the 400th anniversary of the settlers' first landing at Cape Henry on April 26, 2007

APPENDIX 1

Jamestown 400th Commemoration Commission
Inaugural Meeting, Washington, D.C., June 12, 2003

Remarks of Commissioner Alexander L. (Sandy) Rives, **Jamestown 400th Project Director, National Park Service**

It is my pleasure to welcome my fellow members of the Jamestown 400th Commemoration Commission today. The members of this Commission are merely the latest in a long line of illustrious organizers of observances marking the first permanent English colony in North America. Commemorating the founding of Jamestown is a practice almost as old as the independent nation that evolved from her 17th century foundations. Beginning in 1807 and continuing every 50 years since, America has paused to commemorate her founding at Jamestown. Today this body begins its journey towards the 400th anniversary observance in 2007.

The 1807 bicentennial observance of Jamestown's founding was not the responsibility of a federal or state commission, but rather the accounts tell of us a "select committee" made up of citizens from Norfolk, Portsmouth, Petersburg, and Williamsburg that planned the five-day event. Known commonly as the "Grand National Jubilee," the event was attended by some 3,500 participants and featured a regatta of sailing vessels in the James River, a tent bazaar, and a parade. Students from the College of William and Mary gave recitations of odes and orations, while a troupe of actors converted an old barn on the island for use as a theater. Among the dignitaries attending the observance was Jamestown's own Colonel Champion Travis, the surviving member of the Virginia Convention of May 1776, which had been the first to declare for state independence. The events of May 13, 1807, included a procession to and prayers at the graveyard of the church, and an al fresco banquet and dancing at the Travis mansion. Jamestown's bicentennial concluded in Williamsburg with dinner and toasts offered at the Raleigh Tavern.

Fifty years later, the 250th anniversary of Jamestown's founding was marked by a considerably larger event than had occurred half a century earlier. Organized by the Jamestowne Society, this observance drew some 6,000 to 8,000 participants. Sixteen militia companies paraded on the site of America's birthplace, while a like number of steamers anchored offshore, brightly decorated with streamers. Orators at the event included Virginia Governor Henry A. Wise and former President John Tyler, whose address clocked in at a healthy two and a half hours. (I promise you, my remarks will not come close to that today). In his remarks, Governor Wise reflected on the nation that had begun at Jamestown two and a half centuries earlier and now extended from ocean to ocean: "Go to the Pacific now," the Governor told his listeners, "to measure the progression and power of a great people." The anniversary commemoration drew to a close with a great display of fireworks over the James River.

The 1907 Jamestown Ter-Centennial was the first observance drawing on the planning efforts of multiple organizations. The newly formed Association for the Preservation of Virginia Antiquities (APVA) led the way in 1900, passing a resolution at its annual meeting calling for plans to observe the 300th anniversary. Its efforts were eventually joined by the Commonwealth of Virginia and the United States Government, with the General Assembly and Congress providing support and funding for the observance. The majority of the Ter-Centennial events took place not at Jamestown itself, but rather some 50 miles away in the Norfolk area, on the site of today's Norfolk Naval Base. The Jamestown Ter-Centennial Exposition was an international celebration similar in scale to the Philadelphia Centennial of 1876, with public exhibition, cultural events, and perhaps the largest display of naval vessels in American history to that point. The Jamestown site was, of course, not unaffected. The APVA and the federal government constructed a seawall to protect the Jamestown shoreline. A large obelisk, the Tercentenary Monument, was built on land donated by the APVA to the federal government, and the Memorial Church was built on the foundations of the church of 1639.

The 350th anniversary observance of 1957 again brought together multiple organizations with the common theme of planning an observance that would be instructive as well as attractive. Both the state and federal governments established commissions to work together in planning, along with private organizations such as the APVA and the Colonial Williamsburg Foundation. The efforts of these organizations resulted in enhanced visitor facilities, better protection of the historic resources of Jamestown, and a greater appreciation of Virginia's Historic Triangle. In an effort to improve the visitor experience at Jamestown, State Highway 31 and the Jamestown-Scotland Ferry were moved west, off of the island, and the Colonial Parkway, linking the three legs of the Historic Triangle, was completed. The staging area for the observance, known as the Jamestown Festival Park, was established by the Commonwealth of Virginia adjacent to Jamestown on land donated by the National Park Service, and remains today as the Jamestown Settlement. On Jamestown Island, the reconstructed Glasshouse, the Memorial Cross, and Visitor Center were completed and dedicated. Other events included military reviews and flyovers, ship and aircraft christenings, and even an outdoor drama at Cape Henry. The event continued from April 1 to November 30, 1957, with over a million participants, including such dignitaries as Queen Elizabeth II and Prince Philip of Great Britain and U.S. Vice President Richard Nixon.

Remarks of Secretary of the Interior Gale Norton

It is my pleasure to participate in today's ceremonies, marking an important step in the observance of the 400th anniversary of the founding of Jamestown, the first English-speaking settlement in America.

In planning this commemoration, the Commission takes on the task of marking the occasion of one of our nation's most important events. Jamestown was the first permanent English colony in North America. It was the first seat of English government in Virginia and its social and political center for 92 years. At Jamestown, the first English representative government in the New World met, forming the model for the system of government our nation enjoys today. And at Jamestown was recorded the first arrival of Africans to Virginia. Indeed, at Jamestown the peoples of three continents, North America, Europe, and Africa, came together to create a new society whose legacy we live today.

Planning observances to mark the anniversary of the founding of the first permanent English-speaking settlement in the New World is not a new phenomenon. The descendants of those first English settlers and those who followed from other countries and other continents during the next two centuries recognized very early the need to mark what had occurred on the banks of the James River in 1607. Beginning in 1807, when the independent nation that had sprung from Jamestown's modest beginnings was still in its infancy, a commemoration that lasted several days was held at Jamestown to observe the bicentennial of the first permanent settlement and the beginnings of the United States. Every 50 years since then, the nation has sponsored similar observances to note the birthplace of America. And, in every instance, volunteer planners such as you have played a vital role. From the "select committee" of citizens directing the 1807 observance, to the Jamestown-Williamsburg-Yorktown Celebration Commission which preceded you 50 years ago, each of the Jamestown commemorations has had in common the dedication of planners who have successfully overseen the events.

In many ways, the work of the Commission will be similar to the work of those stalwart explorers nearly four centuries ago (though I expect not to hear reports of 80 percent casualties among you a few years from now). The same characteristics that ultimately made the Jamestown colony successful will mark this group's achievements as well. The 104 who set sail for Virginia in 1606 were comprised of volunteers—citizens who, like you, took up the task of their own free will for the improvement of their lives and the lives of others. Ultimately, in the wilderness of Virginia, hard work and ambition alone could not carry the day—success came only with the cooperation and assistance of others, partnerships that you as well will establish. And, of course, the Jamestown colony could not have succeeded without the backing of the Virginia Company of London. So, too, today, four centuries later, will the involvement of the private sector prove to be critical in your efforts.

So once again, let me say to each of you, welcome and thank you for the commitment and enthusiasm you bring to this task at hand. The road ahead is indeed a challenging one, with the eyes of the nation and indeed the world upon you. I close this morning with a reminder to you, taken from the original charter given by the Virginia Company of London to the settlers of 1607. Their words, penned nearly four centuries ago, have as much bearing for you today as it did for our colonial forebears so long ago: "Lastly and chiefly, the way to prosper and obtain good success is to make yourselves of one mind for the good of your country and your own."

APPENDIX 2

Jamestown 400th *Commemoration Commission*
Officers, Members, and Senior Staff

Officers

Frank B. Atkinson, Chairman	2003-2008
Nancy N. Campbell, Vice Chair	2003-2008
H. Benson Dendy III, Vice Chair	2003-2008
Daphne Maxwell Reid, Secretary	2003-2008
Michael P. Gleason, Treasurer	2003-2008

Members

Stephen R. Adkins	2003-2008
Warren M. Billings	2003-2008
Thomas J. Bliley, Jr.	2003-2004
Mary A. Bomar	2006-2008
Suzanne Owen Flippo	2003-2008
J. Steven Griles	2003-2007
Ann W. Loomis	2003-2008
Fran P. Mainella	2003-2006
John L. Nau III	2003-2008
Alexander L. (Sandy) Rives	2003-2007
M. Jordan Saunders	2003-2008
P. Daniel Smith	2007-2008
Malfourd Whitney (Bo) Trumbo	2003-2008

Senior Staff

H. Edward (Chip) Mann, Executive Director	2004-2008
Drema L. Johnson, Democracy Conference Project Director	2005-2008

Jamestown 2007 Steering Committee
Officers and Members, 1996-2008

Stuart W. Connock, *Chair*
Frank B. Atkinson, *Vice Chair*
Colin G. Campbell, *Vice Chair*
A. Marshall Acuff, Jr.
Wayne B. Adkins
Hunter B. Andrews
L. Ray Ashworth
Viola O. Baskerville
John M. Bennett
Peter A. Blake
William T. Bolling
Sandra D. Bowen
L. Preston Bryant, Jr.
Wilbert Bryant
Vincent F. Callahan, Jr.
Emmitt Carlton
Whittington W. Clement
M. Kirkland Cox
Linwood W. Custalow
Rosalyn R. Dance
H. Benson Dendy III
V. Earl Dickinson
Barry E. DuVal
Mark L. Earley
Suzanne O. Flippo
Patrick O. Gottschalk
F. Alec Gould
Peter Dun Grover
John H. Hager
Leroy R. Hassell, Sr.
Robert V. Hatcher, Jr.
Richard J. Holland
Pierce R. Homer
William J. Howell
Heather A. Huyck
Judith Williams Jagdmann
Calvin D. Jamison
Reginald N. Jones
Timothy M. Kaine

William M. Kelso
William B. Kerkam III
Jerry W. Kilgore
Martin K. King
Peter I. C. Knowles II
Elizabeth S. Kostelny
William H. Leighty
Donald W. Lemons
M. Boyd Marcus, Jr.
Martha D. Marks
George Keith Martin
Robert E. Martínez
Ivor P. Massey, Jr.
Daniel McDaniel
Robert F. McDonnell
Thomas R. Morris
W. Tayloe Murphy, Jr.
Thomas K. Norment, Jr.
Alexander L. Rives
Sherwood Sackett
Michael J. Schewel
Cal Simmons
Robert T. Skunda
P. Daniel Smith
Wallace Stettinius
Jay W. Timmons
Edgar A. Toppin
Malfourd W. Trumbo
Wayne M. Turnage
Donald W. Upson
Rovenia Vaughan
Alan M. Voorhees
Jody M. Wagner
Edwin W. Watson
Belle S. Wheelan
W. Bruce Wingo
John Paul Woodley, Jr.
Shirley J. Ybarra

Honorary Members
George F. Allen
Gerald L. Baliles
James S. Gilmore III
Mills E. Godwin, Jr.
A. Linwood Holton
Charles S. Robb
Mark R. Warner
L. Douglas Wilder
Roxane G. Gilmore,
 Honorary Chair (2000–01)

Executive Director
Jeanne Zeidler

APPENDIX 3

Jamestown Commemoration Commission Act of 2000
Public Law 106-565, 106th Congress

An Act to establish the Jamestown 400th
Commemoration Commission, and for other purposes

Be it enacted by the Senate and House of Representatives
of the United States of America in Congress assembled,

SECTION 1. SHORT TITLE.
This Act may be cited as the "Jamestown 400th Commemoration
Commission Act of 2000."

SEC. 2. FINDINGS AND PURPOSE.
(a) FINDINGS.—Congress finds that—
   (1) the founding of the colony at Jamestown, Virginia in 1607,
the first permanent English colony in the New World, and
the capital of Virginia for 92 years, has major significance in the
history of the United States;
   (2) the settlement brought people from throughout the Atlantic
Basin together to form a multicultural society, including
English, other Europeans, Native Americans, and Africans;
   (3) the economic, political, religious, and social institutions
that developed during the first 9 decades of the existence of
Jamestown continue to have profound effects on the United
States, particularly in English common law and language, cross
cultural relationships, and economic structure and status;
   (4) the National Park Service, the Association for the
Preservation of Virginia Antiquities, and the Jamestown-Yorktown Foundation of the Commonwealth of Virginia collectively own
and operate significant resources related to the early history of
Jamestown; and
   (5) in 1996—
      (A) the Commonwealth of Virginia designated the
Jamestown-Yorktown Foundation as the State agency
responsible for planning and implementing the Commonwealth's
portion of the commemoration of the 400th anniversary of the

founding of the Jamestown settlement;

   (B) the Foundation created the Celebration 2007 Steering Committee, known as the Jamestown 2007 Steering Committee; and

   (C) planning for the commemoration began.

(b) PURPOSE.—The purpose of this Act is to establish the Jamestown 400th Commemoration Commission to—

   (1) ensure a suitable national observance of the Jamestown 2007 anniversary by complementing the programs and activities of the State of Virginia;

   (2) cooperate with and assist the programs and activities of the State in observance of the Jamestown 2007 anniversary;

   (3) assist in ensuring that Jamestown 2007 observances provide an excellent visitor experience and beneficial interaction between visitors and the natural and cultural resources of the Jamestown sites;

   (4) assist in ensuring that the Jamestown 2007 observances are inclusive and appropriately recognize the experiences of all people present in 17th century Jamestown;

   (5) provide assistance to the development of Jamestown-related programs and activities;

   (6) facilitate international involvement in the Jamestown 2007 observances;

   (7) support and facilitate marketing efforts for a commemorative coin, stamp, and related activities for the Jamestown 2007 observances; and

   (8) assist in the appropriate development of heritage tourism and economic benefits to the United States.

SEC. 3. DEFINITIONS.

In this Act:

(1) COMMEMORATION.—The term "commemoration" means the commemoration of the 400th anniversary of the founding of the Jamestown settlement.

(2) COMMISSION.—The term "Commission" means the Jamestown 400th Commemoration Commission established by section 4(a).

(3) GOVERNOR.—The term "Governor" means the Governor of the State.

(4) SECRETARY.—The term "Secretary" means the Secretary of the Interior.

(5) STATE.—

   (A) IN GENERAL.—The term "State" means the State of Virginia.

(B) INCLUSIONS.—The term "State" includes agencies and entities of the State.

SEC. 4. JAMESTOWN 400TH COMMEMORATION COMMISSION.

(a) IN GENERAL.—There is established a commission to be known as the "Jamestown 400th Commemoration Commission."

(b) MEMBERSHIP.—

(1) IN GENERAL.—The Commission shall be composed of 16 members, of whom—

(A) four members shall be appointed by the Secretary, taking into consideration the recommendations of the Chairperson of the Jamestown 2007 Steering Committee;

(B) four members shall be appointed by the Secretary, taking into consideration the recommendations of the Governor;

(C) two members shall be employees of the National Park Service, of which—

(i) one shall be the Director of the National Park Service (or a designee); and

(ii) one shall be an employee of the National Park Service having experience relevant to the commemoration, to be appointed by the Secretary; and

(D) five members shall be individuals that have an interest in, support for, and expertise appropriate to, the commemoration, to be appointed by the Secretary.

(2) TERM; VACANCIES.—

(A) TERM.—A member of the Commission shall be appointed for the life of the Commission.

(B) VACANCIES.—

(i) IN GENERAL.—A vacancy on the Commission shall be filled in the same manner in which the original appointment was made.

(ii) PARTIAL TERM. — A member appointed to fill a vacancy on the Commission shall serve for the remainder of the term for which the predecessor of the member was appointed.

(3) MEETINGS.—

(A) IN GENERAL.—The Commission shall meet—

(i) at least twice each year; or

(ii) at the call of the Chairperson or the majority of the members of the Commission.

142

(B) INITIAL MEETING.—Not later than
30 days after the date on which all members of the
Commission have been appointed, the Commission
shall hold the initial meeting of the Commission.
(4) VOTING.—
(A) IN GENERAL.—The Commission shall
act only on an affirmative vote of a majority of the
members of the Commission.
(B) QUORUM.—A majority of the Commission
shall constitute a quorum.
(5) CHAIRPERSON.—The Secretary shall appoint a Chair
person of the Commission, taking into consideration any
recommendations of the Governor.
(c) DUTIES.—
(1) IN GENERAL.—The Commission shall—
(A) plan, develop, and execute programs and
activities appropriate to commemorate the 400th
anniversary of the founding of Jamestown;
(B) generally facilitate Jamestown-related
activities throughout the United States;
(C) encourage civic, patriotic, historical,
educational, religious, economic, and other
organizations throughout the United States to
organize and participate in anniversary activities to
expand the understanding and appreciation of the
significance of the founding and early history of
Jamestown;
(D) coordinate and facilitate for the public
scholarly research on, publication about, and
interpretation of, Jamestown; and
(E) ensure that the 400th anniversary of
Jamestown provides a lasting legacy and long-term
public benefit by assisting in the development of
appropriate programs and facilities.
(2) PLANS; REPORTS.—
(A) STRATEGIC PLAN; ANNUAL PERFORMANCE
PLANS.— In accordance with the Government
Performance and Results Act of 1993 (Public Law
103–62; 107 Stat. 285), the Commission shall
prepare a strategic plan and annual performance
plans for the activities of the Commission carried
out under this Act.
(B) FINAL REPORT.—Not later than September 30,
2008, the Commission shall complete a final report
that contains—

(i) a summary of the activities of the Commission;

(ii) a final accounting of funds received and expended by the Commission; and

(iii) the findings and recommendations of the Commission.

(d) POWERS OF THE COMMISSION.—The Commission may—

(1) accept donations and make dispersions of money, personal services, and real and personal property related to Jamestown and of the significance of Jamestown in the history of the United States;

(2) appoint such advisory committees as the Commission determines to be necessary to carry out this Act;

(3) authorize any member or employee of the Commission to take any action that the Commission is authorized to take by this Act;

(4) procure supplies, services, and property, and make or enter into contracts, leases or other legal agreements, to carry out this Act (except that any contracts, leases or other legal agreements made or entered into by the Commission shall not extend beyond the date of termination of the Commission);

(5) use the United States mails in the same manner and under the same conditions as other Federal agencies;

(6) subject to approval by the Commission, make grants in amounts not to exceed $10,000 to communities and nonprofit organizations to develop programs to assist in the commemoration;

(7) make grants to research and scholarly organizations to research, publish, or distribute information relating to the early history of Jamestown; and

(8) provide technical assistance to States, localities, and nonprofit organizations to further the commemoration.

(e) COMMISSION PERSONNEL MATTERS.—

(1) COMPENSATION OF MEMBERS OF THE COMMISSION.—

(A) IN GENERAL.—Except as provided in subparagraph (B), a member of the Commission shall serve without compensation.

(B) FEDERAL EMPLOYEES.—A member of the Commission who is an officer or employee of the Federal Government shall serve without compensation in addition to the compensation received for the services of the member as an officer or employee of the Federal Government.

(C) TRAVEL EXPENSES.—A member of the Commission shall be allowed travel expenses, including per diem in lieu of subsistence, at rates authorized for an employee of an agency under subchapter I of chapter 57 of title 5, United States Code, while away from the home or regular place of business of the member in the performance of the duties of the Commission.

(2) STAFF.—

(A) IN GENERAL.—The Chairperson of the Commission may, without regard to the civil service laws (including regulations), appoint and terminate an executive director and such other additional personnel as are necessary to enable the Commission to perform the duties of the Commission.

(B) CONFIRMATION OF EXECUTIVE DIRECTOR.—The employment of an executive director shall be subject to confirmation by the Commission.

(3) COMPENSATION.—

(A) IN GENERAL.—Except as provided in subparagraph (B), the Chairperson of the Commission may fix the compensation of the executive director and other personnel without regard to the provisions of chapter 51 and subchapter III of chapter 53 of title 5, United States Code, relating to classification of positions and General Schedule pay rates.

(B) MAXIMUM RATE OF PAY.—The rate of pay for the executive director and other personnel shall not exceed the rate payable for level V of the Executive Schedule under section 5316 of title 5, United States Code.

(4) DETAIL OF GOVERNMENT EMPLOYEES.—

(A) FEDERAL EMPLOYEES.—

(i) IN GENERAL.—On the request of the Commission, the head of any Federal agency may detail, on a reimbursable or non-reimbursable basis, any of the personnel of the agency to the Commission to assist the Commission in carrying out the duties of the Commission under this Act.

(ii) CIVIL SERVICE STATUS.—The detail of an employee under clause (i) shall be without interruption or loss of civil service status or privilege.

(B) STATE EMPLOYEES.—The Commission may—
    (i) accept the services of personnel detailed from States (including subdivisions of States); and
    (ii) reimburse States for services of detailed personnel.

(5) VOLUNTEER AND UNCOMPENSATED SERVICES.—Notwithstanding section 1342 of title 31, United States Code, the Commission may accept and use voluntary and uncompensated services as the Commission determines necessary.

(6) SUPPORT SERVICES.—The Director of the National Park Service shall provide to the Commission, on a reimbursable basis, such administrative support services as the Commission may request.

(f) PROCUREMENT OF TEMPORARY AND INTERMITTENT SERVICES.—The Chairperson of the Commission may procure temporary and intermittent services in accordance with section 3109(b) of title 5, United States Code, at rates for individuals that do not exceed the daily equivalent of the annual rate of basic pay prescribed for level V of the Executive Schedule under section 5316 of that title.

(g) FACA NONAPPLICABILITY.—Section 14(b) of the Federal Advisory Committee Act (5 U.S.C. App.) shall not apply to the Commission.

(h) NO EFFECT ON AUTHORITY.—Nothing in this section supersedes the authority of the State, the National Park Service, or the Association for the Preservation of Virginia Antiquities, concerning the commemoration.

(i) TERMINATION.—The Commission shall terminate on December 31, 2008.

SEC. 5. AUTHORIZATION OF APPROPRIATIONS.

There are authorized to be appropriated such sums as are necessary to carry out this Act.

APPENDIX 4

Jamestown 400ᵗʰ Commemoration Commission
Committees and Liaison Groups

Administration and Finance/Planning Committee
Gleason (co-chair), Rives (co-chair), Dendy (co-chair), Atkinson, Campbell, Griles, Loomis, Nau, Smith, Trumbo

Communications and Outreach Committee
Adkins (co-chair), Reid (co-chair), Atkinson, Billings, Campbell, Dendy, Flippo, Gleason, Griles, Mainella, Rives, Saunders

Democracy Conference Committee
Dendy (co-chair), Nau (co-chair), Atkinson, Campbell, Flippo, Gleason, Griles, Saunders, Trumbo

Development Committee
Campbell (co-chair), Saunders (co-chair), Atkinson, Dendy, Griles, Nau

Digital Production Committee
Adkins (co-chair), Reid (co-chair), Atkinson, Campbell, Dendy, Flippo, Loomis

Editorial Review Committee
Atkinson (co-chair), Billings (co-chair), Adkins, Campbell, Dendy, Gleason, Smith, Trumbo

Education Initiatives Committee
Billings (co-chair), Loomis (co-chair), Adkins, Atkinson, Bliley, Campbell, Dendy, Mainella, Reid, Rives, Smith, Trumbo

Federal Government Liaison Groups
Atkinson, Bliley, Dendy, Loomis, Mainella, Nau, Rives, Saunders, Trumbo
- **White House Liaison Group:** Griles (co-chair), Nau (co-chair), Atkinson
- **Congressional Liaison Group:** Loomis (chair), Atkinson,

Dendy, Griles, Nau, Rives
- **Federal Agency Liaison Group:**   Rives (chair), Atkinson, Griles, Loomis, Mainella, Nau, Trumbo

International Memorials Committee
Flippo (co-chair), Dendy (co-chair), Gleason, Reid, Trumbo

Nominations Committee
Trumbo (co-chair), Bliley (co-chair), Dendy (co-chair), Flippo, Griles, Loomis

Planning and Performance Committee
Campbell (co-chair), Adkins (co-chair), Atkinson, Billings, Bliley, Flippo, Saunders

United Kingdom Liaison Group
(Federal Commission members of the Joint US-UK Planning Committee, later called the "Anglo-American Planning Committee")
Flippo (chair), Atkinson, Dendy, Gleason, Nau

Virginia/Jamestown 2007 Liaison Group
Dendy (chair), Atkinson, Campbell, Flippo, Rives

APPENDIX 5

Jamestown 400th Commemoration Commission
Statement of Cash Receipts and Disbursements
(for the period October 1, 2002, through December 31, 2008)

RECEIPTS
Federal funds:

U.S. Department of the Interior (Commission appropriation)	$ 1,718,100
U.S. Department of State	890,490
U.S. Department of Education	99,200
APVA Preservation Virginia (as fiscal agent)	150,000
Jamestown Yorktown Foundation, Inc. (as fiscal agent)	145,000

Grants and receipts from other organizations:

Commonwealth of Virginia (V400 Fund)	845,711
Jamestown 2007, Inc.	899,002
College of William and Mary Foundation	100,000
Corporate donations	425,070
Jamestown Yorktown Foundation, Inc.	5,017
APVA Preservation Virginia	926
Other receipts and expense reimbursements	99,653
Total receipts	5,378,169

DISBURSEMENTS
Programs:

Democracy conference administration	101,047
Democracy conference events	1,798,365
World Forum international delegates	184,354
International meetings and programs	176,904
Communications and conference promotion	641,096
Educational initiatives	466,321
Legacy gifts and grants	587,444

Administrative:

Archiving	45,378
Audit	35,375
Meeting expense	220,571

Office supplies	76,861
Rent	108,343
Salaries	907,104
Telephone	29,006
Total disbursements	5,378,169

APPENDIX 6

Remarks of Her Majesty,
Queen Elizabeth II
Virginia State Capitol, Richmond, Virginia,
May 3, 2007

Governor Kaine, Members of the General Assembly, Ladies and Gentlemen:

Thank you for your generous welcome to Virginia. Prince Philip and I are delighted to be here in your State Capitol today, designed by that great Virginian Thomas Jefferson and so painstakingly restored over recent years. I would like to congratulate everyone involved in this most impressive project.

As a State and as a Nation you are still coming to terms with the dreadful events at Virginia Tech on the sixteenth of April. My heart goes out to the students, friends and families of all those killed, and to the many others who have been affected, some of whom I shall be meeting shortly. On behalf of the people of the United Kingdom I extend my deepest sympathies at this time of such grief and sorrow.

I visit the United States this week to commemorate the four hundredth anniversary of the landing of a small group of British citizens on a tiny island in what is now called the James River here in Virginia. With the benefit of hindsight, we can see in that event the origins of a singular endeavour, the building of a great nation, founded on the eternal values of democracy and equality based on the rule of law and the promotion of freedom.

But we should always be cautious of hindsight. Four hundred years ago, it was by no means preordained that this venture would succeed. Recent archaeological work has modified our understanding of the original settlement at Jamestown, about the choice of its location and the kind of people who came. While it remains difficult to say what it was about those early years which caught that vital moment in the evolution of this great country, it must surely have had something to do with the ingenuity, the drive and the idealism of that group of adventurers who first set foot on this fertile Virginian soil and the will of the native Powhatan people to find ways to co-exist.

When I visited fifty years ago, we celebrated the three hundred and fiftieth Anniversary largely from the perspective of those settlers, in terms of the exploration of new worlds, the spread of values and of the English language, and the sacrifice of those early pioneers. These remain great attributes and we still appreciate their impact today.

But fifty years on we are now in a position to reflect more candidly on the Jamestown legacy. Human progress rarely comes without cost. And those early years in Jamestown, when three great civilisations came together for the first time—Western European, Native American and African—released a train of events which continues to have a profound social impact, not only in the United States, but also in the United Kingdom and Europe.

Over the course of my reign, and certainly since I first visited Jamestown in 1957, my country has become a much more diverse society, just as the Commonwealth of Virginia and the whole United States of America have also undergone major social change. The "melting pot" metaphor captures one of the great strengths of your country and is an inspiration to others around the world as we face the continuing social challenges ahead.

It is right that we continue to reassess the meaning of historical events in the changing context of the present, not least in this the two hundredth anniversary in the United Kingdom of the Act of Parliament to abolish the transatlantic Slave Trade. But such reassessments should not obscure one enduring consequence of Jamestown. This four hundredth anniversary marks a moment to recognise the deep friendship which exists between our two countries. Friendship is a complex concept. It means being able to debate openly, disagree on occasion, surmount both good times and bad, safe in the knowledge that the bonds that draw us together— of history, understanding and warm regard—are far stronger than any temporary differences of opinion.

The people of the United Kingdom have such a relationship with the people of this great nation. It is one of the most durable international collaborations anywhere in the world at any time in history, a friendship for which I certainly in my lifetime have had good cause to be thankful. That is a lasting legacy of Jamestown, that is something worth commemorating, and that is why I am pleased to be here today.

———————

APPENDIX 7

Jamestown 400th Commemoration Commission
Statement on Virginia Indian Participation in the Jamestown Quadricentennial Commemoration[1]
May 12, 2004

The federal Jamestown 400th Commemoration Commission (Federal Commission) welcomes the decision of the Virginia Indian tribes to participate actively in the commemoration of the 400th anniversary of the founding of the first permanent English settlement in America at Jamestown.

The Federal Commission's statutory purposes include "ensuring that the Jamestown 2007 observances are inclusive and appropriately recognize the experiences of all peoples present in 17th century Jamestown." Thus, highlighting the culture and distinctive contributions of Virginia Indians before, during, and since the 1607 settlement at Jamestown is an important aspect of the Federal Commission's mission.

The 400th anniversary commemoration will be enriched through Virginia Indians' telling their own stories in their own voices. It promises to leave a valuable legacy of enhanced cross-cultural understanding.

The United States of America and its founding principles trace their roots to the Jamestown colony. It is a matter of historical consensus that this landmark settlement might well have failed but for the assistance of the native Virginia tribes. In the succeeding four centuries, Virginia Indians have played a vital role in serving their communities, the Commonwealth of Virginia, and the United States of America.

---

[1] Commission members Adkins, Griles, Mainella, and Rives did not participate in the Commission's adoption of this statement.

The Virginia tribes entered into a treaty relationship with the English Crown in the 17th century and, today, the Virginia Indians enjoy recognition by the Commonwealth of Virginia. During the intervening centuries, however, Virginia Indians were often denied opportunities and basic rights enjoyed by other Virginia and American citizens, and by other sovereign Native American tribes. In recent decades, efforts to remedy these denials have met with some success, and those efforts are ongoing.

The Federal Commission has been asked to comment on the pending question of federal recognition of the Virginia Indian tribes. The Federal Commission is subject to various federal laws that restrict its ability to take positions on pending issues within the legislative and executive branches. In April 2004, the Ethics Office of the Office of the Solicitor of the U.S. Department of the Interior specifically advised the Federal Commission that, under applicable law, the "Commission may not take . . . an official position on Federal recognition of the Virginia tribes." Therefore, the Federal Commission, in accordance with its legal obligations, will take no official position on any pending legislative or administrative action relative to federal recognition of the Virginia Indian tribes.[2] Nor is it the Commission's intention, through this statement, to impact the application of law and fact by the Department of the Interior in the exercise of its statutory responsibilities regarding tribal recognition.

Recognizing the Commission's statutory mandate to ensure an inclusive Jamestown commemoration, and to highlight the contributions of all peoples who came together in 17th century Virginia, the Commission believes that resolution of the differing views surrounding the federal recognition question and the resulting achievement of such recognition by 2007 would constitute an important contribution to the success of Jamestown's 400th anniversary commemoration.

---

[2] Commission members are aware that some congressional supporters and opponents of pending legislation on federal recognition of Virginia tribes have expressed agreement with the ultimate goal of recognition even while disagreeing on the terms and conditions thereof. While pending tribal recognition legislation is supported by Virginia Governor Mark Warner, U.S. Senators George Allen and John W. Warner, Rep. JoAnn Davis, Rep. James P. Moran, Jr., and others, a prominent opponent of the pending legislation, Rep. Frank Wolf, wrote in a commentary published in the *Richmond Times-Dispatch* on March 22, 2004, that he objects to the pending proposal but "want[s] to support legislation to recognize the Virginia tribes." The Federal Commission recognizes its legal obligation to refrain from commentary on the merits of pending legislation, and accordingly has limited this statement to the importance of federal recognition to Virginia tribes—however it may be achieved—in the context of the 400th anniversary commemoration.

The Commission recognizes the importance of the federal recognition issue to the Virginia tribes, including its symbolic value in demonstrating understanding of the distinctive contributions of Virginia Indians before, during, and since the English settlement at Jamestown in 1607 and the important role Virginia Indians have played in the success of the United States of America and the varied communities and cultures that comprise our country.

The Federal Commission, working in cooperation with the Commonwealth of Virginia's Jamestown 2007 Steering Committee and other public and private partners, endeavors to plan and execute an inclusive 400th anniversary commemoration—one that reflects the full fabric of our diverse, yet unified, country and that enhances national and international appreciation of Jamestown's enduring and still-evolving legacies. The Federal Commission welcomes the full participation of Virginia Indians in this commemoration, and the Commission looks forward to working with these tribes to honor the culture and contributions of Virginia's indigenous peoples.

APPENDIX 8

Jamestown 400th Commemoration Commission
Published Commentaries by Commission Members

"When Celebrating Jamestown, Remember America's Mission"
by Frank B. Atkinson
Richmond Times-Dispatch, April 23, 2006

Many private enterprises have produced dramatic advances, and a handful have affected the course of human history. But no entrepreneurial venture has proved as consequential as the Virginia Company of London.

Four hundred years ago this month, a group of optimistic investors and their canny lawyers crafted the visionary charter that brought the Virginia Company into being. They set in motion events that would lead, in May 1607, to the first permanent English settlement in the Americas—at "Jamestown."

The journey they began would change the world.

From that fragile first planting at Jamestown grew a robust Virginia colony, the incubator for ideas and institutions that would define and prosper the American republic—among them, representative government, free enterprise, religious liberty, and the rule of law.

A nation of immigrants, America's cultural diversity also traces its roots to Jamestown, where native Americans, English settlers, and enslaved Africans first came together under the most trying of conditions.

From those harsh beginnings commenced a 400-year-old journey toward making the promise of freedom real for everyone. It is a journey that has challenged and inspired the American people. And in our time it is a journey that has brought liberty and democracy to much of the world.

The United States Congress recognized the transcendent importance of Jamestown and this journey when, in 2000, it created the Jamestown 400th Commemoration Commission and charged it with bringing the anniversary and its significance to the attention of the American people.

The mission is primarily an educational one.

Many Americans, young and old, lack an understanding of their nation's journey. They take for granted freedoms that are strikingly exceptional in the long sweep of human history, and that have been gained and sustained only through centuries of struggle, sacrifice, and service.

The 400th anniversary of the remarkable beginning at Jamestown—*America's 400th Anniversary*—provides a unique opportunity to acquaint Americans with their past and show its connection to their present and future.

To seize this opportunity, our federal commission has focused on a variety of educational initiatives.

Working with state, local, and private partners, we have created a website, entitled "Jamestown—Journey of Democracy" (*www.JamestownJourney.org*), where school teachers across America can access, without charge, a rich variety of lesson plans that weave the Jamestown story into the teaching of civics, history, archaeology, science, and other subjects.

The experiences of all three cultures that came together at Jamestown are addressed in the lesson plans, and the contributors of curricula on the website are as wide-ranging as the materials found there. They include the Smithsonian Institution, National Geographic Society, NASA, University of Virginia Center for Politics, Colonial Williamsburg Foundation, the educational organizations on site at Jamestown, and many others.

More than 1,500 teachers in 49 states, the District of Columbia, and 11 countries have already accessed the educational resources on the website even before major promotional activities commence later this spring. And this fall, the state's Jamestown 2007 organization will host "Jamestown Live!"—an hour-long, live webcast to classrooms across the country focusing on Jamestown's legacies of democracy, diversity, and exploration.

Our commission is also engaging the higher education community through a university-based conference series on the foundations and future of democracy.

The series will begin this summer with an International Youth Democracy Summit at the University of Virginia, and will culminate in September 2007 with the World Forum on the Future of Democracy, an international gathering of scholars and government leaders in Jamestown and Williamsburg.

During the intervening year, seven other university campuses in Virginia will be host to conferences addressing particular aspects of democratic development. One will explore the role of the judiciary in representative democracies. Another will examine the impact of free markets. Others will focus on issues related to ethnic, religious, and cultural diversity. One conference will examine the philosophical underpinnings of democracy, while another will address contemporary challenges posed by globalization, technological advances, and terrorism.

Electronic and written records of the proceedings with be published as the "Jamestown Commentaries on the Foundations and Future of Democracy."

The conference series planning council is being ably led by President Emeritus Timothy J. Sullivan of the College of William and Mary, and will involve respected scholars and governmental practitioners from around the world.

To all who will pause and reflect, it is apparent that Providence has endowed the American people with incomparable blessings and a sacred trust. Freedom is God's gift to mankind, Virginia's legacy to America, and America's mission in the world.

As we mark the impending 400th anniversary with appropriate activities of commemoration, celebration, reverence, and reflection, we should resolve to use the occasion creatively to increase broad-based understanding of the remarkable legacy we share—and of our responsibility as citizens to journey on toward fulfillment of liberty's promise for all.

"Diverse Populace Wove the Fabric of Jamestown"
by Stephen R. Adkins
Richmond Times-Dispatch, May 6, 2007

Amid the hoopla surrounding the commemoration of the 400th anniversary of the founding of the first permanent English settlement at Jamestown, there resides perhaps the greatest potential Virginia has had since 1957 to tell the world the historical facts of those first two decades of the struggles at Jamestown. A story of Jamestown that presents the unvarnished truth will at once delight, sadden, anger, or soothe the consciousness of those who dare to explore its reality.

We have heard all of the nice terms about how the very fabric of the tapestry of democracy—which provides the underpinnings of the greatest republic on Earth—was woven at Jamestown. What we had not heard heretofore are stories of the labors of the very diverse population that directly or indirectly supported those efforts to achieve democracy.

I would not have anyone believe the indigenous peoples who became unsuspecting hosts of the Englishmen always acted with best interests of the settlers in mind. However, based on the sheer numbers of resident natives here in 1607, the colonists could have been wiped out at any time in the first three decades.

Obviously, the hosts saw reasons to allow the colonists to survive.

Perhaps Chief Powhatan was inclined to embrace these strangers and learn some of their technology regarding marine vessels, building architecture, military ordnance, or metalworking. Algonquian culture suggests that he would have wanted to incorporate this powerful people into his own paramount chiefdom.

In any event, without the forbearance of their hosts, the colonists would not have survived.

Things took a serious turn in 1610 when Lord De La Warr ordered the massacre of the Paspehegh tribe. It is safe to assume that a few members of the tribe survived but the tribe as a group ceased to exist. I mention this because Virginia history books do not tell this story—and in fact present most of the attacks by the settlers as provoked, and those by the natives as unprovoked.

The Jamestown journey began in 1607, but in a way it continues today. The federal Jamestown 400th Commemoration Commission has traced the rule of law from 1607 until 2007. Acknowledgments must be made that the rule of law did not always protect those who deserved protection. In fact, for hundreds of years the law injured and suppressed Native people and African Americans. Native Americans' rights were denied to the extent that Native Americans became an invisible minority. The intent behind the rule of law must be applauded, and the progress toward justice for all is ongoing. State and federal governments have moved more and more toward justice—and the surviving Virginia Indian tribes can talk about their history without fear.

The spirit of democracy has become infectious in the intervening years since 1607, and the past 20 years have seen multiple countries embrace a democratic form of government.

Life has not been easy for Virginia's indigenous peoples, but to the person we are proud to be Virginians and Americans. Most tribal members across the Commonwealth are proud to be a part of a commemoration that has provided an opportunity for us to tell our story and to let the world know that descendants of some of the sovereign nations who greeted the settlers on the shores of the Powhatan River (James River) at Tsenacomoco are still here.

Our connection to the British Crown resurfaced as we explored the Treaty of 1677, referred to interchangeably as the Treaty of Middle Plantation or the Articles of Peace. I am confident images of that treaty crossed the minds of the chiefs of Virginia's eight recognized Indian tribes as we greeted Her Majesty, Queen Elizabeth II, as representatives of our sovereign nations this past Thursday at the State Capitol.

It has been rewarding to see the federal Jamestown 400th Commemoration Commission engage academia and Virginia Natives to research history and develop subject matter with attendant lesson plans reflective of Jamestown's rich history. Hopefully, these lesson plans will find their way into classrooms across the Commonwealth and beyond and serve to dispel some of the myths and stereotypes that have shackled Virginia Indians for 400 years.

If one wants to understand what life is like for Virginia Indians, listen to the "Anniversary Voices" music especially prepared for the Jamestown Commemoration:

Remember the Many

We are all part of the sacred earth, every deer, every
stream, every tree.
We have learned to respect all living things, and to live in
harmony.
We are riders on the sands, the sands of time, the Creator's
in the wave, in the shore.
We have been here for more than ten thousand years.
We will be here for ten thousand more!
Stand where I'm standing; take a look at my view
How should I feel? I was here before you.
The time has arrived, recognition is due.
Remember the many who've become the few!

———————————

"Give Thanks for the Gift of Virginia"
by Frank B. Atkinson
Richmond Times-Dispatch, May 11, 2007

The debate over who held the "first thanksgiving" in America has occupied partisans in Virginia and Massachusetts for decades. Massachusetts has the popular advantage. Yet, because "facts are stubborn things," as John Adams famously declared, Virginia retains the superior claim.

But such arguments, like those over the primacy of Jamestown versus Plymouth, miss a much larger point.

On this momentous weekend, when Americans join Virginians in commemorating Jamestown's founding, the point is not who first gave thanks centuries ago, but whether we will first give thanks now, as we usher in America's fifth century.

Millions of years before the three small ships made their way across the Atlantic to Jamestown, another traveler—one celestial in origin—made its way to Virginia from an unknown point in the universe. The three-mile wide object, traveling at 75 times the speed of sound, crashed into the shallow ocean at the site of present-day Cape Charles, Virginia. The largest to impact the earth since the cataclysmic death of the dinosaurs, the meteor produced a tsunami that lapped the Virginia mountains and left a crater in the ocean floor twice the size of Rhode Island and nearly as deep as the Grand Canyon.

This remarkable event, recently discovered by geologists, bears a direct causal relation to Virginia's role as the birthplace of modern America and the cradle of democracy in the modern world.

As the waters of the ocean receded over time, the crater became a vital agent in forming the Chesapeake Bay and its uniquely rich estuary system. Nature and man then interacted in ways that changed the course of human history.

The nurturing Chesapeake estuaries became home to the Powhatan Confederacy, an Indian society that was already highly developed when Englishmen, also attracted to the natural protections and abundance of the Chesapeake region, came to found a settlement in 1607. Without the assistance of the Powhatans in the nourishing bosom of the Bay, the Jamestown settlement would not have survived. But survive it did, and in nearby Williamsburg a century and a half later its heirs worked out their revolutionary ideas and mustered the mettle to assert independence from colonial rule.

The ensuing war ended—history being rich with irony—just down the road at Yorktown, where the Chesapeake and foreign help combined with the colonials' remarkable perseverance to lay a fatal trap for the vaunted British army of General Cornwallis.

Because George Washington chose to return to his serene home on the banks of the Potomac rather than be king—an event destined to rank forever among the most consequential acts of self-denial in human history—a republic took root, and a nation at length was forged.

The question of nationhood was not resolved, however, until rebellious Richmond finally fell to the forces of Union in 1865 after four years of carnage, much of it in the blood-soaked soil of the Chesapeake watershed.

Through that struggle the scourge of slavery, introduced in the Americas on the banks of the James, was ended. And in the crucible of that conflict a new American character was forged—one more faithful to Jefferson's transcendent declaration that all individuals are created equal and endowed by their Creator with the right to life, liberty and the pursuit of happiness.

For more than two centuries, another city on a Chesapeake estuary—the capital that rightly bears Washington's name—has been the locus of decisions that provided hope for people around the world seeking freedom. Among those decisions were the orders that dispatched great vessels from Hampton Roads, near Cape Henry where the English settlers first landed, to the climactic engagements that turned back the tide of totalitarianism and saved liberty.

If we see these and other remarkable events as random dispensations of fortune or fate, then they should occupy us little now. But if we see mankind's remarkable progress toward liberty and democracy as a Providential gift that confers obligation as well as opportunity, then our presence here in Virginia—the cradle of American democracy and *Ground Zero* for an explosion of freedom that has transformed the world—should be cause for profound thanksgiving and solemn recommitment.

The legacies of Jamestown and Virginia—the rule of law, representative government, free enterprise, religious liberty and cultural diversity—are enduring and still evolving. As the fresh breeze of freedom whistles across distant shores, we know that what began when brave pioneers first set foot on Virginia's Atlantic sands is profoundly good, but far from perfect—and still unfinished.

Freedom is God's gift to mankind, Virginia's legacy to America, and America's mission in the world. Giving thanks for that gift is the right way to begin our fifth century on a journey that is still changing the world.

"America's 400th Anniversary: The Native American Perspective"
by Chief Stephen R. Adkins, Chickahominy Indian Tribe
People, Land, & Water, August 2007

We are in the midst of many events in Virginia, the United Kingdom and across this nation commemorating the anniversary of the founding of the first permanent English Settlement in America in May 1607. The culturally diverse history of Virginia has been explored through a number of conferences under the auspices of the Jamestown 400th Commemoration Commission, on which I serve.

During the 400th Anniversary Weekend in Jamestown, May 11-13, 2007, visitors from all over the world—including leaders representing the U.S. government, England, Native Americans, and African Americans—gathered to commemorate the birth of this great republic, the United States of America, which blossomed at Jamestown. What does all this mean for Native Americans, especially Tidewater Virginia Indians?

After all, our troubles began with the landing of the first English settlers in Jamestown in 1607. A methodical process of securing land through the doctrine of discovery began almost immediately. (In fact, the English did not "discover" these lands because American Indians had discovered and inhabited them for thousands of years.)

Colonization sounded the death knell of a way of life for a group of people who had called this place home for several millennia. Our ranks were reduced by 90 percent by the end of the 17th century. By 1610, the Paspehegh, on whose land Jamestown was founded, fell to the sword under the orders of Lord De La Warr and ceased to exist as a tribe. A whole nation was annihilated. This was the nation that befriended strangers and ultimately died at the hands of those same strangers.

Some of the tribal members undoubtedly escaped and found safe haven with other tribes, including my tribe, the Chickahominy. But lands that had been home to native peoples for thousands of years suddenly became off-limits. Linchpins of our culture such as religion and language were set aside. Marginalization of Indians continued well into the 20th century and even continues today.

Against this backdrop, many Natives and non-Natives alike have questioned why any Virginia Indian—even a tribal chief such as myself—would participate in a commemoration of the first permanent English Settlement in Virginia. After having lived on this land for 15,000 years, what is so significant about the last .266 span of time?

The answers are manifold. The fact that we have survived for the past 400 years is ample cause to celebrate. The fact that we have been able to pass along oral history and various components of our culture is worthy of celebration. But the single most important reason to be a part of this commemoration is because we are a part of America and this commemoration is all about America. The commemoration is about telling America's story. In the past the stories of Native and African Americans have been left out, ignored, or overlooked. How could we ignore this opportunity to tell our stories to a world audience?

The federal Jamestown commission, on which I serve, sought input from renowned scholars, tribal leaders, university professors, and others to ensure the picture we painted of Jamestown was accurate. Some of the research revealed factual information that was "new" to all of us. The research showed very clearly how the interactions of the diverse cultures of the early 17th century contributed to the ultimate success of Jamestown.

I applaud the members of the federal commission for not veering away from the objective of commemorating the complete story of Jamestown. Some organizations and individuals challenged and criticized the commemoration activities. However, the commission remained steadfast in its efforts to share and portray the history of Jamestown as honestly and accurately as possible.

From my personal experiences and those of my people, growing up as a member of an American Indian tribe meant living a life marginalized by almost 400 years of anti-Native politics and policies.

I have been asked why I do not have a traditional Indian name. Quite simply: my parents, as did many other Native American parents, weighed the risks and decided it was not worth the risk of going to jail. An article by Peter Hardin in the *Richmond Times-Dispatch* in 2000 describes the documentary genocide the Virginia Indians suffered at the hands of Walter Ashby Plecker, a white separatist who ruled over the Bureau of Vital Statistics in Virginia for 34 years, from 1912 to 1946.

Plecker led efforts to eradicate all references to Indians on Vital Records. The state's legislature enacted the Racial Integrity Act in 1924, forcing all segments of the population to be registered at birth in one of two categories, white or colored. Doctors and midwives faced punishment if they assigned Indian as the racial classification for Native babies born in Virginia in the early- to mid-20ᵗʰ century.

My father and mother traveled to Washington, D.C., in 1935 to be married because the Racial Integrity Act made it illegal to marry in Virginia with the racial designation Indian on your marriage license. Many Native people did not give their children Native names because that too was punishable by up to one year in jail.

In public schools report cards for students were labeled white or colored. For Indian students, lines were drawn through the preprinted racial designations and Indian was penciled in.

On a trip to my brother's high school commencement exercises at Bacone, Oklahoma, in the mid-'50s, I recall stopping at a service station for gasoline. I was a youngster about 9 years old, and I had to go the restroom. I remember asking my Dad, "Where do I go?" because the restrooms were labeled "white" and "black." For me that situation created a real dilemma.

One might ask, "Why would you go to Oklahoma to receive a high school education?" The answer is quite simple. There were no high schools in Virginia for Native people then. In fact, Virginia provided a one way ticket to Oklahoma and tuition to Bacone High School for Virginia Indians.

Our anthropologist says there is no other state that attacked Indian identity as directly as the laws passed during that period of time in Virginia. No other ethnic community's heritage was denied in this way. Our state, by law, declared there were no Indians in the state in 1924, and if you dared to say differently, you went to jail or worse.

My father and his peers lived in the heart of the Plecker years and carried those scars to their graves. The Racial Integrity Act stayed in effect until 1967, for half of my life.

Between 1983 and 1989, eight tribes gained state recognition in the Commonwealth of Virginia. In addition to my tribe, the Chickahominy, these tribes included the Eastern Chickahominy, Mattaponi, Monacan, Nansemond, Pamunkey, Rappahannock, and Upper Mattaponi Tribes. Ironically, while we commemorate the

400th anniversary of America from its beginnings in Virginia, to date no tribes in Virginia have obtained federal recognition.

In 1997, state legislation sponsored by Governor George Allen acknowledged the state action that attacked our heritage. Although this legislation allows those of the living generations to correct birth records, the legislation or law has not and cannot undo the pain and humiliation suffered by my ancestors or the damage done to our documented history. In 1999, the tribes were advised by the Bureau of Acknowledgement and Research (BAR), now Office of Federal Acknowledgement (OFA), that many of our people would not live long enough to see our petition go through the administrative process. We have buried three of our chiefs since then.

Given the realities of the OFA and the damage to our historical heritage suffered by Virginia Indian tribes, six of the tribes, with the support of the current Governor, Tim Kaine, are seeking recognition through the U.S. Congress rather than the Bureau of Indian Affairs (BIA).

We would be hampered in the BIA process by the fact that actions taken by the Commonwealth of Virginia during the 20th century corrupted our written history by altering key documents, intimidated many people, and in several other ways made the tribes fear that we would not fit into the petitioning process.

Against all odds, including a hostile political climate bent on erasing Native peoples from the landscape of Virginia, we, the Virginia Indian tribes, have maintained our cultures and have continued our oral histories. We have maintained an "underground school" that has been our means of teaching our children the history of Virginia Indians, part of our efforts to dispel the inaccuracies of those lessons learned in the public school classrooms of Virginia.

Yet many publications continue to carry romanticized, inaccurate accounts of 17th century history. Sadly many misrepresentations— such as the "discovery" of the "new" world and the characterization of the English settlers as the "first families" of Virginia—go largely unnoticed by non-Native people and are, in fact, given credibility by textbooks used in classrooms throughout Virginia. Moreover, the textbooks have been sorely lacking in subject matter addressing the contributions Natives made to the tenuous beginnings of the "New World."

For example, to historians of the colonial era in the Old Dominion, it is accepted intelligence that the Natives could have killed the settlers at will during the first 10–15 years of their occupation of these lands. However, even after the massacre of the Paspehegh in 1610 at the command of Lord De La Warr, the natives chose not to get rid of the settlers.

Fast-forward to the spring of 2006, and you see a scene replete with diverse participants watching their plan for a meaningful commemoration of the first permanent English Settlement at Jamestown unfold. What distinguishes this commemoration from previous commemorations, aside from the careful use of the term "commemoration" rather than "celebration," is the fact that there was an African American and a Native American presence at the table from the onset.

To the person, every member of the Jamestown commission was determined to mine historical documents and consult subject-matter experts, including archaeologists, anthropologists, historians, educators, and renowned jurists within the United States, the United Kingdom, Africa, and elsewhere, to ensure the factual presentation of the events of the first three decades of English occupation of the "New World."

In July 2006, a delegation of 54 tribal members, recognized by the Commonwealth of Virginia, had the opportunity to visit the United Kingdom as part of the U.K.'s 2007 commemoration activities. For many of us, it was a first-time visit to St. George's Church at Gravesend, the final resting place of Pocahontas, the daughter of Paramount Chief Powhatan and the wife of John Rolfe.

A plaque on the wall of St. George's Church says,

> *This stone commemorates Princess Pocahontas or Metoak daughter of the mighty American Indian Chief Powhatan. Gentle and humane, she was the friend of the earliest struggling English colonists whom she nobly rescued, protected, and helped. On her Conversion to Christianity in 1613, she received in Baptism the name Rebecca, and shortly afterwards became the wife of John Rolfe, a settler in Virginia. She visited England with her husband in 1616, was graciously received by Queen Anne wife of James I. In the twenty second year of her age she died at Gravesend preparing to revisit her native country and was buried near this spot on March 21st 1617.*

For us, who have experienced and know so well what has happened to our people since the days of Pocahontas, the connection we felt to both the congregation and Pocahontas was palpable and real. This feeling of respect and honor in the church congregation suffused the entire Virginia Indian Delegation.

We saw Pocahontas as more than the legend we live behind; we saw her as the first to brave the new world that opened up with first contact by the English, a soul who today can still touch us and remind us of our proud heritage. She is not a myth, for she is still inside all of us, and her death and burial in England remind us of how far and challenging our path has been since she braved that voyage to England.

Much has happened to the Virginia tribes since Pocahontas visited England and the Court of Queen Anne. The story of Chief Powhatan and his daughter Pocahontas is well known across this land. Her picture is in the U.S. Capitol with her English husband John Rolfe. But less known is the plight of Virginia Indians today and the fact that the United States has not formally recognized our contribution.

The 400th anniversary has given us a chance to tell our stories. During the past five years of my tenure on the Jamestown 400th Anniversary Commemoration Commission, I have seen the public visibility of Virginia Indians increase exponentially. I have often said that after 400 years we have grown to understand that if our stories are to be told, we must tell them. And tell them we have. From the State Capitol in Richmond, to the halls of Congress on Capitol Hill in Washington, D.C., to Kent County England, to the halls of Parliament in London, England, and to the shores of the Powhatan River, we have told our stories. We have spoken to audiences who listened in rapt attention to our tale of endurance and survival and who yearn to hear more of the history of Virginia's indigenous peoples, a history of which public school students within the Commonwealth of Virginia have been deprived.

As part of the 400th commemoration of Jamestown, the Virginia tribes will have a much deeper understanding of who we are. After 400 years, we not only see the promised land; we also see a land of promise. We see a land of inclusion, where diversity of thoughts, ideas, and contributions is more valuable than the thoughts, ideas, and contributions of a single, homogenous group.

We hope that the government of the land that we love will embrace us in the same way as the people of England, with whom our last treaty was signed in 1677. At the end of the day I am very proud and honored to be an American and hope that formal recognition of my people by the United States of America will soon be a reality.

———————

APPENDIX 9

Remarks of
President George W. Bush
Anniversary Park, Jamestown, Virginia,
May 13, 2007

Thank you, Justice O'Connor. Laura and I are really happy to join you today. This state is known at the "Mother of Presidents," which reminds me, I needed to call my Mother today. I wish all mothers around our country a happy Mother's Day. And if you haven't called your mother, you better start dialing her after this ceremony.

We're honored to be in Jamestown on this historic day. We appreciate the opportunity to tour the beautiful grounds here. I would urge our fellow citizens to come here, see the fantastic history that's on display. I think you'll be amazed at how our country got started. And I want to thank all the good folks who are working to preserve the past for your hard work, and I appreciate the fact that you spent a lot of time educating our fellow citizens.

Jamestown was the first permanent English settlement in America; it predated the Mayflower Compact by 13 years. This is a very proud state, and some people down here like to point out that the Pilgrims ended up at Plymouth Rock by mistake. They were looking for Virginia. They just missed the sign.

As we celebrate the 400th anniversary of Jamestown to honor the beginnings of our democracy, it is a chance to renew our commitment to help others around the world realize the great blessings of liberty. And so Laura and I are proud to join you. Justice, it's good to see you. There's no finer American than Sandra Day O'Connor, and I'm proud to share the podium with her.

We're also proud to be with Governor Tim Kaine and Anne Holton. I'm proud to call them friends, and I hope, Ms. Kaine, that the Governor recognized Mother's Day. Glad you're here. I want to thank Secretary Dirk Kempthorne of the Department of the Interior; Michael Griffin, the administrator of NASA; members of the United States Congress; members of the statehouse, including the Lieutenant Governor. I appreciate the Attorney General being here. I thank the Speaker for joining us. Most of all, thank you for coming.

I thank the members of the Jamestown 400th Commemoration Commission. Those are all the good folks who worked hard to get this celebration in order. I appreciate the members of the Association for the Preservation of Virginia Antiquities. Laura and I saw members of the Association for the Preservation of Virginia Antiquities digging in dirt. It just so happened we wandered up, and they found some artifacts. I appreciate members of the Jamestown 2007 Steering Committee.

The story of Jamestown will always have a special place in American history. It's the story of a great migration from the Old World to the New. It is a story of hardship overcome by resolve. It's a story of the Tidewater settlement that laid the foundation of our great democracy.

That story began on a dock near London in December of 1606. More than a hundred English colonists set sail for a new life across the ocean in Virginia. They had dreams of paradise that were sustained during their long months at sea by their strong spirit. And then they got here, and a far different reality awaited them.

On May 13, 1607, 400 years today, they docked their ships on a marshy riverbank. Being loyal subjects, they named the site after their King, and that's how Jamestown was born. Today we celebrate that moment as a great milestone in our history, yet the colonists who experienced those first years had little reason to celebrate.

Their search for gold soon gave way to a desperate search for food. An uneasy peace with the Native Americans broke into open hostilities. The hope for a better life turned into a longing for the comforts of home. One settler wrote, "There were never Englishmen left in a foreign country in such misery as we were in the new discovered Virginia."

Looking back, 400 years later, it is easy to forget how close Jamestown came to failure. The low point came after the terrible winter of 1610. The survivors boarded their ships. They were prepared to abandon the settlement, and only the last minute arrival of new settlers and new provisions saved Jamestown. Back in London, one court official summed up the situation this way: "This is an unlucky beginning. I pray God the end may prove happier."

Well, the prayers were answered. Jamestown survived. It became a testament to the power of perseverance and determination. Despite many dangers, more ships full of new settlers continued to set out for Jamestown. As the colony grew, the settlers ventured beyond the walls of their three-sided fort, and formed a thriving community. Their industry and hard work transformed Jamestown from a distant English outpost into an important center for trade.

And during those early years, the colonists also planted the seeds of American democracy, at a time when democratic institutions were rare. On their first night at Jamestown, six of the leading colonists held the first presidential election in American history. And you might be surprised to know that the winner was not named George. As a matter of fact, his name was Edward Wingfield. I call him Eddie W.

From these humble beginnings, the pillars of a free society began to take hold. Private property rights encouraged ownership and free enterprise. The rule of law helped secure the rights of individuals. The creation of America's first representative assembly ensured the consent of the people and gave Virginians a voice in their government. It was said at the time that the purpose of these reforms was, "to lay a foundation whereon a flourishing state might, in time, by the blessing of Almighty God, be raised."

Not all people shared in these blessings. The expansion of Jamestown came at a terrible cost to the native tribes of the region, who lost their lands and their way of life. And for many Africans, the journey to Virginia represented the beginnings of a life of hard labor and bondage. Their story is a part of the story of Jamestown. It reminds us that the work of American democracy is to constantly renew and to extend the blessings of liberty.

That work has continued throughout our history. In the 18th century our founding fathers declared our independence, and dedicated America to the principle that all men are created equal. In the 19th century our nation fought a terrible civil war over the meaning of those famous words, and renewed our founding promise. In the 20th century Americans defended our democratic ideals against totalitarian ideologies abroad, while working to ensure we lived up to our ideals here at home. As we begin the 21st century, we look back on our history with pride, and rededicate ourselves to the cause of liberty.

Today democratic institutions are taking root in places where liberty was unimaginable not long ago. At the start of the 1980s, there were only 45 democracies on Earth. There are now more than 120 democracies, and more people now live in freedom than ever before.

America is proud to promote the expansion of democracy, and we must continue to stand with all those struggling to claim their freedom. The advance of freedom is the great story of our time, and new chapters are being written every day, from Georgia and Ukraine, to Kyrgyzstan and Lebanon, to Afghanistan and Iraq. From our own history, we know the path to democracy is long, and it's hard. There are many challenges, and there are setbacks along the way. Yet we can have confidence in the outcome, because we've seen freedom's power to transform societies before.

In World War II, we fought Germany on battlefields across Europe, and today a democratic Germany is one of our strongest partners on the Continent. And in the Pacific, we fought a bloody war with Japan. And now our alliance with a democratic Japan is the linchpin for freedom and security in the Far East. These democracies have taken different forms that reflect different cultures and traditions. But our friendship with them reminds us that liberty is the path to lasting peace, and that democracies are natural allies for the United States.

Today we have no closer ally than the nation we once fought for our own independence. Britain and America are united by our democratic heritage, and by the history that began at this settlement 400 years ago. Last month some of the greatest legal minds in Britain and America, including Justice O'Connor and Chief Justice John Roberts, came to Jamestown to lay a plaque commemorating our shared respect for the rule of law and our deeply held belief in individual liberty.

Over the years, these values have defined our two countries. Yet they are more than just American values and British values, or Western values. They are universal values that come from a power greater than any man or any country. These values took root at Jamestown four centuries ago. They have flourished across our land, and one day they will flourish in every land.

May God bless you, and may God bless America.

———————

APPENDIX 10

Jamestown 400th
Commemoration Commission
Presidential Documents

"400th Anniversary of Jamestown"
A Proclamation by the President of the United States of
America
The White House
April 6, 2007

Four centuries ago, after a long journey, a small group of colonists
stepped boldly onto the shores of the New World and established
the first permanent English settlement in North America. During
the 400th anniversary of Jamestown, America honors the early
pioneers whose epic of endurance and courage started the story of
our Nation.

The ideals that distinguish and guide the United States today trace
back to the Virginia settlement where free enterprise, the rule of
law, and the spirit of discovery took hold in the hearts and practices
of the American people. Noble institutions and grand traditions
were established in Jamestown. Amid tremendous difficulties, a
determined few worked the land and expanded into the wilderness.
Without knowing it, the colonists who built communities at
Jamestown laid the foundation for a Nation that would become the
ultimate symbol and force for freedom throughout the entire world.

Much has changed in the 400 years since that three-sided fort was
raised on the banks of the James River. Today, we are a strong
and growing Nation of more than 300 million, and we are blessed
to live in a land of plenty during a time of great prosperity. The
long struggle that started at Jamestown has inspired generations of
Americans. Advancing the right to live, work, and worship in liberty
is the mission that created our country, the honorable achievement
of our ancestors, and the calling of our time.

NOW, THEREFORE, I, GEORGE W. BUSH, President of the United
States of America, by virtue of the authority vested in me by the

Constitution and laws of the United States, do hereby proclaim 2007 as the 400th Anniversary of Jamestown. I encourage all Americans to commemorate this milestone by honoring the courage of those who came before us, participating in appropriate programs and celebrations, and visiting this historic site with family and friends.

IN WITNESS WHEREOF, I have hereunto set my hand this sixth day of April, in the year of our Lord two thousand seven, and of the Independence of the United States of America the two hundred and thirty-first.

GEORGE W. BUSH

Letter from President George W. Bush
The White House
February 28, 2005

I send greetings to those preparing to celebrate the 400th anniversary of the Jamestown Settlement.

To understand and love our country, we must know its history. By remembering our past, we honor the courageous and resilient people who established this settlement in the New World. The settlers of Jamestown fundamentally shaped the strong values and traditions that led to the growth of democracy in America. Through my Preserve America Initiative, we are helping foster greater appreciation for our Nation's past and its underlying ideals.

I commend all those involved with the Jamestown 2007 Commemoration for your efforts to celebrate liberty and educate others about the rich history of Jamestown, and for your hard work in support of the upcoming events being planned now. Your dedication shows a deep respect for our founding principles and helps carry our heritage of freedom into the future.

Laura and I send our best wish on this special occasion.

/s/ George W. Bush

———————————

APPENDIX 11

Remarks of Vice President Richard B. Cheney
Memorial Church, Historic Jamestowne, January 10, 2007

Thank you very much, Senator [Chichester]. And thank you, Lieutenant Governor Bolling, Attorney General McDonnell, members of the Senate and House of Delegates, Chief Adkins, distinguished guests, ladies and gentlemen:

It's a special privilege to be with all of you today, as this great legislative body begins the new session, and gathers in a place that Virginians knew as their capital for close to one hundred years.

I want to thank Delegate Melanie Rapp for her efforts to organize this historic session—a tremendous idea, Melanie. And I also want to thank Senator John Chichester for being here today, and Speaker Bill Howell—and Senator Tommy Norment for extending the invitation. I deeply appreciate it.

I've enjoyed visiting Historic Jamestowne and Jamestown Settlement in the past, along with my wife and our children and grandchildren. We were here just last April, I believe. It's an experience that we heartily recommend to others, and that our family looks forward to repeating. Today I count it a special honor to stand with members of the General Assembly as we begin a year of significance and commemoration—to the Commonwealth, and for our country.

It's striking to realize how much of America's story begins with a little three-sided fort, raised on the banks of the James River, four centuries ago. In this place, grand events were set in motion. In this place, great and noble traditions were introduced to the North American continent. So it is fitting that we should know and appreciate all that happened here, the names of those who lived here, and the history, both good and ill, that unfolded here.

Four hundred years ago today, more than a hundred colonists were a few weeks into their journey across the Atlantic. Along with the crewmen and all the provisions they could carry, they were packed in close quarters aboard these three small ships—the *Susan Constant*, the *Godspeed*, and the *Discovery*. These are the ships that landed near this spot. Most of us have seen the replicas, and I doubt any of us would want to spend a day in those conditions, much less the months it would take to make that crossing. But they made it—and because they did, the world would never be the same after the 14th of May, 1607.

The history of our country did not begin on Cape Cod in 1620. That's a great line. A year before that—on July 30th, 1619, just a few steps from this sanctuary—the first representative assembly in the new world was called to order. Indeed, so much of what defines our country—its language, legal traditions, and institutions—have roots in the community that rose in this corner of Virginia. English liberty and law, private property, the spirit of free enterprise, and commerce—all of these are part of the Jamestown legacy.

That legacy also involves struggle and injustice. Of that first group of settlers, the majority would be dead within just a few years. Those who arrived later shared in the hardship and the hunger, and joined in the unending labor of working the land, building communities, and slowly extending civilization into the wilderness. And the story that began at Jamestown covers more than just settlers from England. There were people who had crossed the Atlantic on a very different kind of voyage, held beneath ships' decks—and then kept in bondage, their life's labor stolen from them. And there were the native peoples, who were here first, and who would suffer great loss—the passing of familiar things and the ending of a way of life. Here, it's been noted, we find the beginnings of the cultural diversity that continues to shape our nation's character.

The author James Horn put it well: "At Jamestown, the peoples of America, Europe, and Africa first encountered one another, lived and worked alongside each other, traded and fought one another, survived and persisted."

Since those early years, the people of this land have followed an ever-rising path of liberty and opportunity, justice and equality. On that journey, we have confronted many injustices, and widened the circle of liberty, and become known to all the world as freedom's home and defender.

Jamestown began as a commercial enterprise, but within a generation, Virginia was a colony of the crown. In time, the colonies would be 13 in number, and together they would become the United States of America. Only 20 miles from here was the siege at Yorktown, where Americans won the final battle in the Revolution. The words of the Declaration of Independence came from the pen of Thomas Jefferson—Virginian by birth, founder of its university, member of the legislature, Governor of the Commonwealth, first Secretary of State, second Vice President, and third President of the United States. James Madison of Virginia was Father of the Constitution; and, of course, George Washington of Virginia, the Father of our Country. In addition to these, five other Virginia natives have held our nation's highest office, from Monroe to Wilson. This Commonwealth, and the people who call it home, stand at the very center of American history.

Americans are a people that remember our forebears, and commemorate the signal events of the past. And so there are some places and objects to which we give special care, and guard from the passing of time. Here in Virginia, you've taken seriously the duties of historical stewardship, and nowhere is that more evident than at Jamestown Settlement and Historic Jamestowne. The preservation and the archaeological work in this place are, in a word, superb. The discovery in the 1990s of the original fort, long believed to have been washed into the river, was one of the great archaeological events of our time. And like so much that has taken place here, that discovery is a credit to the patience, sensitivity, and professionalism exhibited here each and every day.

That commitment to good stewardship was shown once more when the congressional delegation of Virginia, along with those of Maryland, Pennsylvania, and Delaware, worked to establish a national historic trail bearing the name of one of the original Jamestown settlers, Captain John Smith. President Bush was pleased to sign the legislation authorizing the John Smith Chesapeake National Historic Trail. This is America's first all-water National Historic Trail—and appropriately it begins right here in Jamestown.

To visit this extraordinary part of Virginia is to gain a deep understanding of the challenges that came along at a pivotal point in our history, and to look with respect on the people who faced those challenges. Only three years after *Susan Constant*, *Godspeed*, and *Discovery* reached this shore, one of the brave souls living here wrote the following words under the title, "News from Virginia."

And I quote:

> Be not dismayed at all
> Let England know our willingness;
> For that our work is good
> We hope to plant a nation
> Where none before hath stood.

Even across the centuries, it is admirable and inspiring that such hopeful words could be written in the year 1610, amid difficulties that our generation can scarcely imagine. And it's a reminder that however important deeds may be, the things of the spirit come first. All the accomplishments of that distant generation were possible only because of human qualities that all of us respect—qualities that all of us would want to be remembered for ourselves: courage, perseverance, loyalty, and trust in Almighty God. Because of those virtues, a young colony was kept alive. And standing here in the year 2007, we can draw a straight line from those early days of struggle and fortitude in a tiny settlement, to the great nation we know and love today.

For that reason, this will be a special year of commemoration and reflection—from America's Anniversary Weekend in May, to the World Forum on Democracy in September. And it will be a particular honor when Queen Elizabeth herself returns to Jamestown, 50 years after she came here on her first visit to America as the British sovereign.

Another great honor comes by virtue of legislation signed by the President. The United States marks this anniversary year with the rarest of tributes—commemorative coins struck by the U.S. Mint. By this extraordinary act of Congress, the nation pays lasting homage to the 400th anniversary of the first English settlement on the North American shore. And we proudly acknowledge Virginia's irreplaceable role in creating the greatest nation on Earth, the United States of America. So today it's my privilege to present the first of the Jamestown Commemorative coins to Speaker Howell and Senator Chichester. The rest of you have to buy your own. So do I. They go on sale here tomorrow.

So, Mr. Speaker, Senator, I ask you to step forward and accept these coins, which I present to you along with the respect of the American people, and the good wishes of the President of the United States. Thank you very much.

APPENDIX 12

Jamestown 2007 British Committee
Final Report, December 2007[3]

Introduction

America's 400th Anniversary marked the fifth major consecutive observance in the USA, during the past 200 years, of Jamestown, the first permanent English-speaking settlement in the New World. The commemoration is held every 50 years and 2006-07 was the first time the event was commemorated in the United Kingdom. Separate reports on the US events are being produced by the Jamestown 400th Commemoration Commission (Federal Commission) and Jamestown 2007 Steering Committee (State Agency).

This report sets out the formation, purpose, objectives and development work of the Jamestown 2007 British Committee (the Committee). It is hoped it will be used as a reference document for any UK planning committee organised to oversee future Jamestown Anniversaries.

Background

In 2007, both the British and the Americans commemorated the 400th anniversary of the founding of Jamestown. As President Theodore Roosevelt observed at the 1907 commemoration, the founding of Jamestown "marks the beginning of the history of the United States of America." It is important to note that the sailing of the three ships from Blackwall, London, preceded the Pilgrim Fathers' arrival in New England on the Mayflower by 13 years. The 400th anniversary provided a unique opportunity to celebrate the Trans-Atlantic relationship and in particular the very special ties between the UK and the USA.

---

[3] The British Committee's report has been reformatted here to conserve space, and the detailed appendices accompanying the report have been omitted from this reprint. A complete copy of the report, including the original text with appendices, may be obtained from the Federal Commission's archives at Colonial National Historical Park at Jamestown.

The Committee was established by the Federal Commission as the official British planning committee for the Jamestown commemorations in the UK. There were early and important meetings held in Richmond in June 2004 and Kent and London in September 2004 where necessary key steps were discussed to establish the British Committee. The Federal Commission sent a high-level delegation to the UK in September 2004 and made a major commitment to joint planning and effort regarding the British activities. The Federal Commission delegation included:

- Frank Atkinson, Chairman of the Federal Commission
- H. E. "Chip" Mann, Executive Director of the Federal Commission
- Stuart Connock, Chairman of the Jamestown 2007 Steering Committee, Co-chairman of the [Anglo-American Planning Committee] and former Chairman of the Jamestown-Yorktown Foundation
- Ray Ashworth, former Chairman of the Jamestown-Yorktown Foundation
- Suzanne Flippo, Co-chairman of the [Anglo-American Planning Committee]
- Don Lemons, Justice of the Virginia Supreme Court

During their September visit the Federal Commission conducted high-level briefings at the Foreign and Commonwealth Office (at which 10 Downing Street was represented), the Education Department, and the American Embassy. Don Lemons, Frank Atkinson and H.E. "Chip" Mann also briefed the legal community at a meeting at Gray's Inn hosted by William Blair. The Federal Commission also met with the following:

- Robert Culshaw — Director for the Americas
- Antony Phillpson — Private Secretary to Sir Nigel Sheinwald
- Anne Jarrett — Head of US Section
- Robert Wace — Royal Households Secretariat
- David French — Westminster Foundation for Democracy

Frank Atkinson, assisted by members of the delegation, made a presentation concerning commemoration plans. The delegation then discussed opportunities for UK participation in key events, including America's Anniversary Weekend (Royal Visit),

Smithsonian Folklife Festival, a UK-based event in December 2006 commemorating the launch of the voyage to Jamestown, and the "Future of Democracy" Conference Series. Advice was received on contacts and plans related to these events. As suggested by Robert Culshaw, a letter signed by Frank Atkinson and Stuart Connock was given to Ambassador Manning in Washington on 5th October 2004, requesting his endorsement of invitation to the British Royal Family for May 2007. Lord Watson was given a copy of this letter and agreed to write a letter to Sir Robin Janvrin, Secretary to Her Majesty the Queen.

During the visit the Federal Commission also met with the prospective Committee Co-chairmen, The Lord Watson of Richmond CBE, International Chairman of the English-Speaking Union, and Sir Robert Worcester KBE DL, Chairman of the Pilgrims Society of Great Britain, to recruit them and begin formation of the British Committee. Alex King MBE, Deputy Leader of the Kent County Council (KCC), was invited by the Co-Chairmen to become Treasurer of the Committee as a result of his work on the development of the links between Kent and Virginia. Kent had initially linked with New Kent County, Virginia, as a result of contact made by John Crump, the Commissioner of the Revenue for New Kent County. The link with New Kent County led to Kent establishing a formal link with the Commonwealth of Virginia in 2005.

With the kind approval of the then Leader, Lord Bruce-Lockhart, KCC offered Executive support to the Committee; Rebecca Casson was appointed as the Executive Director and Bernadette Spence was appointed as the Executive Assistant. The Executive Director managed the Committee's activities alongside her other duties as Head of the Kent-Virginia Development Unit. This unit also provided resource for the Committee in fulfilling its aims and objectives. Following the first formal visit by the Federal Commission, the four initial Committee representatives set about recruiting other Committee members, developing plans and seeking funding.

The Honorable Robert H. Tuttle, United States Ambassador to the Court of St. James, agreed to be the Patron of the Committee following his appointment in July 2005. Sir David Manning KCMG, CVO, Her Majesty's Ambassador to the United States of America, agreed to become Patron of the [Anglo-American Planning Committee in the United States]. Both Embassies were exceptionally helpful and supportive to both the Committee and Federal Commission. Louise Kendall from the Foreign and Commonwealth Office in London was extremely helpful to the Committee in its early development.

In February 2005 Sir David Manning hosted a reception for US-based British businesses at the residence in Washington. Senators Warner and Allen made presentations, along with Ambassador Manning and there was a very effective "pitch" to UK businesses for public relations and financial support. This event was managed by the Federal Commission and over 150 people attended. Alex King and Rebecca Casson attended the event on behalf of the Committee.

Committee Members

A complete list of members of the Committee is [set forth at the end of this report]. All members of the Committee were volunteers. No expenses were paid to members when attending Committee meetings and they received no financial rewards for their involvement in the activities of the Committee.

Many other key contacts kindly supported the committee and its activities during America's 400th Anniversary including Jim Fitzpatrick MP, Minister for London and MP for Poplar and Canning Town, The Lord Astor of Hever DL, Shadow Minister for Defence and Bill Leighty, Chief of Staff to the Governor of Virginia.

Committee Meetings

The first meeting of the Committee took place on 2nd December 2004 at the House of Lords. The final meeting took place on 3rd December 2007 at the English Speaking Union, Dartmouth House, in London. In total there were 12 meetings of the Committee. The English-speaking Union kindly assisted with meeting space, which was secured by Committee member Valerie Mitchell. Other meetings were held in the House of Lords, Portcullis House (offices and committee rooms of Members of Parliament) and the offices of Ipsos MORI (Sir Robert was the Founder of MORI). Committee members attended various Jamestown related events and held sub-meetings to progress projects. Some Committee members also attended Federal Commission meetings and events held in the USA.

Jamestown-UK Foundation Ltd.

Although the Federal Commission had made provision for British activities from their allocated funds, during early meetings with the Federal Commission the leadership of the Committee confirmed that it would be responsible for funding its own activities. Alex King arranged for KCC to pump-prime the Committee and it was agreed early on that a charitable company needed to be established in order to receive and distribute donations.

The Jamestown UK Foundation Ltd. (the Foundation) was incorporated on 18th January 2006. Alex King was elected as Chairman and the other original Directors included Professor Rick Trainor, Simon Walker, William Blair QC and Rebecca Casson. Alison Paines, Principal Head of Charities at Withers law firm (based at 16 Old Bailey in London) together with Richard Cassell, who was responsible for individual donors and philanthropy at Withers, kindly assisted with the establishment of the Foundation by providing pro-bono legal advice. The registered office was agreed as KCC's 'Virginia Room' in Invicta House, Maidstone. KCC agreed to provide the accountancy support for the Foundation via Senior Accountancy Officer Beverly Gibbs. Tom Pelham, Staff Officer to the Deputy Leader of KCC, was instrumental in the support and organisation of the Foundation.

Sponsorship

Scott Prenn, a fundraising company, was employed in May 2005 to work with the Committee and raise funds for the Committee's projects. Scott Prenn's costs were underwritten by KCC on the understanding that, as funds were raised, KCC would be reimbursed. Scott Prenn was helpful in assisting with the early development of the Committee's initiatives such as the Discovery Tour. They also arranged pro-bono legal advice from Withers as outlined above, together with raising some funding. As the Committee progressed and funding was only forthcoming to a very limited degree it was agreed that the services of Scott Prenn were no longer appropriate and a hand over of duties to the Treasurer and Executive Director was completed in April 2006.

On 21st July 2005 the Committee hosted a dinner at St. Stephen's club in London with the aim of making initial contact with potential sponsors. There was good representation from the US including Chief Stephen Adkins, Chief Ken Adams, H. Benson Dendy III (Vice Chairman of the Federal Commission), Virginia [House of

202

Delegates] Speaker Bill Howell, Virginia Supreme Court Justice Don Lemons and Professor Tim Sullivan (President Emeritus of William and Mary College).

In May 2006 a sponsorship brochure was developed by the Committee inviting companies and individuals to sponsor events and contribute to the Foundation. Sponsorship for events and initiatives was difficult to raise. This could be attributed to the limited UK knowledge of Jamestown and America's 400th Anniversary combined with the lack of UK Government funding and support for the commemoration. However, the Committee still secured significant and essential sponsorship, together with pro-bono support. A list of major contributors is given below:

- American Embassy (with specific assistance from Committee member Michael Macy, Cultural Attaché, and continued support from Susan Wedlake)
- British American Tobacco (with specific assistance from Committee member Michael Prideaux and Co-Chairman Sir Robert Worcester)
- City of London (with specific assistance from Committee member Tony Halmos)
- Wolseley
- The Royal Fleet Auxiliary
- Jamestown-Yorktown Foundation (with specific assistance from Federal Commission Vice Chairman H. Benson Dendy III)
- Virginia Tourism Corporation
- Edinburgh House (with specific assistance from Committee member Tony Quayle)
- Selex (with specific assistance from Committee member Alex King)

Companies that showed an interest in America's 400th Anniversary but did not commit sponsorship include: Maxjet, SAGA, Lightmaker, Chaucer Consulting, Fortis Bank and Armourcoat.

The sponsorship brochures were produced with the assistance of David Roder of Red Carrot Design and Print. Red Carrot also assisted with further designs including invitations for the launch event and Discovery Tour promotional material together with printing for the Virginia Indian Festival.

Jamestown 2007 British Committee Initiatives

The Committee developed a series of initiatives to raise awareness of Jamestown and the 400th Anniversary commemorations in the UK. The Co-Chairmen and Executive Director presented the initiatives to 10 Downing Street during a meeting on 23rd February 2006.

A master project plan was developed and presented at each Committee meeting to report on the progress of these initiatives. The following headings were used in the project plan:

Key/Signature Events
* *Virginia Company Incorporation Event*
* *Rule of Law Lectures*
* *"The New World" Film*
* *Virginia Indian Festival*
* *"Journey to the New World" Exhibition at the Museum in Docklands*
* *Discovery Tour*
* *Launch Events*
* *Anniversary Weekend*
* *Smithsonian Folklife Festival*

Royal Participation
Tourism
Education Initiatives
Communities
Communication
Merchandising
European Awareness
Arts, Cultural and Historical Links
* *Twinning*
* *Kent-Virginia Development Project*
* *Association for the Preservation of Virginia Antiquities*
* *Commemorative Stamps*

Committee members were nominated and took individual responsibility for certain projects. Specific and detailed plans were developed for each event. Final details of the Committee initiatives are described below listed in project plan heading and, where applicable, in date order:

Key/Signature Events

• *Virginia Company Incorporation Event*

The Committee hosted a fundraising gala dinner on 20th March 2006 to launch the official UK programme, and to highlight the commemoration to decision-makers and the press. With the assistance of Committee member Tony Halmos, the City of London kindly agreed to sponsor the event (catering, toastmaster and musicians). The City of London was instrumental in the formation of the original Virginia Company in 1606 and the planning of the Jamestown expedition. A total of 185 guests attended the Committee's inaugural event held in the Guildhall of the City of London.

Thomas S. Foley was the Guest speaker for the dinner. Mr. Foley served as the Speaker of the US House of Representatives and Ambassador to Japan. Ambassador Tuttle, Lord Watson, Sir Robert Worcester and Michael Snyder, Chairman of the City of London's Policy & Resources Committee, also spoke at the event. Other notable attendees included Delegate Vincent F. Callahan and his wife Yvonne (both representing the Governor of Virginia), the Rt. Hon. Michael Howard QC MP, then Leader of the Conservative Party, Michael Ancram MP, Shadow Foreign Secretary, Alan Duncan MP and Mr. Carter Branham Snow Furr (with a group from Virginia's First Families).

The Stevenson Brothers, rocking horse makers from Bethersden in Kent, made a Jamestown 2007 rocking horse, which was presented to the Jamestown UK Foundation Ltd. at the gala dinner. The horse is the only one of its kind; it has the Jamestown 2007 logo embroidered on the saddle and a piece of wood from the Discovery ship placed in the base of the stand. The Jamestown horse was shipped to the Smithsonian Folklife Festival in July 2007, where the Stevenson Brothers displayed it during their presentations at the festival to over one million visitors. Following the festival the Governor of Virginia received the horse for display in the Mansion in Richmond until its auction to raise money for Jamestown UK Foundation Ltd.

• *Rule of Law Lectures and Middle Temple Incorporation Event*

Committee member William Blair QC (elder brother of Prime Minister Tony Blair) coordinated with the Inns of Court a series of Rule of Law Lectures. A lecture was hosted by one of the Inns in each quarter leading up to April 2007. The dates and subject of each of these lectures was:

- 8th May 2006: "Due process and the rights of the criminally accused" — Lord Lloyd of Berwick (Inner Temple)
- 7th June 2006: "Economic stability and the creation of stable contract and property rights" — Keith Clark of Morgan Stanley (Lincoln's Inn)
- 18th October 2006: "Independent and stable judicial systems" — Professor Sir David Williams (Gray's Inn)
- 21st February 2007: "The role of leadership in the creation and maintenance of the Rule of Law" — Rt. Hon. Lord Bingham of Cornhill (Middle Temple), former Lord Chief Justice

KCC's Director of Law and Governance, Geoffrey Wild, attended the Lincoln's Inn lecture held on 7th June 2006 and produced a report. The report was approved by William Blair QC and was later posted on the British Embassy website in Washington. Veronica Kendall, the Administrator for COMBAR (Commercial Bar Association), was particularly helpful to the Committee during the lecture series.

The Middle Temple hosted an event on 10th April 2006, the date of the actual anniversary of the Virginia Company charter. The main purpose of the event was to educate both US and UK citizens on the true purposes and motivations for the establishment of the Jamestown Settlement and to highlight the British economic, political and legal antecedents that led to the 1607 settlement. This event was attended by a high-level US-Virginia delegation that included Ambassador Tuttle, [Virginia] Chief Justice [Leroy R.] Hassell, and several key members of the leadership of American commemoration organisations. Sir Robert Worcester attended the event on behalf of the Committee.

- ***"The New World" Film***

The film was released in the USA on 25th December 2005 and in the UK (cut by 15 minutes) on 27th January 2006. The DVD was released in May 2006. Committee member Laura Sandys and Executive Director Rebecca Casson attended the film premiere in Williamsburg in December 2005. Tickets were secured for Committee members and tourism representatives to attend a press screening prior to the film's general release in the UK. A representative of the Federal Commission and British Committee were allowed to see a copy of the screenplay in October 2005. A review of the film written by the Executive Director was published in Kent Messenger Business Film Review.

- *Virginia Indian Festival*

During the 2004 visit to Kent by the Federal Commission it was suggested by Chip Mann that a Jamestown 2007 event in Gravesend, involving the Virginia Indians, would be an excellent event for the Committee to host. This idea was raised by Chip Mann with the Virginia Indians and during a meeting at the British Embassy in Washington on 10th February 2005 Chief Stephen Adkins of the Chickahominy Tribe invited Rebecca Casson to attend the VITAL (Virginia Indian Tribal Alliance for Life) Pow-Wow to discuss a possible UK Virginia Indian Festival.

At the Pow-Wow on 30th April 2005 Rebecca Casson delivered a message and invitation on behalf of the Committee, and Kent, in front of over 1,000 people. The Executive Director met with the Indian chiefs and negotiated with them their participation in the Virginia Indian Festival to take place in the UK in 2006. These negotiations continued throughout 2005 and resulted in a visit to Kent by over 80 Virginians, including the Governor's Chief of Staff. KCC officer Stephen Dukes, supported by the KCC Kent-Virginia Development Unit, managed the visit by the Virginia Indians, the first official visit to the UK in over 250 years.

During his testimony before the House Natural Resources Committee on 18th April 2007 for the Thomasina E. Jordan Indian Tribes of Virginia Federal Recognition Act – HR 1294, Chief Adkins made specific reference to the Virginia Indian Festival:

> After our visit to England I truly believe the Federal Recognition of the Virginia Indian Tribes during the year of the 400th commemoration will make a

significant difference. It will reconcile history in this country between two cultures in a way that honors our history of learning to live together in peace and in love. That is what we want for our people and for our nation. The acceptance of the invitation to visit England to share our culture and history to describe our contemporary lifestyles as both contributors to the American way of life and aspirants to the American Dream and our decision to honor Pocahontas at her grave has strengthened our resolve to obtain federal acknowledgement. It has made us understand that we deserve to be on a level playing field with the other 562 odd tribes who are federally acknowledged. It has made us unwilling to accept being discriminated against because of both a historical oversight and the concerted efforts of our Commonwealth to deny to us our rightful heritage. The aforementioned invitation to visit England was not easy for us to accept. We did not know what to expect, and we were apprehensive. From an overall perspective this visit was destined to be for it brought us into the history we commemorate at Jamestown in a very positive palpable way.

A final report, together with all material relating to the Virginia Indian Festival has been archived and is held at KCC, County Hall, Maidstone, Kent. A summary of the Festival is detailed below:

Virginia Indian Festival dates: 13th – 20th July 2006

The Delegation: A total of 57 Virginia Indians attended the Festival. All of the 8 tribes recognised by the Commonwealth of Virginia were represented. There were 5 Chiefs and 2 Asst. Chiefs amongst the group. In addition to the Virginia Indians, Ben Dendy (Vice Chairman of the Federal Commission), Bill Leighty (Chief of Staff to the Governor) and two members of staff from the Virginia Department of Historical Resources also traveled over for the Festival.

Welcome Ceremony: Hosted by Cobham Hall near Gravesend on Friday 14th July. 73 invited guests in addition to the Virginia Indians attended the ceremony. The Virginia Indians were formally welcomed to the UK by

Allan Willett, Lord Lieutenant of Kent as a representative of HM The Queen. Other dignitaries attending included The Lord Watson of Richmond and Sir Robert Worcester, Co-Chairmen of the Jamestown 2007 British Committee; the Mayor and Lady Mayoress of Gravesham; the Chairman of Kent County Council and the Deputy Leader of Kent County Council. Particularly notable was the presentation to the Lord Lieutenant by Chief Anne Richardson of a golden ring symbolizing the continuing relationship the Tribes have with the Crown and their affection for Her Majesty The Queen. There is no doubt that the prominence given to the Indians by the British Jamestown Committee has been greatly appreciated by them and has raised their profile not only in the UK but also in the USA.

Civic Reception: Hosted by Gravesham Borough Council and held at Fleet Leisure Centre on the evening of Friday 14th July. 140 people including a delegation from Chesterfield County, Va attended the Reception. Harry Smith, Mayor of Gravesham, welcomed the Virginia Indians.

Big Day Out: Community Festival organised by Gravesham BC and held at the Riverside Leisure Area on Saturday 15th and Sunday 16th July. The Virginia Indians were given a dedicated area of their own and opened each day's programme with the recreation of a Pow-Wow lasting 1 1/2 hours. Attendance was double that of the previous year's Big Day Out with around 12,000 people attending over the two days.

Commemorative Service: Held on the morning of Sunday 16th July prior to Big Day Out at St. George's Church, Gravesend. 250 people attended the Service. The Rt. Rev. Dr. Michael Nazir-Ali, Bishop of Rochester, delivered the Sermon.

National Historical Symposium — "Rewriting the History Books": Hosted and organised by the University of Kent at Canterbury on Monday 17th July in Keynes College. The Symposium was attended by around 220 people, and was a combined audience of academics and the general public. Guest speakers were Helen Rountree (Professor Emerita of Anthropology at Old Dominion University, Virginia), Dr. Warren Billings (Distinguished Professor of History Emeritus at the University of New Orleans) and Dr. Peter

Thompson (Sydney Mayer University Lecturer in Early American History at the University of Oxford).

School Visits: A total of 16 schools (8 Primary, 7 Secondary and 1 Special) within Gravesham Borough were visited by the Virginia Indians over two days on Monday 17th and Tuesday 18th July. A total of around 7,000 secondary school and 3,000 primary school children attend the schools visited.   The visit to each school varied but generally involved interaction between the schoolchildren and the Virginia Indians through displays of crafts, music and dance.   A school programme had been developed with each of the schools prior to the visits through the Cultural Beats programme.

Cultural Diversity Seminar: Hosted and organised by Kent County Council on Tuesday 18th July in the Council Chamber at County Hall, Maidstone.   Around 50 invited guests drawn principally from public service organisations involved with cultural issues attended the Seminar.   Guest speakers were Ekanem Hines (Senior Social Worker for the London Borough of Croydon and Chair of Black & Asian Workers Support Group in Croydon) and Patricia Green (CEO of WPG Marketing & Communications Inc., Virginia). The Seminar was webcast giving national access through Kent County Council's website.

Visit to London: Organised for the Chiefs and other tribal representatives by Kent County Council with the assistance of the British American Parliamentary Group, Foreign & Commonwealth Office, VisitBritain and The British Museum. The visit to London included: a tour of the Houses of Parliament; viewing Prime Ministers Question Time from the Distinguished Visitors Gallery; attending a Reception with the Rt. Hon. Michael Martin MP, Speaker of the House; a Parliamentary Lunch hosted by VisitBritain that was attended by around 40 invited guests including a number of Members of both Houses of Parliament; a meeting with David Lammy MP, Minister for Culture, Media & Sport; and a visit to the British Museum to privately view the John White watercolours prior to their first public display as a collection.

Media Coverage: Media coverage of the event was mainly achieved through the press and radio but achieved both local and national media coverage in the UK and national media coverage in the US. National media coverage included articles in the Independent, Observer, Daily Express and wire through the Press Association. Local media coverage included articles in the Gravesend Reporter, Gravesend Messenger, Gravesend Extra, News Shopper, Gravesend Express, Kent on Sunday and Kent Messenger whilst broadcasts also went out on BBC Radio Kent and Invicta FM. Chief Anne Richardson was interviewed for BBC 4's Woman's Hour which was broadcast twice during the week of the Festival, and is available from the BBC's online archive at: *http://www.bbc.co.uk/radio4/womanshour/04/2006_29_wed.shtml*. US media coverage focused on the departure of the Virginia Indians with articles featuring in the Washington Post, US Newswire, Richmond Times Dispatch, Chicago Tribune, Los Angeles Times and Daily Press. A photographer and reporter from Associated Press covered the Festival and filed copy back to newsdesks in the US. Survival International showed great interest in the event and circulated press releases about the visit. The US Embassy interviewed Chief Adkins and Chief Adams for podcast on the Embassy's website.

Costs & Funding: Total cost of the Festival came to £76,630 excluding KCC staff costs. This was a £7,020 reduction on the final budget estimate of £83,650 produced before the Festival. Sponsorship of £69,600 was raised for the Festival. Edinburgh House was the principal sponsor for the Festival. Committee member Tony Quayle was instrumental in this contribution. Other sponsors included London & Continental Railways, Gravesham BC, Land Securities, US Embassy, Diggerland, Comma Oil, Bretts and Graham Webb MBE. In-Kind support for the Festival amounting to around £34,600 was received from Virgin Atlantic, The Village Hotel, Maidstone, host families in Gravesend, Cobham Hall, Gravesham BC, University of Kent, NW Kent Racial Equality Council, Kent County Council and VisitBritain. Gravesham Borough Council was a key partner for the event. The assistance of Jim Wintour, Managing Director and Glyn Thomson, Deputy Managing Director and his team was invaluable.

- **"Journey to the New World" Exhibition at the Museum in Docklands**

The exhibition opened on 22nd November 2006 and ran until 13th May 2007. The 'Discovery', a replica of one of the first three ships to sail to Jamestown, was moored outside the museum and was a major focus of the exhibition. Committee members David Spence, Rick Trainor and David Starkey were instrumental in the early ideas for the exhibition. Hedley Swain and Hazel Forsyth (Museum of Docklands employees) are to be congratulated for their efforts on the exhibition and arranging for the Discovery ship to be moored at the museum. Members of the Committee were invited to the exhibition VIP preview night.

There was an extremely limited marketing budget of around £7,400 for this exhibition, so only a small number of leaflets were printed and distributed. However, the Museum did receive two weeks of free in-car poster space on the Docklands Light Railway in late May 2007 (worth around £12,000) from Serco, which was very welcome, but not ideally timed for the exhibition.

A table showing the number of visitors (measured by magic eye since the exhibition was free) is shown below. Total visits were 15,694, which represented an average of 35.9% of the Museum's visitors over the run of the exhibition.

23 Nov 06 13 May 07	Journey to the New World	Total visitors on those days exhibition was open	Percentage of Museum visitors visiting the exhibition
Nov	836	2055	40.7%
Dec	2475	5519	44.8%
Jan	2007	6101	32.9%
Feb	3272	9194	35.6%
Mar	3206	9480	33.8%
April	2503	7288	34.3%
May	1395	4112	33.9%
Totals	**15694**	**43749**	35.9%

- *Discovery Tour*

It was an early goal of the Committee to have one of the replica ships visit the UK during the commemoration. In May 2005 the Committee sent an official letter to the Federal Commission requesting that one of the replica ships owned by the Jamestown-Yorktown Foundation (JYF) be made available for use in Britain to support the commemorative events it was coordinating. The JYF were having new replicas of the Discovery and Godspeed built, which made this a possibility.

In August 2005 Admiral Sir Jonathon Band KCB ADC, Commander in Chief Fleet of the Royal Navy, agreed that the Royal Navy "should be associated with the British Committee for Jamestown." Officers who provided significant support to the Committee included John Weale, Ken Roberts, Colin Hamp, Andy Ford, Duncan Thomson, Lee Abernathy and Royal Fleet Auxiliary (RFA) Fort Rosalie's Commanding Officer, Captain Ian Gough. The Chamber of Shipping was also very supportive. In November 2005 the JYF Board approved that the replica Discovery ship could be sent to the UK and gifted to the Foundation (and remain in the UK for the rest of its designed life).

On 1st August 2006 the RFA agreed to transport the Discovery from Virginia to Southampton free of charge. The RFA diverted Fort Rosalie to Norfolk, Virginia, in order to collect the Discovery. Contracts between the Foundation and JYF were signed on 21st September 2006 to allow the release of the ship (a separate marketing contract was signed on 16th October 2006). The Discovery left Virginia on 5th October 2006 on the helicopter deck of RFA Fort Rosalie, secured in a custom-built steel cradle. The ship arrived in Southampton on 15th October 2006 ready for transfer to the Museum in Docklands....

Committee member Michael Prideaux and Co-Chairman Sir Robert Worcester were instrumental in securing funding to enable the Discovery to come to the UK. David Redfern, a consultant employed by the Foundation together with Chip Mann, Executive Director of the Federal Commission both contributed significantly to the logistics of the Discovery leaving the USA. Special thanks need to be noted for Tim Kaine, the Governor of Virginia, and Bill Leighty, the Governor's Chief of Staff, for their assistance and intervention with the US Navy. KCC seconded Denise Eden-Green to manage the Discovery

Tour on behalf of the Foundation. A final report, together with all material relating to the Discovery Tour has been archived and is held at KCC, County Hall, Maidstone, Kent. A brief summary of the project is detailed below:

'The Discovery Tour 1607 - 2007' was the UK focus of 'Jamestown 2007', the commemoration of the 400th Anniversary of the establishment of the first permanent English-speaking settlement in Virginia.

Discovery visited eight destinations between 14th May and mid-September 2007 following her extended stay at the Museum in Docklands (see report of 'New World Exhibition'). She was visited, seen on TV and read about in print media, as noted in the next paragraph by an estimated 330,000 visitors. Tourism literature from JYF was distributed at each destination. At Americana International, the Virginia Tourism Corporation and the US Embassy jointly sponsored the Discovery.

Once the Tour was concluded the Discovery was placed in temporary berthing at Ipswich Marina pending consideration of proposals for a permanent home for the ship.

[Media evaluation of the Discovery Tour for the period May 2007 to early August 2007 was based on an assessment of the value of all the newspaper, radio, TV and website reporting by providing equivalent values if the space had been purchased as advertising, and extrapolating these values as editorial using a multiplier of three. The resulting value was £2,041,923.]

The following table shows the itinerary and visitor numbers for the Discovery Tour:

Destination	Event/Profile	Visitor Numbers
Museum in Docklands, Canary Wharf, London Dec 06 – May 07	Discovery was sited in the dock at West India Quay, adjacent to the Museum in Docklands alongside a special exhibition 'Journey to the New World' opened by the US Ambassador and Chairman and members of the Jamestown 2007 British Committee; Journey to the New World. (Note: Visitor numbers are those people who visited the exhibition inside the building; Discovery would have been seen by many more people who work in this important financial district of London.)	15,694
Dover May 07 – June 07	Dover Marina adjacent to De Bradelei Wharf Shopping Centre; exhibition panels were sited in the entrance lobby to the shopping centre.	5,000
Quex House June 07	Local History event	2,500
Chatham Historic Dockyard June 07	International Business Congress (EBN) & local access to Discovery for Dockyard visitors and Schools	9,800

Americana International 2007 July 07	Europe's largest festival of American culture; annual event with high-profile presence by US Embassy (The appearance of Discovery was sponsored by the US Embassy and the Virginia Tourism Corporation)	65,000
Lincoln Brayford Quay July 07	Water festival in central Lincoln — free to attend Hugely successful event – well promoted and received locally. Discovery the centrepiece of the Festival in the middle of the city's waterfront. Good press before, during and after; School visits	25,500
Bristol July 07	Harbour festival – southwest England's largest free event Spectacular event with huge visitor numbers in a place well used to events of this type; Discovery in a prime position adjacent to the SS Great Britain; excellent press; Local group (The Matthew Society) 'adopted' Discovery and provided on-board interpretation and tours	200,000

Ipswich, Suffolk August 07	Maritime festival at historic settler destination; Excellent turn out of BBC and ITV; Visitor numbers verified by supervised survey beside the ship. 4,500 of the visitors also went on board in groups of 12 –15 for a tour provided by re-enactors	9,500
Harwich, Essex September 07	Week-long visit to historic settler destination; School visits and week-end Festival; visits by local dignitaries and residents	11,200
	Total	**344,194**

- *Launch Events*

   Tower Bridge, London (Commonwealth of Virginia):   The Governor of Virginia hosted a Jamestown dinner at Tower Bridge on 14th November 2006 and invited the Committee, together with other VIPs to the event.   This was a good starting point for the Committee's formal launch event on 19th December 2006.

   Museum in Docklands (British Committee):   The Committee hosted the UK launch event at the Museum in Docklands to mark the date the original three ships set sail. Over 200 people attended the event, which was held in partnership with the 'beginyouradventure' campaign, Kent Tourism Alliance, KCC and Virginia Tourism Corporation. Lord Watson, on behalf of the Committee, welcomed everyone to an event of truly trans-Atlantic significance. Other speakers at the event included the Governor of Virginia, Ambassador Tuttle, Jim Fitzpatrick MP, Sir Robert Worcester, David Spence (Director of the Museum in Docklands) and Sandra Matthews-Marsh (Chief Executive of Kent Tourism Alliance).

   Singers from Canterbury Cathedral and re-enactors from the Globe Theatre entertained guests. A Fife and Drum duo from Colonial Williamsburg led the procession with a group of Virginia Military Institute Cadets. Many guests attended from the USA, including members of the Federal Commission and Virginia's First Families.

The Governor of Virginia presented a copy of Graham Clarke's 'Nexus' to Jim Fitzpatrick during the ceremony (the first copy of Nexus had previously been presented by KCC as a gift to the Governor). The Governor also presented Jim Fitzpatrick with the flag that had been flown over the Godspeed, the newest ship in Virginia's fleet and a Proclamation, "A Gift of Friendship in Honor of the 400th Anniversary of Jamestown". This marked the Governor's conveyance of the replica Discovery ship to the Committee/Foundation/British People. Both Andy Fittes and Phil James of Metropolitan Police were particularly helpful with the security of this event, which was kindly provided free of charge by the Metropolitan Police.

Middle Temple (Federal Commission): The Federal Commission hosted a historical black tie dinner on the evening of 19th December 2006 at the Middle Temple that was attended by over 300 guests. The Lord Phillips of Worth Matravers, Lord Chief Justice of England and Wales, was the keynote speaker. Other speakers included: Governor Tim Kaine (who attended with his family); Frank Atkinson; William J. Howell, Speaker of the House of Delegates; David Johnson, the Deputy Chief of Mission at the American Embassy in London (on behalf of Ambassador Tuttle); Stuart Connock; H. Benson Dendy III; Master Treasurer Derek Wood; Sir Robert Worcester.

Lord Watson also spoke on the theme of "Jamestown: The Voyage of English", the subject of his book written especially for the 400th anniversary of America. Copies of Lord Watson's book were distributed to everyone attending the dinner, together with a commemorative clock.

Notable attendees included Deputy Head of Mission for the British Embassy in Washington Alan Charlton, Delegate Vince Callahan, Delegate Kirk Cox, Delegate Adam Ebbin, Jim Fitzpatrick MP, Michael Howard MP, Bernard Jenkins MP, Suzanne Flippo, Dr. Warren Billings, Lord Cornwallis, and Lord Bruce-Lockhart.

Important groups and sponsors were represented at the event, including: Jamestown-Yorktown Foundation (Mr. Ray

Ashworth); APVA Preservation Virginia (Dr. Warren Billings); Order of the First Families of Virginia (Mr. Carter Furr); The Jamestowne Society (Mr. Ken Bass); Sons of American Revolution (Mr. Donald Stearns); Anheuser Busch (Mr. David Dryden, VP & Managing Director UK); Lockheed Martin UK (Mr. Christopher Trippick, Communications Director); James City County Board of Supervisors (The Honourable Bruce Goodson, Chairman).

The colour guards from the Virginia Military Institute and the London Unified Officer Training Corps posted the colours and both national anthems were played. The Reverend Master Robin Griffith Jones, Master of the Temple Church, delivered the invocation. Chief Adkins, Chief of the Chickahominy Tribe, gave the benediction.

The event was managed by the Federal Commission's Executive Director who engaged the assistance of the Committee's Executive Director. KCC's Kent-Virginia Development Unit and Sophia Sidney (daughter of Committee member Viscount De L'Isle) also worked on behalf of the Federal Commission in the UK to assist with the event. Springboard Marketing Ltd. (with specific assistance by Andrew Harfoot and Kate Murrell) coordinated the event on behalf of the Federal Commission.

During his visit to the UK in December 2006 the Governor and his wife stayed at Leeds Castle in Kent, together with the Governor's family and team of staff. This was kindly arranged by Victoria Wallace, the Managing Director of Leeds Castle, and agreed by the Trustees of Leeds Castle Foundation.

- *Pilgrims Society Tour*

On 30 April 2007, 23 members of the British Pilgrims Society led by Committee Co-Chairman Sir Robert Worcester flew to New York, en route to Jamestown, visiting Colonial and Federal Period sites including Trinity Church, Valley Forge, Brandywine Battlefield, Ashlawn and Monticello. They arrived in Williamsburg to spend five days taking part in the Anniversary Weekend, where they were joined by another dozen or so who came for the weekend commemorative events, including the Pilgrims President, former Chief of Defence Staff Field Marshall Lord Inge, KG, and Lady Inge.

- **Anniversary Weekend**

Anniversary Weekend was held in Jamestown, Virginia between 11th – 13th May 2007. The following UK representatives attended:

> **Members of the British Committee:**   Lord Watson of Richmond; Sir Robert Worcester with Lady Worcester; Lord Sandy Bruce-Lockhart with Lady Bruce-Lockhart; Penelope, Viscountess Cobham, with The Rt. Hon. David Mellor PC QC; Lord Cornwallis with Lady Cornwallis; John Haden; Anthony M. Halmos; Paul Henderson with Kay Henderson; Alex King; Professor David Melville (representing Committee member Robin Baker); Laura Sandys with Randolph Kent; Rebecca Casson.

> **Other Dignitaries:**   Norman Ayres; Charles Berkeley of Berkeley Castle; Jill Cochrane with Michael Todd; Amanda Cottrell, High Sheriff of Kent emeritus; Claire Curtis-Thomas, MP with Mr. Michael Jakub - British American Parliamentary Group (BAPG); Mayor Malcolm Eke with Carol Brunger; Jim Fitzpatrick MP with Dr. Sheila Fitzpatrick; Mike More Molyneux of Loseley Park; Richard Shepherd, MP (BAPG); Graham Webb MBE with Amanda Webb.

> **KCC, KTA and VisitBritain Staff:**   Jill Dain; Stephen Dukes with Elaine Dukes; Alison Fraser; Leila Maggs; Sandra Matthews-Marsh; Cheryl Parker; Hollie Snelson; Deirdre Livingstone; Paul Chibeba; Paul Gauger; Rupert Peters; Robert Strickland; Andrew Weir; Andrew Nusca; Gayle Friel; Jaacob Levstein.

At Anniversary Weekend the Committee provided an engraved A4 stainless steel edged case with documents from Jamestown commemoration events held in the UK in 2006 and 2007. Co-Chairman Sir Robert Worcester and Committee member Alex King presented the following documents at Historic Jamestowne: a brochure and CD on the Virginia Indian Festival; a copy of Lord Watson of Richmond's book – 'Jamestown The Voyage of English'; a DVD of over 3 hours of coverage of the Royal visit to Capitol Square in Richmond and as broadcast live by CBS 6 WTVR, along with other reports produced by CBS 6 WTVR and BBC South East in a reporter exchange that preceded the Royal visit; a Kent County Council white horse lapel pin; a Pilgrims lapel pin; a leaflet on *www.beginyouradventure.co.uk.*

The case was added to the Jamestown 400th Time Capsule at a Memorial Service by Sir Robert Worcester, representing the Pilgrims Society (UK and USA), along with 17 other groups including Virginia Indians, the DAR and SAR, and others representing the ancestors who founded and formed America. The principal speaker was Governor Kaine. President George W. Bush completed the Time Capsule the following day by placing documents and memorabilia at the closing ceremonies.

The Committee joined with the Federal Commission to host a VIP reception area located in the Rockefeller Building, in Colonial Williamsburg, sited between the Williamsburg Inn and the Lodge. Each evening the two committees gathered and bonded together with invited guests. The Committee members present were most grateful both for this collaboration and for the courtesy and friendship between themselves and members and staffs of the Commission.

The Federal Commission kindly ensured that Committee members and other UK guests were seated in the front rows of the VIP area during the President's speech at Anniversary Weekend on 13th May. Unfortunately it was not possible for members of the Committee to be introduced to the President during his visit. The Webb sisters from Sevenoaks in Kent were invited to play at Anniversary Weekend. Significantly, they were the only UK band to play at the event entertaining the crowds with songs from their album 'Daylight Crossing' and a special song they had written for the Virginia Indians celebrating the life of Pocahontas.

- *Smithsonian Folklife Festival*

The Federal Commission suggested early on that the UK could join with Virginia at the Smithsonian Folklife Festival in June/July 2007. Alex King MBE arranged for KCC to underwrite the funding for this event in order to secure the UK's involvement. Early meetings were held with the Smithsonian Institution who agreed that Kent, and other UK Counties relevant to the Jamestown story, could be involved in the festival as a partner to Virginia. The Committee encouraged other UK counties and national organisations to become involved with the festival but this support was not forthcoming. As a result of the lack of national UK interest in the festival it was confirmed that Kent would be the sole UK partner with Virginia.

A Memorandum of Understanding (MoU) was signed between KCC, Jamestown 2007 and the Smithsonian Institution in September 2005. The MoU enabled Kent to join with Virginia at the 2007 Smithsonian Folklife Festival and participate in the 'Roots of Virginia Culture' programme. A summary of the festival is listed below. The festival proved to be a huge success for Kent and its participants. A final report, together with all material relating to the Smithsonian Festival has been archived and is held at KCC, County Hall, Maidstone, Kent.

- 38 people represented the county of Kent at the Smithsonian Folklife Festival in Washington DC for ten days between 27th June and 8th July 2007. KCC's Kent-Virginia Development team led Kent's participation in the festival, which provided Kent with a valuable, high profile opportunity to promote itself in the USA and further develop its relationship with Virginia.

- KCC officers Leila Maggs and Hollie Snelson were instrumental to the success of Kent's participation in the festival. They were supported by a team from KCC, and volunteers including: Rebecca Casson, Stephen and Elaine Dukes, Beverly Gibbs, Allison Campbell-Smith, Ian Vickery, Deborah Malthouse and Denise Eden-Green.

- Begin Your Adventure Campaign representatives Jill Dain, Cheryl Parker, David Stainer and Cathy Smith supported the Roots of Virginia Culture programme for the duration of the festival.

- VisitBritain sent a representative to assist for 3 days of the festival.

- The 2007 Festival attracted 1,006,195 visitors.

- The busiest day was 4th July (Independence Day) where 221,118 people crowded onto the Mall. The next biggest day was Sunday, July 1 with 172,145 visitors.

- 25% of Festival visitors indicated they had some "English" ancestry.

- In rating the Festival overall, the Festival uses the same scale and question as used in the Smithsonian museums, asking visitors to rate the overall quality of their experience. The results:

  0% poor
  3% fair
  24% good
  51% excellent
  22% superior

- This is an extremely good showing, on a par with the best museum exhibitions, and among the best results in the Festival's history.

- The Smithsonian website received the highest amount of web hits in its history—over 33,236,357 hits over the Festival period.

- Total sales in the Festival marketplace were $416,507, the third highest in Festival history.

- Festival program books sold out for only the second time in history.

- Total sales through food and beverage concessions were $1,179,018, again the third highest in Festival history.

- Kent participants Marc and Tony Stevenson were featured on primetime breakfast television by Fox news. They were interviewed on the Mall about their rocking horses and why they were attending the Festival.

- Ten Alps (Kent TV) and BBC Radio Kent each visited the Festival for 2 days.

- An estimated 78.3 million people (primarily in the UK) heard about Kent's presence at the Festival. This equates to roughly £728,799 worth of coverage.

- Cross KCC directorate working involving various different divisions of Environment & Regeneration as well as the Chief Executive's Department and Communities Directorate.

- Partnership working was developed with Kent Tourism Alliance, as well as various Kent companies and organisations: Shepherd Neame, Penshurst Place, Canterbury Cathedral, Westenhanger Castle, The Hop Farm, Canterbury Archaeological Trust, Chatham Historic Dockyard Trust.

- Strong relationships were developed with the Smithsonian Institute, Virginia Tourism Corporation, Jamestown 2007, Governor's Office, and British Embassy.

- There were several firsts for the KCC website: first operational blog that was updated daily; updating site remotely from USA; fast turnaround of video content from filming to editing and uploading of files within 24 hours.

- Unique fieldwork was carried out in Kent resulting in the identification of many cultural exemplars in the County. This research had not previously been carried out and is now uniquely held in one place in KCC's archives.

- Relationships have been built between Kent's cultural representatives who have continued to keep in touch following the festival and could develop links to benefit Kent culturally.

- Kent's legacy is significant as the first county in England to be represented at the Festival. Kent was also the first 'joint programme' presented at the festival and has changed the Smithsonian Institution's thinking about how it presents culture in the future.

Royal Participation

Her Majesty opened Parliament on 15th November 2006 and confirmed her state visit to the USA: "The Duke of Edinburgh and

I look forward to our State Visit to the United States of America in May 2007 to celebrate the 400th anniversary of the Jamestown Settlement." Committee Co-Chairman Lord Watson was in his place in the Chamber of the House of Commons as one of the Peers chosen to represent the Upper House of Parliament at the State Opening by Her Majesty.

An e-mail to the Committee was received by the Co-chairmen on that same day, 15th November 2006, from Frank Atkinson, Chairman of the Federal Commission:

> Just a few moments ago, I had the great pleasure of viewing the Queen's Speech at the opening of Parliament during which she announced plans for a state visit to the United States in May 2007 to commemorate the 400th anniversary of the Jamestown settlement.
>
> The announcement indicates that one of the foremost goals of the AMERICA'S 400TH ANNIVERSARY planning organizations will be realized. We know this is due in no small measure to your efforts and those of other members of the Jamestown 2007 British Committee, who have been effervescently highlighting the importance of the Jamestown anniversary and quadricentennial observances for quite a while.
>
> On behalf of all of the planning groups, sponsors and partners on this side of the pond, I want to express our deep appreciation to you and the British Committee for these valued efforts. I trust you will convey these sentiments to the members of the Committee.
>
> We will now set about over here making the necessary preparations for a most extraordinary and enthusiastic welcome for Her Majesty, and we very much hope that you and the members of the British Committee will be on hand to join us in receiving her at Jamestown and Williamsburg next May.

The Executive Director was invited to Buckingham Palace on 23rd January 2007 to provide a briefing on the Committee's Jamestown activities.

On 24th April 2007 Buckingham Palace hosted a media briefing and invited Lord Watson to speak to the press about Jamestown and the Committee's activities. The Executive Director and Denise Eden-Green, Discovery Tour Manager, also attended to answer any questions.

Her Majesty's state visit to the USA took place between 3rd–8th May. The visit included an address to the Virginia Assembly in Richmond, where members of the Committee were present, and a visit to the sites of Jamestown Settlement and Historic Jamestowne where Committee members were presented to HM The Queen, HRH the Duke of Edinburgh and their host, Vice President Dick Cheney. This was followed by a ceremony in the Jamestowne Church where the Queen presented a period chair to Governor Kaine, and then a luncheon in Williamsburg hosted by the Governor of Virginia and Colin Campbell, President of Colonial Williamsburg for the Royal guests and the Vice President. Her Majesty then went on to the Kentucky Derby before finishing her state visit in Washington DC.

The Committee assisted with the coordination of the visit, particularly the part that was spent in Virginia. The Committee's Executive Director was invited to work in the Governor's office for the duration of the Queen's visit. The British Embassy in Washington was key to this historic event, especially Alan Charlton, Deputy Head of Mission and Melanie Hinton, Public Affairs Manager. The following UK representatives were presented to the Queen at Historic Jamestowne on 4th May 2007: Lord Watson; Sir Robert Worcester and Lady Worcester; Viscount and Viscountess De L'Isle; Amanda Cottrell; Alex King; Rebecca Casson.

Tourism

• **British Commemoration Tourism Partnership (KTA/VisitKent)**

The Committee's Tourism activities were coordinated by the British Commemoration Tourism Partnership (BCTP) which was initiated and led by Kent Tourism Alliance (KTA — now VisitKent). In developing the BCTP, KTA formed an early partnership between Kent and partners from East England regions and counties, which produced the 'beginyouradventure' campaign.

The three-year campaign (ending March 2008) attracted over 50 different partners, with an income of approximately £500,000. Aimed at consumers, media and travel trade, the campaign concentrated on relationship building and awareness raising, primarily with US visitors from the eastern seaboard. It benefited from a very strong relationship with the Virginia Tourism Corporation.

A leaflet showing relevant Jamestown related historical/tourism links, a DVD and web site _www.beginyouradvernture.co.uk_ was produced by the BCTP.

Sandra Matthews-Marsh, Chief Executive of Kent Tourism Alliance, was instrumental to the success of this project. The BCTP was the only UK presence in the USA for the Godspeed Sail and Anniversary Weekend events. Committee member Viscount De L'Isle and his wife Lady De L'Isle led the unique BCTP Jamestown trade mission to the USA in October 2005. They both continued their kind support by attending the Queen's visit in May 2007 and the Smithsonian Folklife Festival in June/July 2007. Kent Tourism Alliance Chairman, Amanda Cottrell, also played a significant role in the success of these activities.

A 'Goodwill' Tour, welcoming key delegates from the US, was organised for 3rd-11th April 2006 by the [Anglo-American Planning Committee], led by Suzanne Flippo, Chairman of the committee, and with the assistance of the BCTP partnership.

Although the tourism gains resulting from the BCTP's activities will become clearer over time, initial figures released by KTA accredits the Jamestown and America's 400th Anniversary campaign with boosting Kent's tourism economy by £7.4 million. Media interest has helped the campaign reach 18 million households in the US and UK. The editorial value of the print media coverage has been worth at least £1,000,000.

The University of Nottingham will conduct an external audit of the campaign in March 2008. A separate report of the efforts by BCTP will be produced by VisitKent and held in their Canterbury office.

• *VisitBritain*

Committee member Penelope, Viscountess Cobham was instrumental in gaining VisitBritain's (VB) support for the commemoration.   VB seconded Deirdre Livingstone for approximately 2 days per week and a budget was put aside, for her use, to fulfill her remit to attract visitors to the UK from overseas.   The main theme for VB was the Jamestown 2007 anniversary and ancestral tourism and ancestry.co.uk was secured as a key partner.

VB achieved some excellent coverage in the US market with a PR value generated through print articles and television coverage exceeding $3 million. The advertising equivalent value for print articles was $570,049.19 with advertising equivalent value for television coverage reaching $46,400 — this was from the two TV crews VB sent to England, ABC and CBS network affiliates. The total audience in terms of combined circulation and online visits was 39,359,233. A separate report of the efforts by VisitBritain will be produced by them and held in their London office.

Education Initiatives

Educational elements were present through all appropriate UK commemorative events.   A small educational programme was developed to accompany the Discovery Tour and to complement the Virginia Indian Festival. Committee members John Haden and Dr. Robin Baker of the University of Kent coordinated the educational initiatives on behalf of the Committee.

John Haden initiated and co-authored the following booklets: "Admiral of New England: Captain John Smith and the American Dream" (with the Y7 students of King Edward VI Grammar School, Louth), "Captain John Smith of Willoughby and the founding of America" (with the Pupils of Willoughby and Partney Schools), "Captain Christopher Newport of Limehouse, Virginia and the East Indies" (with the Pupils of the Mayflower and the Holy Family Schools, Tower Hamlets, London), "Mrs. John Rolfe of Heacham, better known as Pocahontas" (with the Pupils of Heacham Junior School), and "Bartholomew Gosnold of Otley and America" (with the Y7 Students of Woodbridge School, Suffolk).

Kent was heavily involved in forming links with Virginia Schools and Colleges, as was Lincolnshire (through the ARIES — American

Roots in English Soil — Project). The ARIES project site www. captainjohnsmith.co.uk promotes the Project and books written by John Haden.

As a result of feedback from the Committee through its education initiatives, the Federal Commission updated their educational website www.JamestownJourney.org to be more user friendly for British teachers.

It was hoped that the Committee could coordinate a national schools competition 'What would you take?' but due to lack of funding and resources this was not possible.

Communities

The Committee hosted a UK communities seminar on 3rd November 2005 to raise awareness of the commemoration. The event was kindly supported by Peter Hilling at the Middle Temple. This event coincided with a visit by the Directors of the Smithsonian Folklife Festival who hoped to recruit other counties to join with Kent and Virginia at the 2007 festival. 57 people attended the seminar in total. The event was coordinated by Springboard Marketing Ltd.

Many approaches were made to the Committee from groups in the UK interested in becoming involved with the commemoration. For example, Sunderland City Council invited the Committee's Executive Director to make a presentation to its international management board 18th September 2006.

Feedback on the Committee initiatives was generally positive. The following quote was received from one contact (Vice-Admiral Richard Norton, Drapers Company):

> I am impressed by the programme you have put together, because everything about the US project seems so distant and so massive that it is hard to see how to interface with it sensibly. Now you have provided us with potential solutions.

A Jamestown community event calendar was developed on the beginyouradventure website.

Communication

Due to US sponsorship complications it was very difficult to get approval from Jamestown 2007 State agency for the continued use of the official logos including the three ships and America's 400th Anniversary logos.   As a result, the Executive Director commissioned the design of UK Jamestown logos using the three ships, including one for the Committee, the Foundation and the 'British Commemoration'.   These logos were used throughout anniversary events, particularly the 'British Commemoration' logo, which was used across the UK by many organisations and groups who held Jamestown 2007 events.

- *Media Promotion*

    A PR company (Ruder Finn) was contracted in the US by the Federal Commission with a brief to assist the Committee through its London office. It was hoped the company could assist the Committee to raise the UK profile of Jamestown. However, due to the limited UK contract time allocated to the Committee this was not as successful as first hoped. The Federal Commission did not renew the contract.

    The Kent-Virginia Development Unit established a media clippings file from the start of Kent's links with Virginia. The clippings file also includes articles on UK Jamestown 2007 activities and America's 400th Anniversary. The file will be kept within Kent's archives with the other Kent-Virginia/Jamestown 2007 British Committee records.

    A PR company was employed by KCC's Corporate Communications department to undertake media evaluation between April 2007 and August 2007. The contract period covered the Discovery Tour, Royal visit, Anniversary Weekend and the Smithsonian Folklife Festival. The media evaluation provided an assessment of the value of all the newspaper, radio, TV and website reporting by providing equivalent values if the space had been purchased as advertising, and extrapolating these values as editorial using a multiplier of three.   Media values for the Discovery and Smithsonian have already been detailed in this report. However, values specifically for America's 400th Anniversary are as follows:

Number of clips across all media (April – August 2007)	Audience in millions	PR value	PR Value with 3 multiplier
140	106.0	£641,609	£1,924,827

A full copy of the media evaluation report prepared for KCC will be kept within Kent's archives with the other Kent-Virginia/Jamestown 2007 British Committee records.

As previously mentioned there was a great deal of media interest in the Virginia Indian Festival and the Discovery Tour but overall there seemed to be limited UK media interest in Jamestown, except for during the visit by Her Majesty the Queen which attracted significant media attention. However, some organisations recognised the significance of the Anniversary and were keen to specifically cover the Jamestown commemoration, including the Committee's programme of events: Kent Messenger Kent Business (Trevor Sturgess, KM Group Business Editor, followed the Jamestown story with many articles featured); CBS6/WTVR (who was the first news station to send a reporter (Greg McQuade) and camera man (Stacy Sacra) to the UK in April 2005 to film about Jamestown); CBS/WTVR (led by Managing Director Peter Maroney, also arranged a 'reporter swap' with BBC South East (Mark Norman) in April 2007); Washington Post; So British; BBC South East (Mark Norman was involved in covering many aspects of the Jamestown stories related to the work between Kent and Virginia); Channel 13 (WVEC); WAVY; WTKR (Hampton Roads); Associated Press; The Daily Press; Virginian-Pilot; British Heritage; The (London) Evening Standard; Life TV; National Geographic; Kent Life (who ran a series of Jamestown articles).

BBC Radio 4's "This Sceptred Isle" ran a series on Empire with two programmes featuring Jamestown and the Virginia company:
http://www.bbc.co.uktradio4/history/empire/episodes/episode18.shtml
http://www.bbc.co.uk/radio4/history/empire/episodes/episode20.shtml

A Time Team special ("Jamestown — 13 years digging") was aired on 1st May 2007 at 9 pm on Channel 4. The Committee assisted Brendan Hughes of Time Team with contacts for the programme.

Media for Anniversary Weekend was significant. The 'Beginyouradventure' campaign featured in USA Today which is the largest national daily paper in the US with a circulation of over 2.5 million.

The BBC aired a documentary on 27th November 2007 showing the Queen's visit to Jamestown.

- *Internet*

  A UK Jamestown website *www.jamestownuk.org* together with an e-mail address *J2007BCakent.gov.uk* was kindly established, free of charge, by KCC on behalf of the Committee. Ian Vickery of KCC designed and co-ordinated the website.

Merchandising

It was hoped that the Committee would design and distribute commemorative products. However, due to lack of funding this was not progressed. Instead it was agreed that as commemorative products were needed (when funding was available) they be purchased from the official Jamestown suppliers (based in the USA). The St. James Chapter of the Daughters of the American Revolution sold their own Jamestown merchandise at the Middle Temple event in December 2006.

European Awareness

The Committee hoped to raise awareness in Europe of the 2007 commemorations. Committee members Lord Williamson of Horton and Alex King led on this initiative. Meetings were held with interested MEPs. The European Business Network Congress was held in Kent on 20th–22nd June 2007 and Jamestown was a significant talking point.

Arts, Cultural and Historical Links

- ### Kent-Virginia Development Project

  The Kent-Virginia Development Project is an ambitious partnership being pursued by KCC to enable Kent to gain maximum benefit through establishing long-term links with the Commonwealth of Virginia. The Committee was able to utilise this project in its task of coordinating the UK's involvement in the 400th Anniversary commemorations to the mutual benefit of both parties.

- ### Twinning

  The Governor of Virginia requested that each County in Virginia with a 'UK' name be linked with a place in the UK. As a result of the increased awareness of the 400th Anniversary commemorations Gravesham was linked with Chesterfield County, Ipswich Borough Council approved a twinning agreement with Jamestown in July 2007, and Sunderland further progressed its links with Washington, DC. Committee member Lord Bruce-Lockhart encouraged the Local Government Association to assist the Committee in this effort.

- ### Association for the Preservation of Virginia Antiquities (APVA)

  The APVA invited Parliament to become the primary benefactor of the re-interment of the human remains within the Memorial Garden to be installed at Historic Jamestowne. This initiative was not progressed due to the lack of funding.

- ### Commemorative Stamps

  The US Jamestown 2007 Commemorative Stamp and Cachet Project requested a special stamp and dual issuance in the USA & UK to mark America's 400th Anniversary. This initiative was supported by the Committee, who secured support from the Royal Household, and lobbied the Royal Mail on behalf of the US Jamestown 2007 Commemorative Stamp and Cachet Project. However, the initiative was not progressed as the results of the market testing conducted by the Royal Mail showed it was not popular enough with the general public.

Conclusion

The Commonwealth of Virginia had been planning America's 400th Anniversary for over eight years through the Jamestown 2007 Steering Committee without any official input from the UK. However, once the Federal Commission was established in the spring of 2003, and the official visit was made to London and Kent in 2004, this helped to kick-start the UK's official involvement. The Committee was pleased to engage with the Federal Commission who proved to be a group of highly supportive and effective colleagues throughout the Commemoration. This engagement also enabled the Committee to build strong relationships with contacts in the Commonwealth of Virginia.

There was no funding for the formation of the Committee or its events from the UK or US Governments. The support and funding provided by KCC was fundamental to the success of the UK commemorations. However, it was still difficult to make maximum impact on raising the profile of Jamestown 2007 in the UK.

As the Committee was only officially formed at the beginning of 2005 this severely limited the planning time it had to encourage UK support and raise funds. However, despite the limited planning time and resources available to the Committee, this report documents the exceptional progress made in reaching and engaging UK communities and media in the Jamestown story.

Recommendations

1.   It is recommended that a copy of this report, with samples of all supporting documentation and items, be kept in the archives at Kent County Council.

2.   It is recommended that a copy of this report be held at the University of Kent Templeman Library.

3.   It is recommended that copies of this report be lodged in the libraries of the House of Commons and the House of Lords.

4.   It is recommended that Committee members keep a copy of this report, post it on their websites and hold it in their organisation's archives as appropriate.

5.   It is recommended that a copy of this report be circulated to key contacts involved with the Committee and the commemoration.

6.   It is recommended that a letter be sent on behalf of the Committee to the Leader of Kent County Council, copied to the Lord Lieutenant of Kent, recognising Kent's significant contribution to the anniversary.

7.   It is recommended that a letter be sent on behalf of the Committee to Frank Atkinson, Chairman of the Federal Commission, thanking the Commission for their continued support of the Committee and its activities over the last three years, without which the Committee would not have been successful.

8.   It is recommended that a letter be sent to HM The Queen enclosing a copy of the report and confirming that the State visit was the highlight for America's 400th Anniversary in both the US and the UK.

9.   It is recommended that a letter be sent on behalf of the Committee to the Governor of Virginia and Federal Commission suggesting early UK involvement for the 450th Anniversary. A copy of the letter should be sent to the Jamestown-Yorktown Foundation, Foreign and Commonwealth Office and the British Embassy in Washington.

Final Summary

Despite the limited time and resources available to the Committee, this report documents the exceptional progress made in reaching and engaging UK communities and media in the Jamestown story. The support provided to the Committee by KCC was unusual given Kent's local government status, a level of support equal to that expected from national government. That assistance, which included providing Executive and KCC officer support to the Committee in managing its projects, was fundamental to the success of the Committee and its activities.

Exceptional ideas developed and directed by the Committee included:

- Establishing the first-ever Jamestown UK Foundation Ltd. charitable company
- Bringing the reproduction ship 'Discovery' from the US to the UK
- Managing the ship's tour of the UK
- Coordinating the hugely successful Virginia Indian Festival; and
- Hosting the historical Launch event on 19th December 2006

Other outstanding successes include partnerships to develop the 'Beginyouradventure' tourism campaign, Rule of Law Lectures and Journey to the New World Exhibition.

The historical events and exceptional projects planned and implemented by the Committee, in great partnership with the Federal Commission, will provide a lasting legacy for Jamestown both in the US and the UK.   The activities and stature of the   committee also enhanced   international awareness of the Commemoration, and facilitated the acceptance of Virginia's invitation to Her Majesty Queen Elizabeth II, as well as promoted the presence of a large British delegation for the Anniversary festivities held throughout 2007, particularly between 11-13 May.

It is important to note that 2007 was the first time for any of the Jamestown commemorations that a British Committee was formed. Both the Federal Commission and the UK have now initiated this important precedent for future commemorations.   These efforts will ensure that when future Jamestown anniversaries are commemorated the Committee's activities will provide a planning framework for many generations to come.

This report was completed and circulated in February 2008.   For any comments or questions on this report please contact: Rebecca Casson, Executive Director, Jamestown 2007 British Committee, c/o Kent County Council, lnvicta House, County Hall, Maidstone, Kent ME14 1XX.

JAMESTOWN 2007 BRITISH COMMITTEE

*The Honorable Robert H. Tuttle, United States Ambassador
to the Court of St. James is the PATRON of the Committee*

Co-Chairmen

THE LORD WATSON OF RICHMOND CBE
Lord Watson is Chairman of CTN Communications and
International Chairman Emeritus of the English Speaking Union.

SIR ROBERT WORCESTER KBE DL
Sir Robert Worcester is the Founder of MORI and Chairman of the
Pilgrims Society.

Members

DR. ROBIN BAKER CMG
Dr. Baker is the Vice-Chancellor at University of Chichester, and
was appointed to the Committee when Pro-Vice-Chancellor at the
University of Kent. Dr. Baker has held significant positions in the
British Council since 1984, including Director (Europe) and Deputy
Director General.

WILLIAM BLAIR QC
William Blair is chairman of the Commercial Bar Association and
specialises in the law of domestic and international banking and
finance. He is a director of Jamestown UK Foundation Ltd.

THE LORD BRUCE-LOCKHART OF THE WEALD, Kt OBE
Lord Bruce-Lockhart has been Chairman of the Local Government
Association since July 2004. Lord Bruce-Lockhart was first elected
to Kent County Council in 1989 and he was Leader of the Kent
County Council from 1997 to 2005. Among other charities and
foundations, Lord Bruce-Lockhart is a Trustee of the Leeds Castle
Foundation.

THE RIGHT HONOURABLE THE LORD CARRINGTON KG
GCMG CH MC
Lord Carrington is a former Secretary-General of NATO, former
Secretary of State for Defence and Foreign and Commonwealth
Affairs and also Minister of Overseas Development.

PENELOPE, VISCOUNTESS COBHAM
Lady Cobham is Deputy Chairman of VisitBritain and Chairman of the British Casino Association.

LORD CORNWALLIS
Lord Cornwallis' ancestor is commonly remembered in American history for his defeat at Yorktown.

EARL DE LA WARR
The Earl's ancestor, Lord Thomas De La Warr, founded the States of Delaware and Virginia.

VISCOUNT DE L'ISLE MBE DL
Appointed Vice-Lord-Lieutenant of Kent in 2003. Owner of Penshurst Place, the Sidney family seat in Kent, since 1552. Algernon Sidney, 1623-1683, an ancestor, wrote "Discourses on Governance" widely read by colonists and used in the drafting of the American Constitution, by J. Q. Adams. Co-chairman of Capital Campaign to raise funds for Hampden-Sydney College, Virginia.

LOYD GROSSMAN
Loyd was born in Boston, Massachusetts and educated at Boston University (B.A.) where he read history and the London School of Economics (M.Sc.Econ). Loyd is a member of the Council and the Court of Governors at the LSE. He was the Chairman of the Museums and Galleries Commission.

JOHN HADEN
With twenty years experience as Head of two secondary schools, John Haden now works part-time as an Adviser to Governors and Heads in primary, secondary and special schools and runs the ARIES (American Roots in English Soil) education and community project.

TONY HALMOS
Tony is the Director of Public Relations for the Corporation of London.

PAUL HENDERSON
Previous Director of Fund Raising & Promotion World Wildlife Fund, Management Consultant, McKinsey & Co and previous owners of Gidleigh Park. Currently a Director of Balls Wood Consulting Ltd. and of Hart Hambleton Ltd.

THE RT. HON MICHAEL HOWARD QC MP

Michael was elected Member of Parliament for Folkestone and Hythe in 1983 and held senior positions in the Cabinet including Home Secretary, and Shadow Foreign Secretary and Shadow Chancellor before becoming Leader of the Conservative Party.

ALEX KING MBE

Mr. King is Deputy Leader of Kent County Council and Cabinet Member for Policy and Performance with responsibility for International activities for Kent. He is also Chairman of Jamestown UK Foundation Ltd.

MICHAEL MACY

Cultural Affairs Officer, Embassy of the United States.

VALERIE MITCHELL

Valerie is the Director General of the English Speaking Union.

LORD POWELL OF BAYSWATER

Lord Powell was for many years Private Secretary and adviser on foreign affairs and defence to Lady Thatcher when she was Prime Minister.

TONY QUAYLE

Managing Director, Edinburgh House Estates Limited.

MICHAEL PRIDEAUX

Director, Corporate & Regulatory Affairs, British American Tobacco.

LAURA SANDYS

Laura founded Capital Entry in 2000, an international business consultancy that assists companies enter new markets. She is Chairman of Opendemocracy.net and a trustee of the Open University Foundation. She is Winston Churchill's granddaughter.

DAVID SPENCE

Managing Director, Museum in Docklands.

DR. DAVID STARKEY

Dr. Starkey is a distinguished media personality and author. Dr Starkey is a Tudor Historian and the UK's leading constitutional and monarchy expert.

PROFESSOR RICK TRAINOR
Dr. Trainor is Principal of King's College London and their Professor of Social History. He was also a director of Jamestown UK Foundation Ltd.

SIMON WALKER
Simon Walker was Director of Corporate Affairs at Reuters Group and now Director of BVCA (British Venture Capital Association). Prior to Reuters he was Communications Secretary to HM The Queen. He is a director of Jamestown Foundation Ltd.

THE LORD WILLIAMSON OF HORTON GCMG, CB
Lord Williamson was Secretary General of the European Commission, head of the European Secretariat in the British Cabinet Office and is currently convenor of the crossbenchers.

JOHN WINDELER
Thirty-five years in banking and insurance, most recently Non-Executive Chairman of Alliance & Leicester plc.

JUDITH WOODWARD
Senior Policy Adviser – Culture Strategy, Mayor's Office, Greater London Authority.

EXECUTIVE DIRECTOR
Rebecca Casson, Head of Kent-Virginia Development, Kent County Council and Director of Jamestown UK Foundation Ltd.

APPENDIX 13

Jamestown 400ᵗʰ
Commemoration Commission
Curriculum Advisory Committee Members

Stephen R. Adkins, Chief, Chickahominy Indian Tribe,
  Jamestown 400th Commemoration Commission
Rhyannon Berkowitz , Virginia Council on Indians, Virtual
  Jamestown
Ann Berry, Historic Jamestowne, APVA Preservation Virginia
Warren M. Billings, University of New Orleans, Jamestown 400ᵗʰ
  Commemoration Commission
Gloria Chernay, Office of Education, Smithsonian Institution
Hon. M. Kirkland (Kirk) Cox, Virginia House of Delegates
Anne Doyle Dale, Jamestown 2007
Rex Ellis, Colonial Williamsburg Foundation
Elise Emanuel, Williamsburg-James City County Public Schools
Laura F. Hawthorne, University of Virginia
Ellen Holmes, NASA Connect
James Horn, Rockefeller Library, Colonial Williamsburg
  Foundation
Pamela Pettengell, Jamestown-Yorktown Foundation
Karen Rehm, Colonial National Historical Park, National Park
  Service
Daphne Maxwell Reid, Jamestown 400ᵗʰ Commemoration
  Commission
Tonia Deetz Rock, APVA Preservation Virginia
Kenneth Stroupe, University of Virginia Center for Politics
Hon. Malfourd W. (Bo) Trumbo, Jamestown 400ᵗʰ Commemoration
  Commission
William E. White, Colonial Williamsburg Foundation
Carolyn Whittenburg, College of William and Mary
James Whittenburg, College of William and Mary
Karenne Wood, Chair, Virginia Council of Indians

Project Coordinator:
Daman Irby, University of Virginia Center for Politics
Civics Curriculum Developer:
Meg Heubeck, University of Virginia Center for Politics

APPENDIX 14

Jamestown 400th Commemoration Commission
Democracy Program Planning Council

Honorary Leaders:

Hon. George H. W. Bush (honorary chair), 41st President of the United States

Hon. William Jefferson Clinton (honorary chair), 42nd President of the United States

Rt. Hon. Tony Blair (honorary chair), former Prime Minister of the United Kingdom of Great Britain and Northern Ireland

Rt. Hon. Margaret Thatcher (honorary chair), former Prime Minister of the United Kingdom of Great Britain and Northern Ireland

Hon. Sandra Day O'Connor, Honorary Chairperson, *America's 400th Anniversary*

Hon. William P. Barr (honorary vice chair), former Attorney General of the United States

Hon. Thomas S. Foley (honorary vice chair), former Speaker of the U.S. House of Representatives and former U.S. Ambassador to Japan

Members:

Timothy J. Sullivan (chair), President Emeritus, College of William and Mary

Stephen R. Adkins, Jamestown 400th Commemoration Commission

Frank B. Atkinson, Jamestown 400th Commemoration Commission

Cassandra Newby-Alexander, Norfolk State University

Lawson R. Bader, Mercatus Center, George Mason University

Warren M. Billings, Jamestown 400th Commemoration Commission

Mary A. Bomar, National Park Service

N. Scott Cole, Longwood University

Colin G. Campbell, Colonial Williamsburg Foundation

Nancy N. Campbell, Jamestown 400th Commemoration Commission

Stuart W. Connock, Jamestown 2007 Steering Committee

244

Hon. M. Kirkland (Kirk) Cox, Virginia House of Delegates
H. Benson Dendy III, Jamestown 400th Commemoration
  Commission
Robert Dortch, Richmond Region 2007
Phillip G. Emerson, Jamestown-Yorktown Foundation
Suzanne O. Flippo, Jamestown 400th Commemoration Commission
Stewart H. Gamage, College of William and Mary
Michael P. Gleason, Jamestown 400th Commemoration
  Commission
Hon. John H. Hager, former Lieutenant Governor of Virginia
A.E. Dick Howard, University of Virginia School of Law
Daman Irby, University of Virginia Center for Politics
Lt. Colonel Richard Iron, NATO Allied Command Transformation
Regina Karp, Old Dominion University
Elizabeth S. Kostelny, APVA Preservation Virginia
Hon. Donald W. Lemons, Justice, Virginia Supreme Court
Ann W. Loomis, Jamestown 400th Commemoration Commission
Robert E. Martinez, Norfolk Southern Corporation
John L. Nau III, Jamestown 400th Commemoration Commission
Hon. Thomas K. Norment, Jr., Senate of Virginia, Jamestown 2007
  Management Committee
Daphne Maxwell Reid, Jamestown 400th Commemoration
  Commission
Hon. John O. Marsh, Jr., former Member of Congress, former
  Secretary of the Army
Gene R. Nichol, College of William and Mary
Alexander L. (Sandy) Rives, Jamestown 400th Commemoration
  Commission
Daniel M. Roberts, Jr., University of Richmond, *A Moment in Time*
Larry J. Sabato, University of Virginia Center for Politics
M. Jordan Saunders, Jamestown 400th Commemoration
  Commission
Rodney A. Smolla, University of Richmond School of Law
Kenneth Stroupe, University of Virginia Center for Politics
Daniel B. Thorp, Virginia Tech
Hon. Malfourd W. (Bo) Trumbo, Jamestown 400th Commemoration
  Commission

Staff:
Drema L. Johnson, Democracy Conference Project Director,
  Federal Commission
H. Edward Mann, Executive Director, Federal Commission
Jeanne Zeidler, Executive Director, Jamestown 2007
Kenneth Ashby and Maris Segal, Executive Producers, Prosody
  Creative Services

William R. Allcott, Jr., Communications Director, Federal
   Commission
Peter Farrell, Assistant to the Chairman, Federal Commission

———————

International Conference Series on the Foundations and Future of Democracy Conferences and Sponsors

"International Youth Democracy Summit," August 7-11, 2006
(University of Virginia, U.Va. Center for Politics, and Presidential Classroom)

"Sustaining Democracy in the Global Age," January 25-27, 2007
(Longwood University and Hampden-Sydney College)

"America's 400th Anniversary: Voices from Within the Veil,"
February 22-23, 2007
(Norfolk State University)

"Markets and Democracy," February 23-24, 2007
(The Mercatus Center at George Mason University)

"Democracy and the Rule of Law," April 11-14, 2007
(University of Richmond School of Law, American and English
Inns of Court, American Arbitration Association, English
Commercial Bar Association, and John Marshall Foundation)

"Democracies in Partnership: 400 Years of Transatlantic
Engagement," April 18-19, 2007
(Old Dominion University and NATO's Allied Command
Transformation)

"We are the Change: Democracy and Diversity in the 21st
Century," April 19, 2007
(Richmond Region 2007, Wilder School of Government and
Public Affairs of Virginia Commenwealth University, and regional
partners)

"Foundations of Democracy," September 5-7, 2007
(Virginia Tech and its Alliance for Social, Political, Ethical, and
Cultural Thought)

"World Forum on the Future of Democracy," September 16-18, 2007
(Federal Commission, Colonial Williamsburg Foundation, College
of William and Mary, and Jamestown 2007)